THE EVERYDAY CATHOLIC

THE
EVERYDAY
CATHOLIC

by

MARTIN HARRISON, O. P.

ROMAN CATHOLIC BOOKS
P.O. Box 255
Harrison, NY 10528

Nihil Obstat.   fr. Hilarius Carpenter, O.P., S.T.L., B.Litt.,
(Oxon.)

fr. Kenelmus Foster,   O.P.,   S.T.L.,   M.A.,
(Cantab.)

Imprimi potest. fr. Athelwinus Tindal-Atkinson, O.P., M.A.,
(Oxon.) Prior-provincialis Prov. Angliae.

Nihil Obstat. Richardus Roche, D.D.

Imprimatur.   ✠ Joseph, Archiepiscopus Birmingamiensis.

Birmingamiae die 21*a aprilis anno* 1947.

ISBN 0-912141-17-4

CONTENTS

PREFACE

St Thomas Aquinas begins his Prologue to his great master-piece, the *Summa Theologica*, with these words: "Because a teacher of Catholic truth ought not only to teach the learned but also instruct the beginners, in accordance with the words of the Apostle: *As unto little ones in Christ, I gave you milk to drink, not meat.*—(I Cor. III 1, 2), we purpose in this book to treat of whatever belongs to the Christian religion in such a way as may tend to the instruction of beginners."

These same words might be used with equal propriety as a prologue to this present work. Not that the author, in any wild flight of futile ambition, sets himself to produce a work of comparable magnitude or sublimity to that of St Thomas; nevertheless he has written a singularly comprehensive survey of "whatever belongs to the Christian religion" and has rendered this essential spiritual food of the mind in a form at once palatable, easily digested and nourishing.

If there is a notable difference between the close reasoning in philosophical terms of St Thomas and the simple, everyday style of treatment to be found in the present volume, this is not so much a reflection on the author as a sad commentary on the normal mental equipment of even educated people today in comparison with the capabilities even of beginners in the time of St Thomas. The *Summa Theologica* has long been the accepted text-book of all Catholic theologians, and it would be a temerarious claim even amongst the most able of them to profess a mastery of that splendid treatise. Nevertheless the teaching therein set forth is urgently needed even by the simplest and most unlettered; it is needed not merely for some measure of appreciation of the mysteries of faith, not merely for an understanding of the formal obligations of religion, but also in its practical application to the needs of everyday life. It is in this latter aspect that the present work shows a peculiar and all too rare excellence.

This is a miniature and simple *Summa* for the work-a-day Catholic, for the tens of thousands of quite ordinary folk who are the pillar and support of the Catholic Church in this country. It is primarily meant for the busy mother of a family, for the hard-working father, for the tradesman, the business girl, rather than for the learned and the highbrow—though there is none that could not profit from its perusal.

There has been much diversity of opinion as to the desirability of rendering the Sacred Scripture into everyday language. There has been much discussion as to the propriety of such a production as *The Man Born to be King*, wherein our Lord is represented as a firm-voiced modern and St Peter speaks with a marked Yorkshire accent. Whatever may be the pros and cons of such controversies, this much is certain: our divine Lord presented his revelation to his listeners in practical everyday terms; he made it quite clear that religion must be equated with living, that the service of God was to be implemented not only in formal acts of worship but in our very eating and drinking, in our daily tasks, and above all in our relations with others. He emphasised the need of unfailing simplicity and continual unselfishness; he required his followers to take up the Cross daily and to discover that Cross in the problems and difficulties of everyday life.

The teaching of our Lord has been set forth by many learned and holy writers in a splendid variety of language and approach. But there was still need for a simple, vigorous exposition in terms of common experience and example. It seems to me that this is precisely what Fr. Martin Harrison has largely succeeded in doing. His language is informal, his illustrations homely. He shows that a saint is not a being of a finer clay, but essentially an ordinary person doing ordinary things extraordinarily well. In reading his book one feels that our Lady might conceivably have been our next-door neighbour, that the Apostles might have been our work-mates, and that there may well be saints amongst our friends and acquaintances. The reader will look in vain for a scholarly treatise, for an obviously scientific analysis of the degrees of perfection; but he may well find something there of more immediate practical value to help him towards "doing the truth in charity" born out of the long experience of a pastor of souls.

HILARY J. CARPENTER, O.P.

1 PREPARING THE GROUND

The most important question in the catechism is the first one: "Who made you?" The answer is equally important: "God made me." Unless this were true the rest of the questions would have no significance at all, since our whole duty to God springs from the fact that we belong wholly and entirely to him as our maker to dispose of us as he may choose. The next question follows on naturally from the first: "Why did God make me?" What was his purpose? The answer gives the reason for our existence: "God made me to know him, love him and serve him in this world, so as to be happy with him for ever in the next." It is a covenant; if we do our part, God will do his without fail. Service merits eternal happiness: refusal to serve entails an eternal punishment through loss of God. The first essential is "to know God" which includes whatever pertains to the laws that control service or the method of living in order to attain eternal happiness. Knowledge of itself is barren unless it leads to love, which in turn demands service as its expression, the service of our whole being; body, soul, mind and strength with nothing withheld. Love is not mere sentiment but a powerful driving force that serves in self-sacrifice. The keeping of God's commandments is the whole test of love for God. "If you love me, keep my commandments." There is no other standard given to us. We cannot love that which we do not know nor serve unless we know the conditions of service. Hence the necessity of knowledge in the first place, which in turn will beget love leading to service. Thus our whole duty in life is comprised in knowledge, love and service which are inseparable, always reacting on one another. We must realise that there is a great difference between knowing 'about God' and 'knowing God.' One may know quite a lot about God and yet 'not know him' in himself or his relationship to us. Thus I may know a lot about a Mr. Smith, where he lives, what he does, what position in society he holds, whether he is clever or not, and a lot of other details about him, but I cannot say "I know him" as I know a friend. In the same way there are many things we may know about God in his perfections and yet not know him as a friend. Children often know God better than adults do; to them he is as real a person as father or mother, and means a great deal to them. This is lost in adults by contact with the material struggle to exist. Hence unless we become "as little children" we cannot enter into the kingdom of heaven. It is only by a study of Jesus himself in the gospels that we can 'know God' since that is one of the objects of his coming—to teach us to know God as our Father and friend in every detail of life.

The acquiring of such knowledge is no easy matter if it is to blossom into a personal love and service. Lessons are not learnt by the mere process of hearing or reading, but by assimilating, studying, and fixing in the heart what is learnt so that it becomes productive when occasion arises for putting into practice the knowledge applicable to the circumstances of the moment. Failure in general, when it comes to dealings in the spiritual life, results from want of preparation before the seeds of knowledge are sown. The truths taught do not fructify into acts of virtue and service because no preparation was made to receive these truths so that they could take root and grow: hence the knowledge of them is barren and unfruitful. We need to prepare the mind and heart to be receptive, to put ourselves in the disposition to learn, to have the desire of acquiring knowledge so as to make it our own in such a way that when opportunity offers it at once springs into appropriate action.

Our divine Master's favourite way of driving home truths was by means of stories or parables about everyday incidents. In one of these he tells of the sower who went out to sow seed, some of which fell by the wayside and was trodden down or picked up by birds; some fell among rocks, sprouted and withered away from want of moisture; more fell among thorns and was choked out; the rest fell on good ground and produced fruit a hundred-fold. The disciples asked the meaning of this and were told that the seed was the word of God, i.e. knowledge; that which fell by the wayside is meant to show how truth is received by those who hear with interest but allow the devil to take it from them lest any improvement is made; that which fell among rocks means that some hear with joy but soon forget through want of thought; that among thorns represents those who allow worldly cares and interests to choke out all good desires; lastly that on good ground points to those who keep the word of God in their hearts and act upon it. Each one of us falls under one or other of these types, and we must find out to which we belong.

It is obvious that the seed is fruitful or barren according to the place on which it falls. Failure to produce fruit lies, not in the seed, but on what it falls. What is it that makes good ground? It is preparation ; and unless we are prepared to receive the word of God, no fruit will result. The failure is in ourselves if the knowledge does not fructify. Some do not want to learn, fearing that it will mean making some change in their lives; there may be some affection for sin about which they do not wish to be reminded or troubled in conscience by hearing the word. Others are eager enough to hear but too indolent to put into practice what they have heard; they like to hear a good sermon but rather for pleasure than profit, so they soon forget what they heard. Many are too occupied with worldly interests, ambitions, plans for improvements in their station in life, pleasures and such like, to be really serious in any desire for knowledge of God. Those who do produce acts of virtue were prepared beforehand to receive and use for their spiritual advancement what they heard.

Before a man goes out to sow the seed, there is much labour to be done. Weeds must be cleared from the ground, the soil ploughed into furrows and left to the weather, then harrowed to break it up until it is soft and friable to a certain depth; it may need some manure or fertiliser added to provide plant food. Not until all this is done will the soil be 'good' and productive of fruit. Applying this to ourselves, we realise the need of effort to prepare the heart to receive knowledge. The weeds of sin must be up-rooted and cast out, whether real sin or affection for sin, which is brought about by true contrition— literally by bruising together to break up into parts—hence contrition ploughs, furrows and harrows the heart, breaking up its propensities to evil. This is the first essential in pre-

3

paration. 'A contrite and humble heart thou wilt not despise.' The prepared heart needs to be made fertile by prayer and the grace of the Holy Spirit directing us to the end since alone we are helpless and need the help of God.

When the seed is sown by hand much is blown away by the wind on to unfruitful ground; we lose the seed by inattention and want of interest, so we must give all our attention, be eager to learn, to know what we must do. Humility is necessary—'The poor have the gospel preached to them.' We must have a poor opinion of ourselves, realising the poverty of our knowledge and our sinfulness. Pride rebels against what is made known or thinks it knows better, not liking to be reminded of what duty means. We need the docility, the teachableness of a child that accepts without question what is taught, trusting entirely to the knowledge of its teacher.

More remains to be done. When the wheat is ripe it must be harvested, then threshed to separate the grain from the chaff; the grain must be milled into flour, the flour baked into bread, the bread chewed and assimilated ere the purpose of the seed is fulfilled. Likewise when we gain knowledge it needs to be threshed in the mind, ground by reflexion, chewed by meditation until it is assimilated and becomes a second nature in action.

Thus do we turn knowledge into love and service, otherwise it is barren and produces no fruit, no change of life, no virtuous acts.

How many sermons have we heard, how much have we read, what lasting results have been produced from the hearing or reading of the word that is to teach us to 'know God'? Must we admit that results are very meagre? If so, then the failure lies within ourselves. We could have achieved so much more had we really learned our lesson. Is it not that we have taken little trouble to prepare ourselves for the seed sown in our hearts? We were not really contrite in truth, not sufficiently humble to learn, not docile and teachable as a child, perhaps too ready to criticise and disagree with what was taught. Maybe we had no real desire to overcome our many faults, to acquire virtue, to sanctify our lives. We need goodwill, desire to profit, eagerness to learn and to put into practice in our daily lives the lessons that are taught in the gospels. It is not just on occasion that we need this knowledge but all through the day; religion must be a part of our daily lives just as much as eating, sleeping, working or playing—yes, even more than these, since it should permeate all that goes to make up life. Too many try to keep work, play and eating as things quite separate from religion, like two parallel lines that never meet but run alongside each other. That is quite a false view. Whatsoever ye do, . . . do all for the glory of God. Only by a sufficient knowledge of our duties, our obligations to God, can we bring forth fruit in abundance, growing out of the knowledge we have obtained, springing into love for God and his service. Only preparation and attention so that we can assimilate what we learn, will lead to spiritual advancement and bring us to lead a life of virtue. 'Prepare ye the way of the Lord.'

II SELF-KNOWLEDGE

'Know thyself!' How very necessary it is to know self as far as it is possible to do so, to know whether any progress is being made in our spiritual state, drawing nearer to God in love daily increasing, overcoming faults, gaining virtues, becoming more holy in God's sight. We cannot know self unless we take some steps to find out, to see ourselves as in a mirror; it is not just a matter of leaving things to work out as best they can; we must study our condition, find out faults, needs, and weaknesses: but through being too absorbed in the cares and toils of a daily struggle for existence we fail to study our spiritual state and need, we have no time to pause so that we may look into spiritual matters. We should realise what original sin has brought about in human nature and how we are affected by it in our attitude to God. Adam's sin was not merely a matter of a sensual enjoyment of a luscious fruit; it was a declaration of the independence of human nature from God; a claim to be self-sufficient in happiness apart from God. Adam made no blind choice when he was tempted, his intelligence was surpassed as a man only by that of Christ and he fully realised all the consequences of his choice. We in our maimed nature are unable to understand fully what Adam did when he claimed independence for human nature. It was akin to Lucifer's defiance of God and differed only in that human nature can change its choice and by God's help repent, which is impossible to angelic nature. As far as we are concerned it implanted in human nature this declaration of independence of God and self-sufficiency for its happiness and hence an aversion from God which can only result in failure to attain to happiness. This is seen in the futile attempts man makes to order his affairs. Each age sees a renewal of these; Humanism, Rationalism, Socialism, Communism, are all futile attempts to realise a perfect human state of happiness apart from God. Hence life is one continued struggle of the flesh against the spirit. The spirit is willing to subject itself to God: the flesh demands independence in rebellion against God. Though baptism gives grace and creates a new man within us, it does not destroy the old man;

6

so there is a continual opposition between the two. We must know then that our chief difficulty is to subdue this rebellion of the old man in claiming independence, and to foster the submission of the new man created in Baptism. Growth in holiness is just the suppression of the rebellious flesh by the submission of the spirit to the laws of God. We cannot know whether any progress is being made against the tendencies of maimed human nature unless we study ourselves in the light of this knowledge.

In the parable of the Unjust Steward, our Lord remarks that the children of this world are wiser in their generation than the children of light. One way in which this worldly wisdom is shown is by the efforts made in business to find out the exact state of everything in the conduct of affairs so that a full and complete knowledge is obtained. At times a notice is seen outside some business concern stating that it is closed for stock-taking. What does this mean? It means that the firm having closed its doors to the outside world and ceased its normal business activities, has retired within itself to hold a rigorous examination of its state. The stock is examined to see whether any goods are missing or not accounted for and why this is so, where the missing goods have got to; the books are all scrutinised to find out whether there is loss or profit—if profit, how it can be increased; if loss, how it was caused, how it can be avoided; in what way the business may be improved and increased. When all these items have been thoroughly examined, then the exact state of the business is laid bare, the true position is known, and decisions are taken to make its concerns more successful. Surely this is a very wise proceeding.

Would it not be wise to apply this method to our spiritual concerns? After all our chief business in life is our spiritual progress — 'What shall it profit a man if he gain the whole world and suffer the loss of his soul?' Our chief business is growth in holiness, a closer relationship with God, the increase of sanctifying grace, the elimination of faults and the perfecting of virtue; it is the business of a lifetime. Would it not be most profitable to pause from normal activities and hold

7

a rigorous inspection of our chief business, to close for stock-taking, shutting out the world and ordinary pursuits for a time, however short, in order to find out just how we stand in relation to God? To find out our spiritual state, our profit, or loss; where improvement is needed; to 'know self'? However, like Martha busy about many things, we forget that 'one thing is necessary' and we let things slide instead of being busy about that one necessary thing.

Before commencing his public life, Christ retired into the desert alone for forty days that he might prepare himself in prayer for the great work he came to do. After the Ascension the disciples retired to the upper room where for ten days they persevered in prayer waiting for the coming of the Holy Ghost. They were not wasting their time; they were 'realising themselves,' preparing for the divine mission they were to undertake. Each year Religious Orders and the Clergy make a 'retreat' shutting themselves off from the normal activities of their lives so that they may take spiritual stock of themselves. If such persons dedicated to the service and work of God find it necessary to retire for awhile to examine their spiritual state, how much more necessary is it for those to do likewise who are occupied so much with the affairs of the world having little time to devote to the soul and God? No doubt it is difficult for such busy people to set aside time to make a long retreat, but it would not be difficult to give up an occasional Sunday for self-examination, for reading spiritual books of value to the soul and their spiritual state. How many ordinarily good people do more than make a daily examen of conscience, if that? How can anyone 'know himself' unless some effort is made to look into his spiritual affairs and try to profit by what is discovered? Can we say whether we are making any sort of progress at all, making any headway against our chief faults? How can we know if we do not make any effort to find out? Are we growing stronger against temptations, more persevering in prayer, going to the sacraments more frequently, gaining a greater personal love for God, or are we just drifting along anyhow?

We cannot answer such questions unless we pause awhile,

draw apart for a time from worldly concerns to ponder over our state. So many are content to leave their spiritual affairs to chance, to let matters drift so long as they are not conscious of actual mortal sin, to feel that all is well without regarding daily faults which do not appear mortally sinful but which prevent all real progress. This is not the way to repress the rebellious tendency of human nature, which is our legacy, that 'proneness to evil from childhood' that besets one and all. If this is all the care we take of our souls, no progress will be made in the chief business of life—the saving of our souls. Woe to us if we find ourselves spiritually bankrupt because we did not take the trouble to find out the true state of our souls, because we did not 'know ourselves' at all.

Having taken stock and found out how things stand, then comes the work of deciding what must be done to effect improvement. In other words good resolutions must be made. First, though, a word of warning! It is no use making a general resolution to 'be good in future'; it will mean nothing at all in the end. What is needed is some practical and definite work to be done. One good practical task is worth a host of indefinite intentions to improve. We cannot become good suddenly; it is a slow and laborious process, step by step to better ways of life.

There are several things to be considered. First, is what I intend to do compatible with my state in life? It is no use deciding to go daily to mass, if business affairs make it impractical. Again what we intend to do must not give trouble to others, e.g. will it entail someone else getting up earlier to call me for mass? Will my new resolution bring about any real improvement in my spiritual state? Most of us have a 'besetting sin,' some fault which is more prevalent than any other. Here is something definite to work on—little by little to lessen the number of times we fall until we have mastered the fault. There will be many lapses at first but gradually by prayer and perseverance we shall make progress and in the end overcome this evil tendency. Again we must not undertake too many things at the same time. One fault is enough to watch at once and if it is our worst fault, we shall gain strength by a persistent endeavour to overcome it and find it more easy when the time comes to rid ourselves of some other fault. We must learn to walk before we can run; a bad habit is not overcome just because we have made a resolution to destroy it; there will be many lapses at first.

Thus the business of improvement is the work of a lifetime and cannot be accomplished in a few weeks or months. Adam's rebellious claim to independence is strongly rooted in human nature, and therefore in us, and our total submission to God is not easily won but is a laborious process needing much grace from God through prayer. If when we are called to our last account we have approached as much as in us lies with the help of God to perfection, God will be satisfied with our efforts and we shall hear his 'well done good and faithful servant' and reap the reward of our labours. Prayer and watchfulness must be our chief aids; knowing our great weakness and proneness to evil, we must lean on God and by the grace of the Holy Spirit progress steadily in making complete submission to the Will of God. 'I can do all things in him who strengtheneth me.'

III ORIGINAL SIN

To understand the difficulties that are to be met in the spiritual life it is necessary to have as clear an idea as possible of original sin and its consequences in human nature. To picture Adam as he was created by God in a state of innocence and friendship with God together with the privileges he enjoyed, is beyond our imagination. He was the perfect human being with all his faculties and emotions completely dominated by his soul and under full control; he was the most intelligent man (save Christ alone) that has existed, with a clear perception of good and of truth, his magnificent intelligence working freely and unaffected by any uprising of passion, unclouded by any darkness of ignorance or error. It is difficult to understand how he was deceived by temptation so as to commit sin—a sin that brought dire ruin to human nature centred in Adam as its head and source—and disobey God's command. First Eve, then Adam, succumbed to the wiles of Satan and ate the forbidden fruit! Many miss the whole point of this temptation. It was not merely a desire to gratify the pleasure of taste; for that was under perfect control—Adam was not as a boy tempted to rob an orchard for some luscious fruit; it was something far more subtle that could appeal to an intelligence such as Adam possessed. Let us study this temptation.

Satan asks Eve why they do not eat of all the trees in paradise. Eve replies that they are commanded not to eat of the tree in the midst of paradise lest perhaps they die. Then Satan says: 'No, you shall not die the death. For God doth know that in what day soever you shall eat thereof your eyes shall be opened: and YOU SHALL BE AS GODS KNOWING GOOD AND EVIL.' God had commanded that they should not eat of this tree as a sign and token of their surrender and submission to his will as their Creator and Supreme Good. Good they already knew; evil they would know only by the experience of it in themselves. Human nature in Adam desired to be independent—to be as 'like unto God' as it was possible for him to be, imitating God in the knowledge of good and evil. St Thomas Aquinas explains that

11

Adam desired the knowledge of good and evil so that by his own natural powers he might decide what was good and what was evil for him; also that by his own natural powers he might obtain his ultimate happiness. In both ways he desired to be equal to God in so far as he was willing to rely on himself in contempt of the divine rule (II^a II^{ae} 193.2). It meant that Adam wanted to be self-determinate, to decide for himself what was good or evil without reference to the law of God. It was a terrible sin of pride. Satan and Adam both committed the same sin in willing to be independent of God and self-determinate. But in Adam this was not merely a personal sin; it was a sin committed by him precisely as head and origin of the whole human race. Therefore this desire for independence infected human nature, this perverse ambition of self-determination which repeats itself through the ages, this desire of man to be the arbiter of his own destiny and happiness by his own natural powers. Truly their eyes were indeed opened and like God they knew evil but by the experience of it in themselves and they could not rid themselves of the awful results in their nature.

This terrible disaster was appalling in its consequences. Man's complex nature, unified by the control of the spirit, was now no longer 'one'. St Thomas Aquinas says 'The equilibrium of a composite body being destroyed, the composed elements disperse in different directions, each gravitating to its own proper end. So the harmony set up by original justice being broken, the diverse faculties of the soul tend each to its own object regardless of the interests of the person as a whole'. Adam now felt the revolt of his lower nature against the spirit which could no longer satisfy the craving for pleasure in the various elements of his complex nature. 'The flesh lusteth against the spirit,' desires could no longer be controlled or checked; knowing good, Adam could no longer bring it about. He felt the revolt in his members; his intelligence, clouded by passion, darkened by ignorance and error, could no longer give him a clear idea of truth; he could no longer do the good he willed to do.

St John in his first epistle (II, 16) sums up the wounds

in human nature thus: 'All that is in the world is the concupiscence of the flesh, the concupiscence of the eyes, and the pride of life.' These are the chief difficulties against which we have in our fallen nature to contend, these the poisonous roots that make us prone to evil from childhood, which remain rooted in us even after baptism has reconciled us to God.

Concupiscence of the flesh is the hunger for pleasure and satisfaction of desire in the flesh; it is the revolt against pain, toil, hardships and mortification; it is resentment against the disabilities of nature and loss of happiness caused by sin. Man yields to the demands of his lower nature in the vain hope of stilling the clamour for satisfaction in his lower appetites and instincts.

Concupiscence of the eyes is the inordinate desire for fame and glory from creatures, the desire to extol one's self apart from God. Knowing his own emptiness and futility, man hungers to raise himself up, to feel that he is 'somebody of importance,' to enjoy a greatness that is false. This desire seeks gratification in ambition that causes injustice, broods over injuries, wishes revenge, brings about bloodshed, wars and oppression. Wealth is sought as a means of attaining a spurious glory among men, or anything that will serve to gain some semblance of power and importance.

Pride of life is the worship of SELF. It makes self the centre of being rather than God. Man is forced to worship something but finding God too remote, too abstract, too hidden, he turns to self and seeks independence of God. No longer centred in God as its proper object, human nature strives to be self-sufficient, to be its own standard of morality and truth.

Original sin is seen repeating itself through the ages in systems designed to promote human happiness by natural powers, such as in Humanism, or Rationalism, and in our own times by Atheistic Communism or Nazism, etc., which banish God from human concerns, hoping to achieve lasting happiness yet proving such hopes to be futile and useless, as is only too obvious. Pride of life again displays itself in the independence man claims for his own private judgment in what he shall

13

believe or not believe of divine truths, resulting in a confused multitude of religious beliefs. It rejects the divine authority of the true Church as contrary to its own independence of thought; denies the infallibility of Christ's Church as depriving man of his right to private judgment on what he shall accept or deny as Truth, and thus man chooses a 'church' of his own making rather than submit to authority and yield up his independence to God.

Satan and Adam were alike in the sin of pride which claimed independence, but whereas angelic nature could never change its decision, human nature fortunately, by the grace of God, could change and regretting its fatal mistake could repent, though utterly unable of itself to escape from the result of such a mistake. Baptism, through the mercy of God, restores the relationship of man with God but does not take away the disorders caused by sin in human nature. These poisonous roots remain, as we know to our cost. These must be renounced at baptism, as the enemies of the soul. But they remain to afflict us and render it difficult to give our total allegiance to God.

This unhappy state of man is summed up by St Paul (Rom. VII, 19—23) thus: 'For the good which I will, I do not; but the evil which I will not, that I do. I find then a law that when I have a will to do good, evil is present within me. For I am delighted with the law of God according to the inward man; but I see another law in my members fighting against the law of my mind . . . Unhappy man that I am, who shall deliver me from the body of this death?' To his bewilderment such was the state in which Adam found himself and which was all that he could pass on to human nature in the children of his flesh.

We know from sad experience how the wounds that human nature incurred are our lot, creating evil tendencies within us. The flesh revolts against the spirit, pleading for the satisfaction of its hunger for pleasure with insistent demand. We are longing for the esteem of men rather than the esteem of God; resent injuries and seek revenge; desire wealth and power to feel greatness and importance among men; and look for vain glory and praise from men. How difficult it proves to obey the laws of God when they seem to interfere with our independence to live our lives as we would, how much we become self-centred and resent self-sacrifice to avoid sin. Such is our unhappy legacy from Adam who, by his declaration of independence, caused revolt in his members, through losing the dominion of the soul over his complex nature, and found himself unable to remedy his unhappy state. Prone to evil from our childhood we realise the truth of St Paul's words and find 'another law in my members fighting against the law of my mind.' Yet only by realising this evil which results from sin and by standing up to the difficulties thus created can we hope by the grace of God to face up to the long protracted struggle throughout life in the endeavour to gain the mastery over evil tendencies, and learn to control the flesh by the higher faculties of the soul. The understanding of our unhappy state is necessary to explain so many of our tendencies to evil. To know why we do evil things rather than good and be ever on the watch for these insidious uprisings of evil that we may crush them ere they cause us to fall headlong into sin. Chastity, Poverty and Obedience, the three religious vows, are powerful antidotes to these tendencies. Yet not to all is the grace given to make such a sacrifice, but all have a promise in baptism to renounce the flesh, the world and the devil.

IV THE REDEMPTION

Though Adam repented of his terrible sin, he found himself totally unable to escape from the fatal results. To save him from utter despair, God, in his divine mercy, promised a redeemer who would atone for all sin and make it possible for man to achieve the purpose of his creation of being eternally happy with God. In this hope and expectation of a divine redeemer, Adam and Eve began life anew but in very different circumstances in which they and their progeny were to work out salvation in looking for the promised redemption. As the ages passed, man drifted further and further from truth; the greater number set up for themselves false gods which they worshipped through fear or from hope of advantage, losing completely all idea of the promised redemption. Only among the chosen people and a few other individuals, did the idea of one God continue, and even among the Israelites, in spite of prophets sent by God to unfold gradually the characteristics by which the Redeemer might be known when he appeared, a complete misunderstanding arose because they formed their own idea of the kind of redeemer they needed and the sort of redemption that would suit them best. It was that deep-seated independence in human nature that wanted to settle what was best for itself, the awful result of original sin.

Needless to say man's idea of the redeemer was in total contrast to the intention of God. The Jews, though they sighed for the redeemer, had yet no idea of the true kind of redemption that was needed by human nature to bring back to man the possibility of true happiness in spite of the disabilities in his nature caused by sin. They detested the political domination of the Romans over them, they wanted to be a great, powerful and independent nation, rich in worldly wealth; so to them redemption meant freedom from subjugation to Rome, and to be a great independent people. When Jesus, the Redeemer, came he disappointed them, since instead of preaching a crusade against the power of the Romans and leading them to throw off the hated yoke, he taught an inner

16

revolution of the spirit, a change in their interior lives by true love for God and one's neighbour. Jesus taught the brotherhood of man in which all were united in the true worship of God; he taught self-sacrifice and the service of others, to love God in the spirit and not merely to offer him a formal observance of the Law outwardly, whilst having no real interior submission to his will. That sort of redemption was of no use to them; they wanted a change for the better in their outward circumstances, not a change themselves, in their own hearts towards God; they were quite satisfied with their outward formal observances of religion, hence they rejected him and brought about his death—'He came unto his own and his own received him not.' They utterly misunderstood the purpose of the Redemption as planned by God for the true betterment and happiness of mankind.

The spiritual transformation of human nature is the chief object of the Redemption but the greater number of mankind still expect the Redemption to change their external circumstances and bring happiness without any need of change in their spiritual nature. To man, redemption has always tended to mean something different from what it has meant to God. In religion men look for some code that will allow them to please themselves without displeasing God; it is that same spirit of independence showing itself. There cannot be any such code. Man cannot make any compromise with God; he cannot make any concessions to God that will leave him free to follow his own will in some matters. Mankind has lost its way to happiness. The chief source of unhappiness is not pain or suffering, but fear; and they fear to trust God. If men practised true religion they would be happy.

Christ came not only to offer the supreme sacrifice of atonement for sin, but also to teach men so to live life as to find real happiness therein. God alone, as man's Creator, can know the purpose of his creation and the way his creatures must live in order to be happy. When Christ came, he chose that state of life which would be common to the greatest number of men, and which could be adjusted to cover all other states of life. The greater part of his life was spent as a working man, toiling with his hands, living in the sweat of his brow; but it was a perfectly natural human life also, and therefore a perfectly happy life. In other words he lived as God intended that man should live, since Christ fully carried out the purpose of man's existence in being utterly subject to the will of God. We have become so used to the idea of Christ as the 'Man of Sorrows' that we have lost the idea that he was also the 'Man of Happiness.' Christ in his manhood was always happy in spite of toil and hardships, and this was quite apart from the beatific Vision which he always enjoyed. Christ was always happy because he lived a perfect human life as it should be led in accordance with God's purpose in creation. Christ came to show man how to live in the way intended by God and so to find happiness. The whole christian way of life taught by Christ is the perfect method of being happy because it brings man into his true relationship with God. Yet so many have missed this idea of religion, thinking it simply a means of getting rid of sin, instead of getting rid of sinfulness as well. If the christian religion does not control and permeate life entirely, then it fails to produce the result of happiness as it should. There can be no compromise with God; it must be all or nothing. The mission of Jesus was not merely benevolence, not to rescue man from adverse circumstances, not just to secure his well-being, but to teach him how to be happy in spite of pain, toil and hardships. He was not just an humanitarian come to cure evil; he came to bring about a total change in the spiritual outlook of man.

Because redemption means to man something different from what it means to God, we find the Jews, and modern christians also, asking the same kind of question: 'Lord what must I do to be saved?' This question implies the idea that salvation can be assured by means of some extra external observance. They want some formula to act as surety. 'Do this, and you will be saved.' Offer some additional sacrifice, do some special good deed, and all will be well. Thus a young rich man comes to our Lord asking 'Lord, what must I do to be saved?' Our Lord bids him sell all he has, give it to the poor and follow HIM. Obviously the young man hoped for some

special external work that would secure his salvation, but
the answer he received was a disappointment and he went
away sad. Similarly a lawyer asking the same was informed
that to love God above all things and our neighbour as ourselves was the only formula possible. That was not what he
wanted either. That meant a change in spiritual outlook.

Modern christians still look for some external work that
will make them sure of salvation. The real question is not
'What must I do' but 'What must I be,' and our Lord answers
'Be ye perfect even as your heavenly Father is perfect.' But
the modern christian thinks this is asking the impossible.
Nothing but the whole-hearted acceptance of the rule of life
as taught by Christ, implying a complete change in the interior
spirit, a total reversal of human values in real following of
Christ in his method of life, will ensure salvation which also
includes happiness for man on earth. It is sometimes said
that christianity has failed, but it has never been tried as a
system of life by the majority. Those individuals who have
accepted whole-heartedly the spirit of Christ made their lives
divine—they are the real super-men, yet intensely human;
we call them Saints. To the many christianity will always
seem wanting because it seems to fail in bringing the promised
redemption as they expected it; but the real failure is in their
own misunderstanding of it, and the partial acceptance of
what pleases them in it. They want to compromise with God.
They will accept the mercy of Christ but not his justice; they
accept his benevolence but not his self-sacrifice. The harsher
portions of his doctrine appal them as totally contrary to
what human nature desires. When Christ says 'Let a man deny
himself' it goes against the grain, it strikes at his very independence and fails to impress him as a way to happiness because
it is so directly opposed to fallen human nature. Again 'Happy
are the poor in spirit, the meek, the peacemakers, the clean
of heart.' Impossible, says man, to find happiness in that,
since the world, that is to say the common opinion of human
society, counsels the very opposite; to be happy one needs
be wealthy and powerful, to stick up for self, to grab all at
any price. If christianity says the opposite then it cannot give
happiness.

But the christian has promised to 'renounce the world' i.e. its counsels and methods, so contrary to the will of God. If the way to salvation and happiness is 'by the narrow road,' how can it appeal to human nature? Man is afraid to trust God; though he will accept the smooth and easy, he rejects the hard and difficult in Christ's teaching. He fears too much, he cannot cast himself wholly on God's infinite love and care for his creatures. Christianity—the gospel of Christ—must be accepted unreservedly and completely if it is to be true 'redemption' for man. There can be no compromise; it must be all or nothing.

Even catholics fail to utilise life properly because they will not allow themselves to be enlightened by their faith in many of the ordinary issues of life, social, political and economic. They profess to be catholics, but do not put their religion into full practice. They still cling to private judgment in many matters affecting their religious values and think the Church behind the times, because she still proclaims SIN as the great enemy of mankind. Redemption must mean the total change in spiritual values, the whole-hearted acceptance of Christ's system of life—a real following of Christ in self-denial and carrying the Cross.

V   RELIGION

When 'religion' is spoken of, how many people really understand what the term means or in what religion consists? Many confuse it with external worship, without knowing anything of the interior attitude to God which religion really means and without which it is mere sham. To such people religion is just a matter of going to church services, being visited by a priest, or receiving financial assistance when in need, forgetting that religion is something deeply rooted in the soul, affecting every action, and controlling the whole of life. When sorrow or distress appear, they fly to what they imagine to be religion, expecting to find comfort and consolation only to find no relief at all; they visit the priest, but his words leave them cold and unaided, so religion is condemned as a failure, as being of no use in need. They do not understand that the failure is in themselves, having a mistaken idea of religion and its uses; they have treated it merely as an external affair, kept like a bottle of medicine to be used as needed, or like an overcoat to be put on when it is chilly. No wonder it has little or no effect. They accept all the truths of religion, believe what they are taught in a superficial way, but it means little more than words and phrases without much understanding of them, not being a real part of daily life. They have no religion in the true sense. Religion should be the mainstay of life, the one thing to which we cling when all else has gone—friends, riches, health, pleasures. When these are gone, religion should mean everything to us; if it does not, then our religion is not true and real.

Job gives us an example of true religion. God allowed him to be deprived of all his wealth, afflicted by the devil, to lose his children in death, to be tormented by ulcers, taunted by his wife for his trust in God, to be accused of crimes by his friends, yet in spite of all he remains patient, trusting in God because his religion is real and true. His one answer is 'The Lord hath given and the Lord hath taken away, blessed be the name of the Lord.' Could we imitate such patience, have perfect trust in God, were we so afflicted? It would depend on whether our religion was true or sham.

What does religion mean? It is that belief, that confidence, which binds the spiritual nature to God, conscious of complete dependence on him. It is wholly interior in the inner depths of the soul, rebinding the spirit to God. In a secondary way it includes acting in accordance with that belief in God by the practical expression of outward observances springing from the recognition of relationship with God. This includes personal conduct, doctrines, duties, and the ritual of services of adoration, founded on the interior relationship. The acts are the outward expression of religion—they are the body, religion is the soul animating them. It is possible to act in a religious manner by the performance of external rites, by attending to duties imposed, and yet not have that interior attitude to God which is the essence of religion. Suppose one were stranded in a desert place without any church, no services of religion, no sacraments or religious rites, would that one still have 'religion'? If religion is true and real, the loss of the external acts should make no difference—the interior attitude should remain the same, namely union with God.

Religion consists in the attitude to God which spiritual union creates and from which spring all the external manifestations in acts of devotion and service. Man is a composite being formed of body and soul, made in the likeness of God, which likeness resides in the soul through intelligence and free will. Since this likeness lies in those two faculties, that rebinding of the soul to God, the essence of religion, can rest only in these two powers. It consists in knowing God by the intelligence, and loving him with the will. The combining of the two produces that service which constitutes the external observances of religion. Unless such service springs from the mind and heart (or will) it has no reality. Hence what pertains solely to the body and is shared by brute creation does not enter into the essentials of religion which rests in the highest faculties of man; it is not in the imagination, nor in sensible emotions—these may enter into the externals, but only as being part of man's whole nature. Many think themselves religious when they feel what they call devotion; if this feeling

22

is absent they judge themselves to be wanting in religion. The love of God is judged as the love for creatures; affection is a physical feeling towards husband or wife, friend or lover, and because a similar feeling is not experienced towards God, it is thought to be non-existent. Such emotional persons expect religion to make them feel comforted and supported in time of crisis, and when they do not feel such emotions blame religion as being of no value. Such people have no real religion but merely emotional tendencies towards God which not being under control at will, are valueless.

True it is that God does sometimes permit a 'sensible devotion' to be experienced which gives joy and happiness in his service, but this is incidental and not essential. Sometimes it is felt at the beginning of our turning to God, and perhaps never again. Many of the saints suffered from 'spiritual dryness of soul,' as the absence of all sensible pleasure in religion is called, but they persevered in loving service thus proving the truth and reality of their love for God. True religion lives in the mind and will, independent of all sensible emotions or feelings.

Religion then is not merely the observance of external duties: these must spring from and be vivified by the internal spirit. The pharisees are examples of external observance without interior religion; particular about the minute external observances, looked upon as the holy ones of Israel, yet condemned as hypocrites because found wanting in that interior disposition of submission to God which is the essence of all religion. In the gospel of St Matthew we read: 'The Scribes and Pharisees have sitten in the chair of Moses. All things therefore whatsoever they shall say to ye, observe and do; but not according to their works do ye, for they say and do not. For they bind heavy burdens and lay them on men's shoulders but with a finger of their own they will not move them. For they make their phylacteries broad and enlarge their fringes. And they love the first places in the synagogue and to be saluted in the market place and to be called Rabbi.' This is a condemnation of external observance without interior spirit; they are called hypocrites because they pretend

23

to be outwardly holy but in the soul they have no real religion, not being bound to God by knowledge, love, and service. So with us also if we are content with the outward signs alone; If we are content with nothing but the external observance and have no real bond with God to vivify our works our religion is vain. St James says: 'If any man think himself to be religious, not bridling his tongue, but deceiving his own heart, this man's religion is vain. Religion clean and undefiled before God and the Father is this: to visit the fatherless and widows in their tribulation; and to keep one's self unspotted from the world.' (I, 26, 27).

Is it not true that so many apparently religious people have little guard over the tongue? They go to Mass, the sacraments, and spend long periods in prayer, but discuss their neighbour in a critical and unfriendly manner. It seems to be a failing of so called 'pious people' not to mind their own business but to judge others, bringing odium on their 'piousness' by such uncharitable conduct. They can see the mote in a neighbour's eye but not the beam in their own eyes. Anyone not bridling his tongue, that man's religion is vain! The Apostle describing real religion, clean and undefiled, says nothing about religious observances, but simply demands acts of charity to a neighbour in need, and keeping one's self unspotted from the world, in other words keeping the commandments of God, the only criterion of love—'If you love me, keep my commandments.'

This then is the essence of religion; to know God through the intelligence: to fix the will on God by complete submission to his will; from these will spring our service proving the reality of our love for God, the keeping of his commandments, and the observance of the external rites commanded by God's Church as a part of the service of the whole being of man, body and soul. Be mindful though that these external observances are of themselves barren unless we are united to God in spirit and in truth. St John says: 'My little children, let us not love in word nor in tongue, but in deed and in truth.' External observance is not 'the end'—the object to be attained —but the 'means used' to strengthen us in grace and that essential union with God without which all else is lifeless and meaningless.

VI   THE NECESSITY OF RELIGION

A reasonable man is bound to admit the existence of a God, all-powerful, all-perfect, the supreme Being independent of all, on whom all else depends for its existence—the Creator. Admitting this, another step must be taken. Becoming conscious of another's existence, a man contracts some duty to this other, he must at least wish him well; if asked a civil question must give a civil answer. With fellow-workers a closer relationship is involved, since these cannot be ignored without failing in social duty. At home, the relationship becomes more sacred. As soon as a child is able to recognise his parents when reason wakes, he must recognise that he has received life from, been cared for, loved and provided for, by these same parents who are his natural refuge. Therefore he must show to them love, reverence, and obedience. Love and reverence must remain throughout life, neglect of these will be condemned by all right-thinking men. Yet these parents were not this child's creator, they were instruments used by God; they did not form his features, give him power to speak, to hear, to know, to love. God alone gives him existence as a reasonable being, and as such, his first reasonable duty is to admit this and to recognise that he has certain definite obligations towards his Creator which cannot be ignored and which he is bound to fulfil.

God has a definite purpose in creation and human beings have a very definite purpose in this scheme; hence we must know why man was made. In creation, we find that Nature obeys laws or follows instincts which never fail: the sun pursues its course with revolving satellites, tides rise and fall, animals follow their instincts. Man is bound also by certain natural laws, e.g. if he falls from a height, he is bound to drop until something prevents any further motion. But in many things he alone is free to choose how he will act. He finds there is a distinction between good and evil and by his free choice of one or the other, he fulfils, or fails to carry out, the purpose of his creation. As a reasonable being he has the duty to fulfil in creation of freely choosing to do good, and to

25

reject evil. This duty is 'religion' and is the bond between himself and his Creator.

Is it possible to lead a 'good life' without religion? If the purpose of man is to serve God consciously and of his own free choice, the man who does not attempt to do this cannot be 'good.' Many have no religion at all, but if these are consciously ignoring God, they cannot be 'good.' Reason must be subject to God if it admits his existence. A 'good' life is one in which man tries to find out and to practise his duty to God, his neighbour, and himself. Religion is the sum total of the truths and duties by which man's life is lived in accordance with the purpose of God. We find dogmas, precepts, and rites; dogmas are 'the truths taught'; precepts are the laws governing conduct, practical duty; rites are the outward expression of belief and service. On all these men disagree, hence are found sects warring against each other as to doctrine and morals, causing religion to be disparaged because so many are at variance on these points. In a small town may be found four or five chapels, two or three churches, all disagreeing on essentials, and a man may say that the voice of God cannot be heard among so many discordant teachings, so why bother about any religion? That is not a reasonable attitude; it does point to the necessity of religion among men. It is a remarkable thing to find so many chapels or churches in a small town; it indicates that religion is 'a universal fact' throughout the world which has been continuous since the beginning of man, when Cain and Abel were urged by their very nature to offer homage and sacrifice to God. The only explanation of this universality of religion in time and place is that human nature needs religion as an essential part of existence. Man craves for perfect happiness, and religion is the only thing that holds out any promise or attempt to lead this craving into its true course, i.e. towards God who alone can satisfy this natural craving for happiness to be fulfilled. Religion is necessary because we have a definite duty to God as our Creator. It is the link between us and God, the expression of our attitude to God. A man without religion is not acting reasonably but unjustly, because he does not pay his debt to his Creator.

26

What does a man reasonably owe to his Creator?

1 *Adoration.* By this is acknowledged the truth that God is the Creator and that all things belong to, and are dependent on, God alone. Man depends on God for his existence, and for its continuation, for every action, and final fulfilment. For a man to live as though he were an independent being is to pretend to be something which he is definitely not; to attempt to live without God is folly. Though all things depend on God, man has the faculties of intelligence and free-will; he is therefore bound to acknowledge God's sovereign dominion by a free and conscious act of adoration, not for himself alone, but for all created things on earth.

2 *Thanksgiving or gratitude.* By creating man, God became his benefactor from whom all gifts ultimately come so that there is nothing possessed by man which he has not received from God. By means of parents man receives his life and natural gifts, care, education, and love, but God gives him intelligence to know truth, power to love and enjoy, and all spiritual gifts. Only by an act of extreme folly could anyone claim life, condition, or happiness, to be their own unaided work, boasting of parentage, of qualities of mind and body as though he alone by his own efforts had chosen and brought about such conditions. No reasonable being can deny the obligation of returning thanks to God for favours received.

3 *Contrition.* There is nothing fine in sin! Unfortunately it is only too easy for anyone to sin, and all do at times. It is easy to live in a state of indifference to religion and its claims if one is thoughtless enough; the difficulty is not to sin. There is a duty to God, to one's neighbour, to one's self; the law of God is the eternal wisdom which insists that man shall carry out the purpose of his creation; if he refuses this with full knowledge and consent, he sins grievously. It is useless to speak of sin to one who refuses to admit that God has rights over man, or who considers sin only as an act that harms a neighbour. A man in whose life God has no place is guilty of injustice, ingratitude and folly. Since all sin at times, the duty of a man conscious of sin is contrition and repentance.

4 *Supplication.* God knows our needs, he does not require

27

to be told, he gives without the need of co-operation on our part, yet he has commanded us to pray—'Ask and you shall receive.' It is reasonable to use the power of prayer, to obey this command. God foresees all, knows all—prayer does not change God, but it changes us, making us fit to receive benefits. The humblest act of prayer is worship of God. If we pray for a fine day, or for help to find work, we make a practical acknowledgement of trust in tne power of God and dependence on him, for both the forces of Nature and the fickle will of man are ruled by God. Supplication fulfils the duty of acknowledging dependence on God for our needs.

Religion is the whole man; it is his nature to manifest his feelings by outward action. So religion must be expressed by the whole of man's being, body and soul. Man does not live as an isolated being, he must associate with his fellows, hence social life follows, implying not only personal rights but public duties. Merely individual religion is unreal; it is not sufficient to protest personal devotion, there is a duty to meet together for social worship. He who condenms social worship says: 'I will work, play, and feast with my fellows, but I will not worship God with them.' Such an attitude is unreasonable; society owes worship to God and must make public acknowledgement of that fact; it cannot be left to individual taste. Had God left no instructions, then the Public Authority would have the duty of determining the time and place of such worship. Man is bound to adore, to thank, to ask pardon, and to pray; the expression of these is a social duty as well as a personal one. Moreover a teacher is necessary. Man may find things out for himself or he may be taught, but few can find out their full duty to God, so a teacher is needed. Many claim that each must form his own mind about religion by private judgement; hence the chaos that exists about fundamental truths. Only the Creator can teach why man was created. God alone can tell how he wishes to be worshipped. If God has taught us, then that teaching is of strict obligation; our duty is to find the authority for handing on such teaching with divine sanction. The Bible, though hotly disputed on many points, professes to be a record of the fact that God did teach man. Christ came claiming divine authority to teach, proved it by miracles and by his resurrection from the dead. Any fraud in these matters would have destroyed christianity. Many teachers have risen setting themselves up as authorities to teach religion. A reasonable man must try to find out which is the authority guaranteed by God to have divine sanction as the teacher of divine truth.

We must know God as Creator, adore him, repent of evil, and ask for needs to be supplied; as a member of society man must express dependence by social worship and as a reasonable being follow the true religion. Man must give to God his 'reasonable service.'

VII GOD

From the dawning of man's existence there has been an innate recognition of some Being, or Beings, transcending in power and nature everything that man felt about his own power and nature. Something in man forced on him the idea of a power controlling and ordering his existence which he was powerless to alter, so that he was compelled in one way or another to acknowledge this higher power. To escape from evils, or to obtain benefits, man felt the urge to make offerings for self-protection from evil or deliverance from calamity; also to obtain some benefit which he was unable to procure for himself. This seemed to point to more than one Supreme Power, otherwise how account for good and evil? Thus man felt that there must be powers of evil as well as powers of good, so he came to believe in many deities. With this belief came the idea of offering sacrifices to propitiate these good or evil deities, especially those hostile to man, by the slaughter of animals or the fruit of the earth, and in extreme cases by the sacrifice of human beings. Thus were instituted gods expressing various ideas of necessities, dangers, or fruitfulness in Nature.

The Chosen People, who held to the one true God, feared him; he was the awful Being who would punish, whose very Name must not be uttered, who visited disobedience with death, whose law must be obeyed in fear and trembling. That was one view of God, though by no means a complete one.

To know God, his perfection, his relationship to us, is our first and chief duty. Our knowledge of God depends therefore on our ideas of him. We all believe in one God, but we have not necessarily the same ideas of him, and our own ideas express what God means to each of us personally. Hence it is a very personal question 'What is my idea of God?' That depends on our personal knowledge. Though we all believe in one infinite all-powerful, all-knowing God, does the word 'GOD' express an identical idea in each mind? As far as revealed truth is concerned we may answer 'Yes,' but much is left for us to discover for ourselves in Nature, in the works of God, in our own experience, so that the idea of God may differ widely in each mind apart from revealed truths.

1 *'Master, thou art a hard man and reapest where thou hast not sown.'* That is a prevalent idea of God, that of a tyrant who must be obeyed, whom like slaves we serve grudgingly under pain of eternal punishment with a service which consists mostly in not doing those very things which are most attractive and easiest to our nature, in which we delight and expect to find happiness, things he made enjoyable to us only to forbid them. He demands much that is irksome and difficult to nature. A God who made ten commandments to deprive us of contentment in life; who delights in pain and suffering; who, like a cat watching a mouse, is ready to pounce and strike with sudden death and hell anyone who dares to sin against his hard laws.

This is an extreme view, yet expressing more or less what many feel about God. What sort of love will spring from such a concept? It will be a poor sort of love unworthy of the name, being forced by fear, a service of slavery, like that of slaves under the bondage of sin. They who try to serve God in this way attempt to live on the border line of sin, trying to serve as little as possible, trying to keep just short of sin, failing miserably in the attempt, yet fearing to be struck by death and damnation. There could be no happiness in such an idea of God. Not many perhaps would have so extreme a view, but many are unconsciously tinged with such ideas.

How unworthy is such a concept of God! How utterly at variance with the true idea of a God infinitely merciful and indulgent to his creatures.

2 *'I will arise and go unto my Father.'* God—our Father! This is another idea of God and the only true one: fatherhood, with all the loving care which such a title involves; one to whom we are in truth children, to be loved though wayward and disobedient, to be cared for, provided for in all the needs of life, guided through difficulties, protected from dangers; one who turns all to our good, knowing what is best, turning even

31

pain and sorrow into benefits; who, should he punish, does so with loving mercy but to draw us back again to himself, in whom alone we can find lasting happiness. Certainly he has forbidden certain things to us, all too attractive to fallen nature, not because he would deprive us of joy but because such things are harmful and, if permitted to us, would make life impossible. The ten commandments are proof of his infinite wisdom and loving care. Take one away, and life would become chaos. If children were not obliged to obey and honour their parents, there could be no family life, no discipline, no authority. If killing were allowed there could be no sanctity of human life, all would go in fear of being murdered. If stealing were permitted we should be obliged to spend all our time protecting our possessions. If we could say what we chose, no one's character would be safe. Need we say more? It is self-evident that these commandments make life livable and give us peace. Yet how often for the whim of a moment we disobey these reasonable laws. Does God watch us ready to strike if we sin? 'God wills not the death of the sinner but rather that he be converted and live.' Our own experience proves that we receive mercy or long ago we should have been punished. How many times have we sinned and been called back to repentance? May it not be that God takes us when we are best prepared to go to judgement? It would certainly be in accordance with his mercy. How little we understand the wonderful providence and fatherly care of God. Life goes smoothly on, we have all we need, but seldom reflect whence all comes. If for one instant God withheld his care, we should become non-existent. We must learn all we can of God's infinite love and goodness to wayward man. Whence shall we learn this?

Philip said to Jesus: 'Lord show us the Father and it is enough for us.' Jesus saith: 'Philip, he that seeth me, seeth the Father also.' By the study of the life of Christ on earth, we learn of God. Can we read of the wonderful kindness shown to sinners, the compassion which cured the sick and maimed, of his hunger for men who did not believe his word, and reading not understand the infinite love of Jesus for men? His gentleness, self-forgetfulness for others, the readiness at all times to help others, present to us a picture of what God is in himself. We do not always understand that Jesus by his words and acts was teaching us 'to know God.' He himself told us that what he was doing with all this kindness, this compassion for human weakness was showing us the reality of God himself: 'The Father, who abideth in me, he doeth the works.' It is as though Jesus had said: 'I am showing to you what God is; what I feel for men is what God feels for men; what I do to relieve human affliction is what God does; if you know me, you know God himself.' Could we ever doubt the infinite love and compassion of Jesus for men? Could he have given greater proofs of love? 'Greater love than this no man hath, that he lay down his life for his friends.' God laid down his life for us, to give us the greatest possible proof of his infinite love for fallen men. Did he not say: 'My desire is to be with the children of men?' He gave us himself to be the food of our souls, our daily bread to strengthen us against our own human weakness, promised to be with us all days to the end of the world. Whatever he did was done for us, is still done for us, by God himself. To know Jesus Christ is to know God; we cannot separate the two, for God is one, indivisible. The human love of Jesus for men is the expression of divine love itself. Only by meditating on the life and love of Jesus, can we come to a fuller knowledge of the love of God for his creatures. Through Jesus we learn a truer deeper idea of the perfection of God, of his infinite lovableness, and thus are led to a truer devotion and submission to his service.

Everything round us speaks of the wonder of God. The beauty of nature, the hills, trees, running brooks, the colour of flowers in bloom, the charm of young things, all teach us something of the wonder of God since he is the source of all beauty and attraction, other things being mere faint reflections of the attractiveness and lovableness of God, since all of these things come from him alone. God is love!

Since the idea we nave of God necessarily influences our service of him, it is obvious that we must form the truest possible concept of God, and this in turn depends on our knowledge of all his infinite perfection. God is not a hard taskmaster mercilessly driving us like slaves, but an infinitely loving Father. Between these two concepts of God there are many shades of variation, one of which forms the personal idea in the mind of each of us. We must ask whether our idea approaches the true one of God's fatherhood or whether it tends towards the idea of tyranny. We must meditate chiefly on the life of Jesus, and by a personal love for him, be attracted more and more to a real personal love for God, transcending all other attractions in life. Only thus shall we truly love God with all the power of our being, and by a loving childlike service of him, win for ourselves the eternal happiness of the vision of God in heaven. 'I will arise and go unto my Father.'

VIII THE LOVE OF GOD

'Thou shalt love the Lord thy God, with thy whole heart, and with thy whole soul, and thy whole mind, and with thy whole strength. This is the first commandment' (Mark XII, 30). Since God made us and we are his, he has above all others the right to our love; he has a further right because of his infinite love for us, his many gifts, and the desire he has for our eternal happiness. Love for God is a strict obligation and we must love him: (1) *With our whole heart*. This means sincerely and thoroughly, excluding any rebellion by desire or affection contrary to his law—'He that loveth father or mother more than me, is not worthy of me.' (2) *With our whole soul*, i.e. with all the faculties we have, memory, understanding and will, subject to the divine law, and all our sensible and vital powers must act in accordance with his ordinances. (3) *With all our mind*, by love, understanding and will so that love is reasoned and deliberate, and the intelligence submissive to his revelations by faith. All our thoughts and intentions should be directed to God. (4) *With all our strength*, so that our bodily powers are used according to his will. All our actions should be for his service, subjecting all passions and emotions to his commands.

All this means that God must hold the supreme place in our love so that he comes first in all; we must prefer him to all else and be willing to lose all rather than act against him, or cease to love him. The love demanded is efficacious and sincere keeping the whole being loyal to God in himself, and in his image, man's neighbour. Most people need to be reassured about the nature of the love of God. So much are we influenced by feelings or emotions that we are apt to judge of our love for God by fleeting emotions and often we hear it said: 'I do not feel that I love God.' Because of this, it is feared that the love of God is not real and sincere. There appears to be a great contrast between the love we have for God and the love we have for parents, friends, and others. This contrast gives the impression that our love for God is not as great as it ought to be. We 'feel' love for human beings;

we do not 'feel' love for God; therefore we conclude that God does not hold the supreme place in our love. The reason is because love for other human beings is usually, at least in part, a physical love causing reflex action within us, such as a quicker beating of the heart, excitement at the approach of the beloved, great joy in the presence of the loved one; yet we do not experience these emotions in the love of God since it is spiritual. The physical feelings need not enter into it at all. The love of God may be described as an unemotional act of the will putting God in the first place so that no other love can influence us to do what is contrary to God's law. The real test of love has been given to us by our Lord himself: 'If you love me, keep my commandments.' That is the acid test of love for God, the standard by which it must be judged.

It may happen that we have a great love for some person so that we feel ready to do anything for him, but the test comes when there is a temptation to go against the law of God for the sake of the beloved. Suppose a youth in love with a maid is asked by her to go walking on a Sunday morning which would entail his missing mass, what will he do? Will he choose to go for the walk to please her, miss mass and displease God; or will he refuse to go walking, displease the maid but do his duty to God by going to mass? His choice will show at once whom he puts first in his love. If it does happen that the demands of two loves run contrary to each other and there is a temptation to disobey God to please the human lover, then comes the test of love for God: 'If you love me, keep my commandments.' If we do our duty to God by resisting the temptations then we put him in the first place; if on the other hand we choose to please the human being, then God is put in the second place and we sin against him; we do not love him with our whole heart. What we 'feel' does not in the least matter; it is what we do that is the test.

Two kinds of love can be distinguished: (a) affective love and (b) appreciative love. The first is contented and happy to love without questioning WHY? or considering any motive for loving. It might be described as an emotional warmth of feeling which may vary, or even cease if the one loved prove

36

to be disloyal or dishonourable. It is probably the commonest type of love, and accounts for the frequent changes in affection of persons towards each other. It rests on the unstable foundations of feeling or emotion, being a non-reasonable love which may be excited by a fancied attraction in some other. What is called 'love at first sight' is of this type, since it can have no foundation in reason or knowledge. True love depends on knowledge, and will either increase or decrease as knowledge becomes more informed as to the qualities of the person loved. Appreciative love is the deliberate choosing and adhesion of the will to an object that is good to the intellectual perception—it definitely depends on knowledge in the first place. It is a calm, even cold, attachment based on judgement and esteem; if the esteem holds supreme place, the love will also be supreme. As knowledge increases, so will the love increase provided the first judgement was based on a correct estimation of the one loved.

It is this latter type of love which we must give to God. It may easily be less intense than affective love, not so ready to sacrifice self, may not bring any emotional joy, but it is lasting and reliable. It is also much more earnest, because deeper and more reasoned, bringing a firm adhesion of the will to the beloved. There may be little or no emotional feeling in it, no physical reflexes—it might be called cold and deliberate since it depends entirely on an act of the will. Hence appreciative love is an act of the will independent of emotion but formed by knowledge inducing a reasoned judgement. That is why we are told that God made us 'to know him' in the first place and through knowledge the will is moved to act and adhere to him or 'to love him.'

True love is active, not merely passive, and needs to express itself in action, therefore 'to serve.' 'If a man give all he has for love, he counts it as nothing.' Love is the most powerful of all motives, leading to self-sacrifice and finding joy even in suffering for the beloved. Hence our whole duty is 'to know God, to love him and to serve him' by keeping his commandments.

What then does it mean to love God above all? In the first

place it means that hatred of God such as is felt by those who wish there were no God, must be unthinkable, abhorrent to us. Next it means the total avoidance of mortal sin by which a creature is preferred to God. Mortal sin is the total aversion of the soul from God, and though it may not be hatred of God, yet it is utterly opposed to friendship with him. Actual love for God may be (a) the love of gratitude by which we love God 'for our own sake' because of his goodness to us. There is something of self-seeking in this love since the motive is that we benefit by God's goodness to us; it is selfish in that we love for what we get rather than for the lovableness of God in himself; or (b) the love of friendship or charity by which God is loved for himself alone with no thought for self. God deserves to be loved in this way since everything that we find good and lovable in creatures, everything that can attract us or that we admire in others, is but a faint reflection of the attraction and lovableness of God, who is the source of all the qualities that attract our love to creatures. If we find creatures lovable, much more ought we to find lovableness in God, the source of all perfection of whatever kind it be.

Hence in love for God, no account need be taken of the absence of any feeling or emotion; we do not need to 'feel' that we love God, for the emotions are no criterion of love for God. The real test is always: 'If you love me, keep my commandments.' That is the standard by which our love will be judged, by which we ourselves can judge how great or how little love we have for God. It is an act of the will founded on knowledge which deliberately chooses God before all and puts him first always. It is the absolute opposite to mortal sin. It may seem cold and calculating to us, who are swayed so much by our emotions, so apt to judge by what we feel and thereby to imagine that we have but little love for God; but the test is our submission to his will: 'Thy will be done.'

True, at times we may feel some spiritual joy or consolation but this is no test by which to judge our loyalty or reliability, our steadfast adherence to God, since at the next temptation we may fail and sin against God through human weakness. The absence of emotional feelings is known as 'spiritual dryness' and was experienced by many saints, but none the less their love was real and true. Indeed this unemotional state which chooses to put God in the first place no matter what it costs, to resist all temptation, to do penance for sin, to suffer and yet cling to God steadfastly and faithfully, is what proves the truth and reality of love for God. Such must be the love we give to him: to put God first and never count the cost, to suffer all rather than be unfaithful or disloyal in the slightest degree.

'If you love me, keep my commandments.'

IX   THE HOLY TRINITY

Of all mysteries the Unity and Trinity in God is the most difficult to explain or understand; it appears to be contradictory. The feebleness of the human mind is unable to grasp so marvellous a truth. Were it not that God himself revealed this truth, no man would dare propose the statement that the same thing should be one, yet three. Only by degrees was this revealed; so stupendous a truth had perforce to be unfolded little by little to finite understanding, so that the mind could be accustomed to the idea of more than one Person in God. To the Jews, God had always been one, terrible, almighty whose very Name must not be uttered by men. In the Sermon on the Mount, our Lord speaks many times of 'Your father who is in heaven' showing the fatherhood of God to men. He goes on to claim this father as his own: 'Every one that shall confess me before men, I also will confess him before MY father, who is in heaven,' 'I came to do the will of my father.' He next proclaims: 'The father and I are ONE!' Philip saith to him: 'Lord show us the father and it is enough.' Jesus saith to him 'Philip, he that seeth me, seeth the father also. How sayest thou show us the Father? Do you not believe that I am in the Father and the Father in me?'   Thus was unfolded the dual personality, that of the Father and the Son, two Persons yet one with each other, inseparable, co-equal. What a revolution in thought! Later our Lord speaks of another Person: 'I will ask the Father and he shall give you another Paraclete that he may abide with you for ever: the Spirit of Truth, whom the world cannot receive because it seeth him not, nor knoweth him.' 'But the Holy Ghost whom the Father will send in my name, he will teach you all things.' So was the idea of yet a third personality instilled into the minds of the disciples. The full idea of the Trinity was taught when the final commission was given to the Apostles: 'Going therefore, teach ye all nations; baptising them in the name of the Father, and of the Son, and of the Holy Ghost.' What a marvellous truth! God—One and Three—the Holy Trinity.

How explain what cannot be explained? How in the feeble

human tongue, which has so many limitations in expression, seek to expound so sublime a mystery? Yet haltingly we may attempt to find some sort of explanation of the unexplainable, though we must speak in terms of time of what knows not time.

It is true to say that I know myself better than any other human being can know me; in my mind I have an idea of myself, my nature, my aspirations, my talents, my limitations, all that is 'ME.' I might call this idea of myself 'the child of my mind, begotten in my mind,' as we speak of an invention as being the child of a man's brain. If I wish to give outward expression to this idea, this image of myself, I must express it in words, in sound, which momentarily has a separate existence of its own but which is 'ME' expressed and perceptible to others—a 'word-image' of myself.

Let us apply this notion to God the Father. He has a perfect idea of himself, his capabilities, perfections, all that he IS, begotten in his own divine intelligence, duplicating himself in the minutest perfection, so that it is a completely perfect image. To this image, he gives a separate expression in the 'WORD,' as we read in the Gospel: 'In the beginning was the Word, and the Word was with God, and the Word WAS God.' Hence there was the perfect image of the Father, the Word expressed, begotten in the intelligence of the Father so that he is the 'Only Begotten Son.' This image of the Father was the Father anew in all perfections. Whatever could be said of the Father could equally be said of the Word who was a perfect duplicate of the Father but with the sole difference of relationship of Son to Father, exactly the same, but separate in personality; as the Father is God, almighty, all-holy, all-perfect, omniscient, so also is the Son in every minutest detail.

In thus endeavouring to explain this mystery, the terms of time have had perforce to be used as though the Father first existed and subsequently expressed himself in the Word. But any such impression of an interval or lapse of time is contrary to revealed truth. From all eternity there was no single instant when the Father had not this perfect idea or image of himself, not a moment when this Word was not expressed. There was no beginning in begetting the Word, who is eternal as the Father, who was, is, and always shall be.

To return to the example of self, just as I know myself, so because of this knowledge, I love myself. It is a fact that each one loves self with an absorbing love; it is natural for us to do so. If that 'word-image' of myself could exist as a separate reality apart from me, I should love it, because it is 'myself' in another form. My 'word-image' would also love me in the same way, because the two are identical; this love would be flowing continually between my image and myself.

Applying this truth as far as may be to God, the Father loves himself and all his own infinite perfections; hence he is impelled to love the Word, his second self, his only begotten Son. The Father loves the Son with an infinitely perfect love. Likewise the Son loves the Father in an equal and identical manner; this mutual love which needs two for its existence is eternal between the Father and the Son. This Love, which is neither the Father, nor the Son, has a separate Personality yet is essentially identical in every particular with the Father and the Son, having the same nature, attributes and perfections of both, and this personified love of God the Father and God the Son is the Holy Spirit, the Holy Ghost, the third Person of the Blessed Trinity, himself God, for God is Love. So we have the divine Trinity, three yet one, differing only by relationship or mode of existence—God begetting, God begotten, God loving and loved, the Father, the Son, and the Holy Ghost.

That there should be three persons in God with but a single nature is of course no mystery. There are not merely three but millions of human persons with but one human nature. But that each of these three Persons in God should be God in his entirety, that they should not only share the nature of God as a man shares with other men in human nature, but should each absorb (as it were) the whole of the divine nature in his person; here is the profound mystery of faith that no amount of reasoning or thought can begin to understand.

Why did God reveal this astounding mystery? Surely not just to puzzle us, to test the submission of our intelligence to him? God does nothing in vain. This mystery was revealed because the Holy Trinity is so intimately connected with all our life. To God the Father is ascribed the attribute of power, the Father almighty; to the Son begotten in the divine intelligence that of wisdom; to the Holy Ghost that of love.

These three are inseparable: power, wisdom, love. We cannot have power acting alone, it must be in conjunction with wisdom, because of love. Nothing ever happens to us which is not the will of all three, the whole of our life is ordered by them. Everything that happens in the world does so by power, guided by wisdom, and influenced by love. Always we can go on unafraid in perfect trust and confidence in the goodness of God who because of his infinite love for us permits only what is for our good; even the mistakes of men are turned into good for the whole world by the wise, loving power of God.

If we live by faith and believe in the Holy Trinity, we must accept all that comes as being in some way for our ultimate good. How could it be otherwise when infinite wisdom directs, infinite love permeates, all that is brought about or permitted by infinite power? Should not this be our comfort in distress, when all seems dark and foreboding in the future, when temptation presses hard, to know that we are sustained by power, wisdom and love in all things? The thought of the Holy Trinity should be our help in all the trials of life. How can we be anything but grateful for whatever comes upon us; why criticise or complain when God visits us with pain or hardship knowing that it is in some way, hidden perhaps from us, for our real good and eternal happiness? Shall we not walk in confidence, even through the valley of death, with perfect trust in the Holy Trinity that guides us through all, though to us it be obscure?

The revelation of this mystery was given that it might be our hope, giving confidence throughout life, helping us to believe that nothing but what is good can befall us because power, directed by wisdom and infused with infinite love, is guarding us from all real evil. Our life is so intimately connected with this greatest of mysteries that it is essential for us to realise its truth and the influence it exerts over our whole existence. Let us thank God that he has made known to us the wonder of himself and break forth into praise of the Holy Trinity.

Glory be to the Father and to the Son and to the Holy Ghost, thrice blessed Three in One.

X THE MYSTICAL BODY OF CHRIST

Writing to the Corinthians (XII, 27), St Paul insists: 'You are the body of Christ and members of member.' He had illustrated his meaning by using the human body as an example. He points out diversities of operations, ministries, graces, showing how the various members of the Church have their special duties. He continues: 'For as the body is one and hath many members and all the members of the body, whereas they are many, yet are one body, so also is Christ. For the body also is not one member but many. If the foot should say because I am not the hand, I am not of the body, is it therefore not of the body? And if the ear should say because I am not the eye, I am not of the body, is it not therefore of the body? If the whole body were the eye where would be the hearing; if the whole body were the hearing, where would be the smell? But now God hath set the members every one of them in the body as it hath pleased him; and if they were all one member where would be the body? and the eye cannot say to the hand I need not thy help, nor again the head to the feet I need not thy help.' Thus St Paul shows how all the members depend one on another that there might be no schism in the body but that the members might be mutually careful of one another: 'and if any member suffer anything, all the members suffer with it; and if any member glory, all the members rejoice with it.' In this way we are given an insight into the meaning of the Mystical Body of Christ.

Men need to know the purpose of their lives and the laws by which they must order their lives, but can do so only by revelation from God. Men have to live not merely naturally, but super-naturally with a life that is above that of their human nature and comes as a grace from God alone. Hence there is need of the TRUTH to know God, the WAY in which to love and serve God and the LIFE to live according to the law of God. By offering the sacrifice of atonement, Christ regained for the human race that heaven should be re-opened to it: moreover he brought the gifts of the truth, the way, and the life that were needed. He gathered together a body of disciples,

44

taught them and gave them a commision to teach these truths, promulgate laws and administer sacraments by which the life might flow into the souls of men. This commission was extended to all nations and was to survive till the end of time. These followers, united under the primacy of Peter, were to be one body, and in that body to receive infallible teaching because Christ would be with them, and to receive the life-giving sacraments through Christ. Hence Christ says: 'I am the WAY, the TRUTH, and the LIFE.' He does not say 'I have' but 'I am.' Christ is the LIFE, that life which must live in all men, if they are to attain to heaven. Christ must live in men, as in St Paul who could say: I live, now not I, but Christ liveth in me.' Christ must live in us; we must live in him. In our body we find a clue to this life. The body is composed of individual cells living together the life of the body; the body is living in the cells which live with the life of the body but there is but 'one life.' The body is not a number of distinct cells each with its own individual life, but one life vivifies the whole, each cell sharing in the one life. In a similar manner we must be in the Mystical Body of Christ as the cells in a human body, and Christ must be the 'ONE LIFE' flowing through and vivifying each and every cell, or individual, who together form the mystical body which is the Church.

St Paul works out this idea clearly. Christ living on earth had a human body through which he worked among men; he taught with his lips, healed with his hands, made atonement with his body; but all this was done by God himself. Though Christ had two natures, one human, the other divine, he had only ONE personality, the divine personality of the Son of God. Nature gives the source or principle of action. Thus if it is asked 'What is crying?' the answer would be 'the shedding of tears,' that is the nature of crying. Personality gives the responsibility of action; so if it is asked 'Who is crying?' the answer might be 'the child is crying,' i.e. the child is responsible for the crying. Action belongs not to the nature, but to the personality, hence it is the divine person, Jesus, who is God, that acts and is responsible for all the actions of his human nature.

45

Christ has left this earth in human form, but he still works among men—not in his physical body, but in his Mystical Body of which he is the head and the life. This Mystical Body was brought into life in the Upper Room by the power of the Holy Ghost, who is the soul of the Mystical Body which is the Church.

The Church then is Christ's body linked to him really, inseparably, as a body to its head. Life flows through the Church as life flows through the human body; as man lives in his individual cells, so Christ lives in the individual cells of his Mystical Body. His Church is mysteriously, yet really, his body. To become a member of the Church means being built into his body, being 'incorporated' in him. Once we are thus incorporated we are cells in the Mystical Body and Christ can live in us. Hence Christ considers that whatever is done to one of the members is done to himself. Christ says to Saul the persecutor: 'Saul, Saul, why persecutest thou, me?' Saul asks: 'Who art thou, Lord?' Christ answers: 'I am Jesus, whom thou persecutest.' Thus Christ declares that the Church is his body. He does not ask why do you persecute the Church, but why do you persecute 'ME?' In striking the body, you strike at the head; Christ and the Church are one person. Just as the tongue speaks if the leg is struck and I ask 'Why do you strike me (not my leg)?' So when any member of the Church is injured, Christ speaks as though it were himself injured. All this follows from the perfect unity between Christ and the Church, for which he prayed 'that they all may be one, as thou Father in me and I in thee: that they also may be one in us.' 'That they may be one as we also are one. I in them, and thou in me that they may be made perfect in one.' No closer unity could be imagined. That is why Christ so desires that charity be the distinguishing mark of his disciples, why we must love one another even as Christ has loved us. Hence the words—'I am the way, the truth, and the life,' mean that 'to be in the way' we must be in him; to possess truth, we must possess him; to have the life, he must live in us and we in him. As all men were incorporated in Adam by nature, so all men are incorporated in Christ by supernature, not by birth but by baptism: 'Being baptised in Christ, we have put on Christ.' So all needs are met by incorporation in the Mystical Body; we share in Christ's atonement, are reconciled to God, and heaven is thrown open to us.

This Mystical Body is a growing body; it has as members not only those living on earth, but also all who have died, in the supernatural life. A new member is a new cell, so this body is continually growing as a human body grows until full development is reached, to which point the Mystical Body is also tending. There is a purpose for the whole race, as for the individual. Thus the Church presents a double aspect. In so far as it is Christ living in men for the teaching of truth and moral law, for the giving of life in the sacraments, it is perfect: in so far as it consists of human members living the life of the body, or not living by it because of sin, it is always short of perfection. Hence we have to live our life not as isolated units, but as members of a living Body united with Christ and with all men in the world, or beyond death, who love God because all are members of Christ's Body. We are also 'one with each other,' one member can help another. If the foot be hurt, the hand can tend it; so in the Mystical Body, we help each other by prayer, teaching or by sacrifice.

Within this Body, death makes no difference. The dead are not less members, but rather living more intensely in the life of Christ in which we all share. By baptism we are built into this Body. We speak of baptism as re-birth and birth means entry into life. By birth we enter into the life of man; by re-birth in baptism we enter into the life of Christ; equally the life of Christ enters into us: 'Unless a man be born again of water and the Holy Ghost, he cannot enter into the kingdom of heaven.' Thus the member of Christ's Church is not an isolated unit; he is a living cell in a living body and as such has a special relationship with Christ, whose life flows through every cell of this Mystical Body so long as that cell is living in the supernatural life of grace. This life may be flowing fully, partially, or not at all, according to the state of the individual cell, since a member though retaining faith, may not be vivified by charity because of sin.

One thing stands out clearly and that is the complete unity that must exist in this Body founded on the rock that is Peter. There is only 'One Lord, one Faith, one Baptism.' All must believe the same teaching, observe the same moral law, and receive the same sacraments—the way, the truth and the life— in communion with the See of Peter, Christ's Vicar on earth: 'He that heareth you, heareth me.'

To realise this truth is to understand the personal relationship that exists between each member of the true Church, to live in him and by him, so that with St Paul we can each one of us exclaim:

'I live, now not I, but Christ liveth in me.'

XI THE MYSTICAL BODY—IN THE MEMBERS

Our divine Lord himself teaches the truth of the unity that must exist between himself and his members in the Mystical Body, by using the vine as a simile. He says (Jn. XV. 1): 'I am the true vine . . . abide in me and I in you. As the branch cannot bear fruit of itself unless it abide in the vine so neither can you unless you abide in me. I am the vine, you are the branches: he that abideth in me, and I in him, the same beareth much fruit: for without me, you can do nothing. If anyone abide not in me he shall be cast forth as a branch and shall wither, and they shall gather him up and cast him into fire and he burneth.' This teaching plainly shows how much we depend on the Christ-life flowing through each member. We are to receive all our life from him; we cannot bear fruit unless the divine sap of the true vine is flowing through us: 'I am the LIFE.' True, we may be attached to the vine and yet be a dead branch that receives no life from the vine; the sap does not flow and there can be no fruit since we are powerless apart from Christ to do any good of ourselves.

Reverting to the human body as the example, it is possible for certain cells in the body to cease sharing the life of the whole. A limb may become partially or wholly paralysed and though still attached physically to the body cease to live the life of the body; being no longer controlled by the head, it has no common function with the rest of the body and the healthy cells; to all intents and purposes it is dead though still attached. A worse state may occur, like a condition of cancer, in which some cells break away from the life of the body, and live a life of their own, preying on and destroying other cells, absorbing these into the same diseased state, thus affecting the whole body. In a similar manner in the Mystical Body, individuals are found who, because of mortal sin, have ceased to be vivified by the life of Christ which, by their own act and choice, has ceased to flow in the soul. They are spiritually paralysed by the loss of charity; they are still attached by faith to the Mystical Body but are no longer living the life of that Body, receive no benefits from it, and this state will persist so long as the state of sin persists.

Just as the human body can be restored to health and cured of illness by proper remedies thus regaining full participation in all the bodily functions and life, so the soul by the remedy of sincere repentance, a turning back to God, can be restored to charity, and the life of Christ once again flows through that soul which now shares in full the life of the Mystical Body. Unless there is such return to health by repentance, this dead cell must inevitably be cut off from the Body and lose God for all eternity. An even worse state arises when an individual member becomes as a cancer in the Mystical Body, not only losing his own life but dragging others with him into his own deadly sickness. This is brought about by scandal or bad-example, by heretical teachings, inducing others to forfeit the life of Christ and to participate in the death of sin. No wonder is it that Christ so strongly condemns the sin of scandal: 'Woe to the world because of scandals. For it must needs be that scandals come but nevertheless woe to that man by whom the scandal cometh. If thy hand scandalize thee cut it off.' (Matt.: XVIII. 7).'Whosoever shall scandalize one of these little ones that believe in me, it were better for him that a millstone were hanged about his neck and he were cast into the sea' (Mark IX, 41). Woe indeed to the sinner who by his example, or by his teaching, like a cancer in the Mystical Body, destroys the life of Christ in other cells of the Mystical Body of Christ.

Since the well-being or illness of each cell affects in some way the whole body, so the acts of the individual member have an effect on the whole Mystical Body for good or evil, causing greater or less perfection in the whole. Hence we are told that 'there is joy among the angels on one sinner doing penance.' The reinvigorating of a single cell that has been ailing causes a corresponding healthiness in the whole body, and that is what the repentance of one sinner means, giving joy to the angels. Thus the good actions of an individual member bring a blessing on the whole body, even as the evil actions deprive it of perfection or health. If the finger gently scratch an irritating spot on the leg, it brings relief to the whole body; so a kindly act to another member brings a corresponding blessing to the whole of the members. We have Christ's declaration for this: 'Whatsoever you do to one of these the least of my brethren, you do it to me.' The whole body is benefited or damaged by our act. Again in St Mark (IX, 40) : 'For whosoever shall give you to drink a cup of water in MY name because you belong to Christ: Amen I say to you he shall not lose his reward.' In giving a description of the Judgment, Christ brings this out very clearly, showing how we shall be judged by the way we treated him in the members of his body. He declares (Matt.: XXV, 34): 'Then shall the King say to them that shall be on his right hand: Come ye blessed of my Father, possess you the kingdom prepared for you . . . . for I was hungry and you gave me to eat, thirsty and you gave me to drink, naked and you clothed me . . . Then shall the just answer Lord when did we see thee hungry and gave thee to eat, thirsty and gave thee to drink, etc. Then the King shall answer them: Amen I say to you as long as you did it to one of these my least brethren, you did it to me. Then he shall say to them also that shall be on his left hand: depart from me ye cursed . . . for I was hungry and you gave me not to eat, thirsty and you gave me not to drink . . . Then shall they also say: Lord when did we see thee hungry and gave thee not to eat, or thirsty . . . or naked . . . and ministered not to thee? Then shall he answer them saying: Amen as long as you did it not to one of these least, neither did you do it to me.'

Could we find any statement more impressive to show how Christ identifies himself with each least member of his Mystical Body? Whatever we do, either good or ill to the least member, Christ takes it as being directed to himself. Therefore everyone must love his neighbour as himself, i.e. no one may be excluded from charity under any circumstances; we must be ready to serve all. Though a limb be paralysed, it is yet the care of the body to be treated with tenderness because of its very affliction and helplessness, even though it cannot feel such care; so we must treat all men with kindness and charity lest we offend against Christ himself, and the ailing members need all the tenderness we can bestow on them. When we begin to realise all the implications of the Mystical Body, how

Christ identifies himself with each member, we understand the reason for the command to love our neighbour as ourselves and that everyone without exception is our neighbour as an actual, or at least a potential, member of the Mystical Body. So the Church lives by the life of Christ flowing through each cell or individual member, one of another, so that all can say with St Paul: 'I live, now not I, but Christ liveth in me.'

The greater the realisation of this truth, the fuller the knowledge of the idea of the Mystical Body of Christ, the more we appreciate the dignity of being a member of it, the more we feel our personal responsibility to the whole Church, understand the value of our meritorious acts and have a higher ideal of the duty of charity towards all men, and especially to those 'who are of the household of the faith.' We also have a new idea of personal relationship with Christ himself. Moreover the Holy Ghost is better appreciated because he is the 'soul' of the Church, which is the Body of Christ. Not only does the Holy Ghost dwell in the Church and in each of the just as in a temple, but he is the principle of cohesion, of movement, of life. 'Know ye not that ye are the temples of the Holy Ghost?' The Church was fully constituted on the day of Pentecost when the Holy Spirit, descending on the Church, vivified it, unified it and strengthened it. Thus the Church was constituted with Christ as the head, the Holy Ghost as the soul, and the individual members as the body. There was 'one body and one spirit.' As St Augustine says: 'What the soul is to the body of man, that the Holy Ghost is to the Body of Christ, which is the Church.'

Great indeed is the dignity of the members of Christ's Mystical Body, and all would grow in personal holiness if all could but realise how intimately each and everyone is united to Christ the head. All would assume a new aspect, our charity would become full of meaning; we should recognise in each other a membership of one united body in which each individual is to be cherished, to be helped by prayer and good works, to be served in all kindness with the avoiding of all the uncharitable and harmful spirit of criticism of others.

Just as each member of the human body cares for the well-being of the whole, directed to this by the head, so we ought to be ready and prepared to serve and help all others in any way in which they may need our assistance, or at very least we must refrain from anything in any degree harmful to another. Hence is laid on us the precept to love our neighbour as ourselves, because we are one with Christ and each other in one united body. Hence the new commandment: 'That you love one another even as I have loved you. By this shall all men know that you are my disciples, because you love one another.'

'I live, now not I, but Christ liveth in me.'

XII THE HOLY SOULS

To be a member of the Mystical Body of Christ imposes certain obligations among which is a practical belief in the communion of saints, which to many is little more than a formula of words. The Church, which is the Body of Christ, comprises three distinct parts: the Church triumphant in heaven; the Church militant on earth; and the Church suffering in purgatory—a trinity that is also a unity, united in one communion with definite obligations of mutual regard and aid, passing continually between the parts. Does belief in this communion amount to more than a pious sentiment? Does it produce action, a recognition of duties to be done? If we really accept this communion of saints, then we must realise its true functions.

Probably we pray to certain saints for whom we have some devotion shown by the choice we make of them as intercessors for us with God, whom we ask for favours to be obtained by their prayers. But do we go beyond this? Each member works for the whole body; all members share both joy and pain; toothache makes the whole body feel miserable, though the pain is felt in one member only; if the ear is delighted with music, the whole of the body is pleased. So must it be in the Church; each member working for the good of the whole, mutual sympathy should exist among all the members. St Paul writes: 'If one member suffer anything, all the members suffer with it; or if one member glory, all the members rejoice with it.' Thus the saints in heaven are not indifferent to our condition, they are ready to intercede with God for our benefit, to beg for the favours we ask, to rejoice in our good works. All the members share in the good works, the spiritual help of prayers, and the sacrifice of the Mass. The saints alone need no help. Just as people in a country share in the institutions supported by the country, hospitals, homes, law-courts, etc, so in the Church all the good works of individuals benefit the whole Church. Do we understand our grave duty in taking our share in the obligation to help all who are in any need? What do we do for the Holy Souls in purgatory? They are just as much members of this mystical body as ourselves; we can help them. We must suffer with them, show practical sympathy for them; we have indeed a grave duty to them, since God in his infinite mercy gives to us the power to lessen their suffering and shorten their period of banishment from heaven by good works which supply satisfaction for such penalties due to sin as they may be paying to God. There is no need to go into the doctrine of purgatory; we accept its existence, know it as a place of intense suffering beyond any suffering we can feel in this world, suffering that is measured not by time as we count it, but by intensity of pain. Just as an hour of pain can seem so much longer than an hour of pleasure, so duration of suffering in purgatory is marked by its intensity; what we term a day may be as a hundred years to these suffering souls.

Every sin must be atoned for, paid to the uttermost farthing. Though the guilt of sin is washed out by repentance, yet the penalty remains to be paid off. Many souls leave this life burdened by a debt of punishment for sin, which must be satisfied ere they can enter into eternal joy. 'Nothing defiled can enter heaven, yet some will be saved so as by fire.' The fire of purgatory burns out the penalties or remains of sin by intense suffering. Thousands daily pass into these cleansing flames. Are they no concern of ours, these members of Christ's Mystical Body? 'Have pity on me at least, o my friends, for the hand of the Lord hath touched me.' 'It is a holy and a wholesome thought to pray for the dead that they may be loosed from sin.' Do we suffer mutually with these souls as members of the one Body? Do we strive to lessen the period or the intensity of their sufferings? If not, then our belief in the communion of saints is mere sham, a form of meaningless words; we are ignoring a grave obligation.

Possibly it is the lack of a 'personal interest' in these souls. We think of them vaguely as dead people who mean little to us; we do not know them, have no interest in them, hence they are forgotten. Those who have lost a loved one have a personal interest; it means something to them, but after a time even this fades and little more is done. We forget our grave duty to give unceasing help because it seems all so vague and indefinite and we are more attracted by definite things that have a personal appeal. A terrible catastrophe in a far-off land has little effect on our feelings, but some awful happening in the home-town fills us with horror though it may be in fact much less than the happening far away; it is something definite to us so we are affected by it. Hence we must bring these suffering members of the Mystical Body out of that vague undefined state and make them definite and personal to us. Thus we single out some special saint in heaven as a patron or protector, though our knowledge of the saint is probably little; but we pray to St Joseph, St Christopher, St Anthony, St Therese, as the case may be, and so we are in some way connected definitely with a saint by prayer and mutual interest. In the same way, we can choose some particular soul in purgatory and become its patron and helper, directing our efforts daily to help this particular soul. What soul is there to be adopted in this definite manner?

(1) *The soul nearest to release.* Always there will be one soul whose cleansing is almost done, and one prayer of ours may send such a soul rejoicing into eternal happiness and the vision of God. Think you that soul will forget what we have brought about by our timely help? We have raised up for ourselves an intercessor before the face of God! Another soul will then be the next for release, so our efforts need never cease as long as we can pray.

(2) *The most forgotten soul!* A soul that looks in vain for an interested friend, for whom never a mass is offered, never a prayer said for its special help. What a work of charity to take such a soul under our care and pray daily for aid in its need.

(3) *The soul that has been longest in suffering* (as we regard time). We can only reckon by the passing years, but what must be the dreariness of waiting in suffering ever hoping for release from pain by the effort of some one living in the world! What gratitude will be felt by such a soul for whatever may shorten the period of banishment!

(4) *The soul that had some common interest with us,* the one most devout to our Lady or, if we prefer it, to our own special loved

saint, or the one who bears our own name, one who held the same position in life, who did the same job. Surely it is not difficult to find a bond that would induce us to remember our duty to the suffering souls. Thus we can lift these souls from a vague unreality to a definite position in our interest and so keep in mind the needs of these suffering friends of Christ. The Church never forgets. In every Mass, in the Divine office, there are petitions continually rising to God for these suffering members. In many churches the office for the dead is said week by week. November is set apart as a month of special remembrance; but the obligation on each one of us extends throughout the year, each prayer means some help.

How can we assist these souls? By prayers, especially by gaining indulgences that are specially allotted to the souls in purgatory, by having mass offered for them or at least contributing with others to have mass offered by means of the Holy Souls Box which is to be found in every church. The giving of the offering itself has a certain satisfactory value as being an act of self-sacrifice on our part. We do not know the effect of Holy Mass on any one soul, since the Mass is offered in the manner of a suffrage, which means that God allots so much effect as is consistent with his divine justice. This is obvious since the effect of one Mass fully applied would release every soul instantly from purgatory.

This may be an answer to those who think the rich have a better chance in purgatory, because of the number of masses they may be able to have offered for them. The 'relief value' of £100 left for masses for a certain soul may not equal the 'relief value' of the offering for a single mass which some poor person has scraped together by personal self-sacrifice for some soul. God is just, and money cannot 'talk' in the next world; like the widow's mite, it is the personal sacrifice which counts most with God.

How long will a soul remain in purgatory? We do not know; God has revealed nothing of that. Until a soul is canonized by the Church there is no certainty of its state, hence we should place no limit to our prayers for any soul. Should the particular soul for whom we pray be no longer in need of help, then God will give the benefit of our good works to some other deserving soul.

Charity urges us, duty compels us, self-interest at least should persuade us to carry out faithfully our duty to the suffering members of Christ. Should we forget or neglect these souls in need, it will be but just that we in our dire need should also be forgotten. Each soul is a potential advocate before the throne of God for our own needs; they will not forget those who helped them when in suffering and pain.

'I believe in the communion of saints.' Let this not be a mere empty phrase; turn it into action for the benefit of the Holy Souls, the friends of God entrusted by his mercy to our care.

'Eternal rest give unto them o Lord, and let perpetual light shine upon them. May they rest in peace.'

XIII MASS AND CALVARY

To understand the Holy Sacrifice of the Mass, it is first of all necessary to have a clear idea of what is meant by a 'sacrifice.' In the catechism a sacrifice is defined as 'the offering of a victim by a priest to God alone, in testimony of his being the sovereign lord of all things.'

Now whilst this is true, it leaves obscure the very essence of sacrifice, which is the interior disposition of soul in the one who offers the sacrifice. St Thomas Aquinas teaches that the 'offering of a sacrifice is for the purpose of signifying something: the sacrifice which is offered externally signifies the internal spiritual sacrifice in which the soul offers itself to God. Sacrifice is twofold; of the two, the first and most important is the interior sacrifice i.e. the disposition and acts.'

St Augustine also writes: 'Every visible sacrifice is a sacred sign of an invisible sacrifice.' Hence, just as a sacrament is an outward sign of an invisible grace, so a 'sacrifice' is an outward sign or symbol of an inward sacrifice consisting in the disposition of the soul to God as Creator, Sustainer and final End. Being primarily a sign, it is what the sign expresses that is most important, and mystical or symbolic death can be as much a token of interior sacrifice as physical death. Sacrifice therefore is the sign or symbol appointed, or accepted, by God to show the disposition of utter surrender and total subjection of man's being and powers to God's will.

In the old law, God appointed certain sacrificial rites to be the sign of man's surrender to himself. These rites consisted chiefly in the offering of some victim which, being slain on the altar, represented the total surrender and subjection of man to the ownership of God, including the power of life and death over man himself. The outward sacrifice would have no meaning or value unless it expressed this subjection to God by the one offering the victim. It is this interior disposition of soul which gives the value to the outward sign or symbol called sacrifice.

Moreover all these sacrifices of the Old Law were acceptable to God only as relating in some way to the perfect sacrifice which was to be offered on Calvary. We find a different type of sacrifice in that of Abraham as contrasted with that of Melchisedec. By command of God, Abraham prepared to offer his son Isaac to God in token of Abraham's perfect submission to God and though this sacrifice was not completed by the slaying of Isaac, because God stayed the hand of Abraham, it was yet a perfect symbol of submission to God. Melchisedec offered bread and wine, which were equally acceptable to God as the sign and symbol of the same subjection to him on the part of Melchisedec. In both sacrifices, so different outwardly, the same interior submission is shown i.e. the total submission of the offerer to God. These two sacrifices typified Calvary and the Mass.

We may now consider the Mass as the renewal of the sacrifice of Calvary. Pope Leo XIII declared that 'Mass is not an empty or bare commemoration of his (Christ's) death, but a true and wonderful, though unbloody, renewal of it.' St Paul writes to the Corinthians (XV, 28): 'When all things shall be subdued unto him, then the Son also himself shall be subject unto him that put all things under him, that God may be all in all.' In a foot-note the Douai Version explains the text thus: 'The Son will be subject to the Father according to his human nature even after the general resurrection and also the whole Mystical Body of Christ will be entirely subject to God, obeying him in everything.' That is most important in view of the meaning of sacrifice. The sacrifice of Calvary was the outward visible sign of the interior submission of Jesus Christ to his Father. In his human nature Christ was utterly surrendered and totally subjected to his heavenly Father, 'obedient unto death.' Adam by his disobedience had involved the whole human race in sin, which is the opposite to 'sacrifice,' for sin is non-surrender, the refusal of subjection, disobedience to God. Therefore only the 'perfect obedience,' which means total surrender and subjection, could atone for sin.

This disposition of surrender and subjection to God was always perfect in Jesus from the beginning of his human nature, and will continue the same through eternity. The most perfect expression of this surrender is acceptance of death itself in obedience to the divine decree. The sacrifice of Calvary was the outward sign and symbol, carried to its utmost limits, of that interior disposition of Jesus, the utter surrender and total subjection of his human nature to his heavenly Father which can never change. It was shown in the agony in the garden when Christ prayed 'Yet not my will, but thine, be done.'

Throughout his life, Jesus protested: 'I came to do the will of MY Father who is in heaven.' In the shedding of his precious blood, which was the cause, by his own will, of his death, Christ gave a perfect proof of his submission to God, and by that utter surrender of himself, 'obedient even to death, the death of the Cross,' he atoned for the disobedience of mankind in every sin.

It was necessary that the Mystical Body, the Church, should offer sacrifice in token of subjection to God and this could be done only by Christ as head of the Mystical Body ever offering himself anew in sacrifice. This could not be done by the same outward sign, which was the physical shedding of his blood on the cross; hence a new acceptable sign must be chosen to signify this same unchanging total surrender of Christ 'obedient unto death,' which will persist eternally. This is well expressed by Pere Gillet, O.P. who writes: 'All the value of the external Passion comes from the internal Passion; the sacrifice of the Body and Blood of Christ has its source and explanation in the sacrifice or total surrender of his will to that of the Father . . . On the altar, as on the cross, we have the same invisible sacrifice of the loving will of Jesus Christ completely immolated to the will of the Father.' Christ having once suffered on the cross, dying by the shedding of his precious blood, could not repeat this death in the same manner. As St Paul writes (Rom: VI, 3-11): 'Christ rising from the dead dieth now no more, death shall no more have dominion over him. For in that he died to sin, he died once, but in that he liveth, he liveth unto God.' Yet in Christ still remains that same disposition of soul which was the interior sacrifice, the very essence of the external sacrifice of Calvary, and which will persist eternally because in his human nature he will always remain 'obedient unto death,' that is to say totally surrendered to his Father.

Since the external sign of sacrifice entailing physical suffering and death cannot be repeated, the new sign expressing this same surrender is provided in the sacrifice of the Mass, which is the external symbol or sign of inward obedience unto death, by the symbolic separation of the body and blood which in the physical sense was the effective cause of death on Calvary. It is obvious, therefore, that Mass is not simply a memorial, but a real renewal of the sacrifice of Calvary, the difference being one of external manner only, showing the same interior sacrifice which is the essence of both outward sacrifices i.e. the completion of the total surrender and utter subjection of Christ in his human nature to God the Father.

If we contrast the two external methods of this one identical sacrifice we find in both the same acceptance of the sign by God, the same priest offering the sacrifice, the same victim offered, and the same essential interior sacrifice of complete surrender. Hence in the essentials the two sacrifices are identical, the sole difference being in the manner of offering, in the external sign or symbol; in the one there is the actual shedding of blood causing physical death; in the other a mystical shedding of blood, and a mystical death, symbolised by the separate consecration on the altar and the apparent separation of the body and blood. Both of these external sacrifices are, and are so accepted by God, the sign and symbol of the internal submission of Jesus Christ to his eternal Father. Hence we are taught by the Council of Trent that the Mass is *one* and *the same* sacrifice as that of Calvary.

As to the effects of the two sacrifices, Calvary was the actual atonement for all the sins of the world, past, present and yet to be committed till the end of time, by the awful suffering and death of Christ willingly accepted under obedience by him as the innocent victim of sin. The Mass is the practical application of this infinite atonement to the individual soul, since each one must work out his own salvation by the interior disposition of soul in submission to God, united to that of Christ in the Mass, through whom alone our own submission can have any value in the sight of God. Mass is the only acceptable and perfect way in which we can give to God that testimony of his being the creator, sustainer and final end of all men, that adoration which is due to him as the supreme Being, that sorrow and repentance for sin so needful to each one, and that thanksgiving which we all owe to God for the multitude of his favours to his undeserving children.

Truly God has given us a wonderful way in which to offer ourselves to him in union with his only begotten Son in the sacrifice of Mass. If we obtain a fuller and richer knowledge of all the meaning of the Mass, a better understanding of its relation and identity with Calvary, then shall we have a greater devotion to this holy sacrifice, a finer realisation of the duty we owe to God in honouring him in the only sacrifice worthy of him that can be offered.

'And in every place there is a sacrifice, and there is offered to my name a clean oblation, for my name is great among the Gentiles, saith the Lord of Hosts.'

XIV THE SACRIFICE OF THE MYSTICAL BODY

It is necessary that God be worshipped by sacrifices. There is in man the instinct to sacrifice to a superior Being, hence all primitive religions have some kind of sacrifice. God must be adored as the supreme Being, the Creator to whom all are subject; be thanked for benefits; be asked for favours; and appeased for sin. This can be done only by sacrifice and to supply this need Christ instituted the renewal and continuance of his death on Calvary that man could offer an acceptable sacrifice to God in fulfilment of his duty to the creator of all things.

Moreover, since Christ had formed the Church as his Mystical Body, it was necessary that all its members should be united to him and share in a sacrifice that would fulfil this duty of worship to God; this means is provided in the holy sacrifice of the Mass. St Thomas Aquinas teaches that 'The head and members are as one mystical person, and therefore the satisfaction of Christ belongs to the faithful as being his members.' That is what the Mass must mean for us, the total surrender of self to God by obedience to the divine will. We offer 'self' in union with Christ, since only by union with him can our sacrifice have any value in the sight of God.

So many have little or no understanding of this; so many go 'to hear Mass,' an expression which seems to mean for them almost the same as 'to see Mass.' Mass is not an opera or play performed for us as an audience, but our own personal sacrifice of self. The priest offering is simply the representative of the mystical person offering Christ himself who is both priest and victim; he is the instrument by which the external rites are enacted on behalf of all the members, but Mass is the sacrifice of all. This is shown by the words used for example in the *Orate fratres*—'Pray brethren that my sacrifice and YOURS may be acceptable.' And this idea is repeated throughout the Mass. It is the sacrifice of all the members, but especially of those present before the altar.

St Gregory says: 'During this holy function we must offer ourselves with sorrow of heart as a sacrifice; for when we commemorate the mystery of the Passion of our Lord, we must imitate that which we celebrate. The Mass will be a sacrifice for us when we have offered ourselves to God.'

In the Encyclical on Reparation, Pope Pius XI writes: 'With the august sacrifice of the eucharist must be united the immolation of the ministers and also the rest of the faithful so that they too may offer themselves a living sacrifice to God. Hence St Cyprian says "the sacrifice of the Lord is not offered with its complete effect of sanctification unless our offering and our sacrifice corresponds to the Passion." The more perfectly our oblation and our sacrifice correspond to the sacrifice of Christ—in other words, the more we sacrifice self-love, our passions, and crucify our flesh, the more abundant will be the fruits of propitiation and expiation which we receive for ourselves and for others.'

St Peter bids us 'Be . . . a holy priesthood to offer up spiritual sacrifices acceptable to God by Jesus Christ.' St Paul (Rom.: XII, 1) writes: 'I beseech you by the mercy of God that you present your bodies a living sacrifice, holy, pleasing unto God, your reasonable service;' and again: 'Those that are Christ's have crucified their flesh with its desires.'

From this we understand what the Mass must mean to us. A sacrifice is the outward sign of the interior sacrifices and in the Mass we have the external symbol of the interior sacrifice of the Mystical Body of Christ which means that Christ is offering himself anew, giving the sign of his utter surrender and total subjection to his heavenly Father. He is still obedient unto death; but that obedience now means that each individual member of the Mystical Body unites with Christ in self-surrender and subjection to God. If the head surrenders, the whole body surrenders with it. Mass therefore must be the outward sign expressing the internal sacrifices of surrender to God of each individual member of the mystical body, and each member shares in every Mass offered. Yet this surrender is not complete on the part of the members, so that the Mass is thus prevented from being a perfect sacrifice of the whole Mystical Body. On the part of Christ it is a perfect sacrifice since his subjection in his human nature to God is perfect;

on the part of the members the sacrifice is more or less imperfect as the self-sacrifice is more or less imperfect in the individual members. Something is withheld from God; we continue to want our own way in some things, or retain some inordinate affection to sin; so we fail in total surrender of self to God and make our sacrifice imperfect; we are not completely one in mind and heart with Christ. Hence we do not receive the full benefit of the Mass. Nothing can obtain so many actual graces, especially sorrow for sin, as the Mass; but these graces are in proportion to our spirit of self-sacrifice, to our conformity with Christ. To go to Mass should signify that we intend to unite ourselves completely with Christ, offering ourselves unreservedly to God so that not only the head but the body also, each individual member, is completely subjected to the divine will.

This perfect state of submission throughout the whole Mystical Body will be fulfilled only when the whole body is rejoicing with Christ in the happiness of the vision of God, where nothing can be withheld, but where every will must be in perfect conformity with the divine will. If this is not our disposition of soul when we offer our Mass we have missed the significance and the value of the holy sacrifice. We must ask ourselves whether we simply 'hear mass' as spectators, or whether we 'offer mass' as we are bound to do in fulfilment of our duty to God, as the outward sign of our interior disposition of self-surrender. We fail in subjection by ill-feeling or resentment felt against another, by want of charity or kindness to others in their spiritual or temporal needs, by inordinate affections to worldly things, by self-gratification in a way not pleasing to God, by want of patience in trials or in acceptance of any crosses, by want of obedience to lawful authority, and in all the many ways in which we cling to our own selfish desires rather than submit to God.

Furthermore this disposition of surrender and subjection to God must not be a mere passing phase, lasting only for the duration of Mass. We must 'live the mass' throughout the day; in other words our disposition of subjection must persist always. 'I came to do the will of him that sent me'; that must also be our disposition at all times, so that our will is one with God's will. Whatever we do must be done to please God; joy or sorrow be willingly accepted as being God's will for us. Our Lord was 'obedient unto death' and that was his normal disposition; it must be ours also.

St Peter bids: 'Be ye subject therefore to every human creature for God's sake: whether it be to the king as excelling, or to governors as sent by him for the punishment of evil-doers and for the praise of the good, for so is the will of God . . . servants be subject to your masters . . . for this is thanks-worthy.' All lawful authority as sent from God is to be obeyed; children must obey parents and teachers ('he was subject to them'); workers must obey employers; all must be subject to the State in civil affairs, to the Church in religious matters—all proper authority in its own proper sphere is to be obeyed. In this way we 'live the Mass' and in no other way can so swift a progress in spiritual holiness be attained.

To sum up this idea of the Mass as the sacrifice of the Mystical Body, Christ our head expresses his internal sacrifice, i.e. his utter surrender and total subjection of his human nature to God, by the external act symbolising his death by the mystic shedding of blood in the separate consecration of the body and blood on the altar, showing his continual and abiding disposition of 'obedience unto death.' We, his members, offer this same sacrifice by uniting our own surrender to God as creator and final end to that of our head, Christ, through whom alone our self-sacrifice obtains any value. The Mass must be for us the outward sign of our own interior submission to God. This sacrifice is perfect only to the extent of the perfection of our own self-surrender to God, and the graces received will be in proportion to this self-surrender on the part of each one. This subjection to God must not be a passing disposition of soul, but enduring and abiding, lived day by day, in obedience to all lawful authority, through willing acceptance of trials or crosses, by referring all to God and striving to promote God's honour and glory. Unless the Mass means this to us we have missed its meaning.

Many who go daily to Mass fail to make any progress in

spirituality because they do not surrender themselves wholly to God; they remain too critical of others, uncharitable in their judgments, proud in their own conceits and clinging to their own prejudices and opinions. They are in fact 'pious frauds,' since they publicly declare their complete surrender and subjection to God, yet retain the right to criticise and pass judgment on the actions of their neighbour, remain proud and vain, failing in fraternal charity to others. 'He that loveth not his brother, whom he seeth, how can he love God whom he seeth not, and this commandment we have from God, that he who loveth God, love also his brother.' (1 Ep. of St John, IV, 20-21). We must submit wholly in all things to God, otherwise our offering is imperfect, incomplete, failing to bring to us all the graces that God so desires to impart.

'I beseech you by the mercy of God, that you present your bodies a living sacrifice, holy, pleasing unto God'—'Be you a holy priesthood to offer up spiritual sacrifices acceptable to God'—'Those who are Christ's, have crucified their flesh with its desires.'

XV THE BLESSED SACRAMENT—OUR FOOD

'There hath stood one in the midst of you that you know not.' How truly may this be applied to the Blessed Sacrament, Emmanuel, God with us, ever present on the altar; how little this wonderful gift is understood or appreciated, the mystery of the real presence of Jesus, true God, true Man, whose delight it is to be with the children of men.

Primarily this sacrament was instituted to be the food of the soul. 'My flesh is meat indeed and my blood is drink indeed.' This food is a vital need of the soul, just as much as ordinary food is a vital need of the body, and unless we make the fullest use of this sacrament as a food we do not realise its chief purpose. 'Unless you eat the flesh of the Son of Man and drink his blood, you shall not have life in you.'

Pope Pius X urged the need of frequent holy communion and decreed that children, as soon as they know the difference between this holy food and ordinary bread, must receive this holy sacrament. Parents are bidden to take the utmost care that their children receive holy communion very often, if possible daily. Their very innocence makes them fit to receive, and there is no better means of keeping them innocent than by the frequent reception of this heavenly food.

How many receive as often as they might? Few go daily, not many even monthly. The Church has not said how often we should receive, but she has set a limit to frequency and to rarity. We may receive once each day; we must receive once a year; between these limits we are free. Why is it that so very few receive frequently? Is it through a mistaken notion of what is necessary? Two conditions only are laid down for daily communion: (1) to be free from mortal sin—venial sin need not prevent us, so long as there is no affection for it and we are sorry for it; (2) a right intention, i.e. to receive from love and desire of increasing in holiness. The fast from midnight must of course be kept.

Two dangers are to be guarded against: staying away from indifference, or receiving merely from routine. Each communion should be unique, recognised for the wonderful privilege it is. Daily communion should not blunt our perception, custom should not stale, this sacred gift. What poor excuses are put forth as reasons for refraining from communion. One will say: 'I'm not good enough.' Of course not, nor ever will be; not even our Lady was 'good enough,' but for that very reason this food was given because our very weakness needs the strength that it alone can give. This sacrament was not instituted for angels, but for fallen man, weak, pitiful, prone to evil, and sinful, that he might gain strength to overcome his evil propensities and many enemies. The more sinful a man, the more he needs this source of strength to resist his temptations.

Some have ceased from frequent communion because others have sneered that communion made them no better—how foolish! The question may well be not whether we grow better, but whether frequent communion keeps us from getting worse. It is not easy to keep good; we need every help possible. It would be better to admit the truth that it is often want of love that keeps us away from the altar, the weakness of our desire; we are swayed by self-love, would rather have that cup of tea before going out, have that extra hour in bed; laziness, self-indulgence and such like are oftentimes the real reasons of neglect, or want of interest in the welfare of the soul, by preferring to pander to the desires of the flesh. Thomas a Kempis bewails the fact that many will suffer all sorts of dangers and difficulties to visit some famous shrine, will have great devotion to a miraculous picture, but neglect the real presence on the altar, because he is so easy to visit, so near at hand. We are much the same! We queue up in the rain for an hour to see some play or picture, go to any trouble to do what we really want to do, but cannot go to communion because it interferes with our convenience. Yet we profess to believe that Jesus Christ, true God and true Man, is really and truly present in this sacrament.

What wonderful promises our Lord has given to those who receive him. 'This is the bread which came down from heaven that if any man eat of this bread he shall live for ever, and the bread that I will give is my flesh for the life of the world.' Mark those words: 'If any man shall eat, he shall live for ever!' (Jn.VI.59). Is that a meaningless statement, or a definite promise? It could not have been put more plainly. Our Lord does not promise meaningless things nor speak haphazardly. Again he declares: 'Amen I say to you except you eat the flesh of the Son of Man and drink his blood, you shall not have life in you. He that eateth my flesh and drinketh my blood hath everlasting life and I will raise him up on the last day.' Surely another wonderful promise! He that eateth 'hath everlasting life,' as though it were already an accomplished fact; it is not simply that he will save his soul, but he already possesses everlasting life. Is that a meaningless expression? Not that having once received we may do what we please, but that those who, sincerely anxious to lead a good life, faithfully receive this life-giving food, have already begun to participate in the eternal life of God even in this world. 'He that eateth . . . hath everlasting life.' A pledge of future glory is given to us! Surely this should act as a spur to make us receive the Blessed Sacrament as often as we can, and so make certain of eternal life.

There is another aspect of the Blessed Sacrament. Our Lord is there a prisoner in the tabernacle, there because his delight is to be with the children of men, our friend and our brother. In speaking of a friend the book of Ecclesiasticus says: 'Go to him early in the morning and let thy foot wear the steps of his door.' It would be well to apply these words to the best, the truest friend we have, to Jesus himself. There behind that little locked door he awaits our visit, the lone lamp telling of his presence, God with us. Yet how much he is left alone, neglected.

Do we recognise him as a friend? He who so loved his friends on earth, held them so dear to his human heart. He knew the need of a friend who was forsaken in dire need. He awaits us as our friend, but we pass him by seeking consolation among human friends so much less able to give comfort in distress. It is an unwritten law that we visit friends or lose them. Shall we show the divine friend less courtesy? To so many he is something impersonal. Look at the altar; there we see flowers, candles, a crucifix, and we know the Blessed Sacrament is also there though hidden from our eyes. Do we think of the Blessed Sacrament as 'one of these things,' inanimate? Do we think of 'it' or of HIM? There is an immense gulf between the alive and the lifeless. Jesus is alive, the very source of life; the presence there is a living one interested in our daily joys or sorrows, ready to give solace to those in need. 'Come to me all ye that labour and are burdened and I will refresh you.' We visit some for business reasons, but friends we visit with eager joy, shall we do less for him? How eager we ought to be to visit him daily if possible, to give some small share of our time to him—our best, our truest friend.

Is our reverence for him true reverence? Is it the reverence of fear such as a small boy has for a policeman? We do not fear our friends! We reverence friends not from fear, but because of love and esteem. That is the reverence he needs from us, the reverence that springs from love and knowledge. Familiarity with a real friend does not breed contempt. Why should familiar reverence with Jesus be any different? He knew that at times accidents would happen to that heavenly bread entrusted to the keeping of man, but that does not make him angry should it occur; only should an enemy in mortal sin dare to receive him, would he consider it an insult to his divine majesty. Let us have no servile fear, but the true reverence of familiar friendship. We need not so much more faith, as a greater realisation of the wonder of this tremendous mystery.

We need to get into closer contact with our friend. What does it matter if we are afflicted with distractions and worries? He knows all our difficulties, our weakness, our desires, even our want of love for him. But he is there waiting to refresh and help us, to share in our interests, our plans, our joys, to console us in sorrow and distress, to give aid in difficulties, to strengthen us against our own weakness and many temptations.

Most of all, though, let us have a true knowledge of the primary reason of the institution of this sacrament. It is to be our food, our strength, our pledge of future glory; that is what must impress us most, and that is the chief use we must

72

make of this life-giving food. To receive him, who is Lord of all, into our sinful soul that it may gain strength from his power, holiness from his infinite sanctity, that he may live in us, and we in him, in a wondrous union beyond our understanding; what a mystery of divine condescension and love for sinful man! How can we find any excuse for not making the fullest use of this sacrament, we who through our sinfulness and fatal weakness so much need all the strength which it alone can give. Think of the wonderful promises he has made to those who are faithful in using this daily bread as the food of the soul!

'He that eateth this bread shall live for ever.'

'He that eateth my flesh and drinketh my blood hath everlasting life and I will raise him up in the last day.' (Jn. VI.55).

XVI BLESSED SACRAMENT—PEACE AFTER VIOLENCE

On entering the presence of the Blessed Sacrament there is felt a sense of peace and tranquillity, far removed from the excitement, toil, and turmoil of the world busy about its affairs. Here we can capture peace and rest for our weary souls. The little flickering light of the lonely lamp bids us call to mind the living presence of our God and Saviour, Emmanuel, God with us, the lonely prisoner of the tabernacle.

Here is no hint of violence, of pain or suffering, of mangling, bruising, blood and death. All is calm, peaceful, and silent. Here is a life that knows no change, can know no change; here is peace after victory over death. Yet this is the calm that follows after the storm, when the violence of warring elements is stilled and turbulence is at rest. Before this peace in the living presence of the Blessed Sacrament could be achieved, how much there was of mangling, bruising, bloodshed and death. It is all too easy for us to forget the suffering and sacrifice of which this sacrament is the memorial.

The Blessed Sacrament is not simply the body and blood of Jesus Christ, much less is it only the appearance of bread or wine; it is the union of both. The union of the invisible substance of the body and blood of Christ with the visible sacramental veils of the outward appearances or 'accidents' of bread and wine makes that divine sacrament of sacraments which has come to us, in both its invisible and its visible elements, through the portals of death and violence.

'Amen, amen, I say to you, unless the grain of wheat falling into the ground die; itself alone remaineth. But if it die, it will bring forth much fruit' (Jn. XII, 25). Before the white pure host could be prepared, the grain of wheat had to fall into the earth and there itself die that more grains might be produced; only by its own immolation and destruction could it bring forth fruit in abundance for the preparation of the sacrificial bread. Again, these grains produced, this fruit of the wheat brought forth by the death of the seed, must be crushed, bruised, and ground into powder by the weight of the rolling mill-stones ere it can become unleavened bread, white and pure, in readiness for the act of consecration.

For the wine is needed the full ripe cluster of grapes, which must be trodden in the wine-press, mangled, crushed, destroyed by trampling feet, that the juice, the very life-blood of the grapes, may flow forth to become wine; these grapes had to shed their blood and die that they might become the wine of the sacrifice.

Our Lord himself is crushed as in a wine-press by his agony in Gethsemane, weighted down by the awful burden of sin pressing heavily on his all-innocent soul until in bitter agony he must sweat blood, suffering as the grapes in giving forth the juice, to prepare himself for death. Then must his body be torn, bruised and mangled by the scourges, so that again his precious blood flows forth to fall upon the earth. With violence was he crowned with piercing thorns forced upon his brow with jeers and taunts in mockery of his rightful kingship over men. Burdened with a heavy cross, his altar of sacrifice, he was driven forth to bedew the way to Calvary with his blood, until on the hill he was nailed to the cross and left to die in anguish on this tree of scorn. Drop by drop, he gave his precious blood in grievous suffering until he released his soul in death, having given every last drop of his blood for our salvation. The victim of infinite love for sinful man, the Lamb slain who takes away all the sins of the world, the scapegoat who died that men might live.

All has come to us through violence, bloodshed and death, both the visible sacramental veils and the hidden substance which is the body and blood, soul and divinity of Jesus, the Son of God. Under circumstances strange indeed was this precious gift given. The disciples timid and fearful, knowing that one of them was to betray the Master, were affected by the strange mood of their Master, Jesus, sorrowful unto death yet possessed by an intense love for these uncouth and self-willed men whom he had chosen to be his own. To these he gives a new commandment 'that you love one another even as I have loved you.' He warns them of their dangers and prays for them; the whole atmosphere was full of strange forebodings and unrest, of unknown fears and suffering. During this unrest and anxiety, Jesus takes bread into his sacred hands and giving thanks lifts his eyes to heaven, blesses the bread and breaks it saying 'Take ye and eat of this for THIS IS MY BODY.' Likewise in a similar way he takes the chalice saying 'Drink ye all of this for THIS IS THE CHALICE OF MY BLOOD WHICH SHALL BE SHED FOR YOU.' 'Do this in commemoration of me.'

This is to be the perpetual memorial of my sufferings, of bloodshed, of violence, of agonising death; this is my last will and testament, my last and best gift to men, the token of infinite love crucified for the sins of the world. Truly the Blessed Sacrament has come to us through violence and death; but now Christ lives in peace and quietude, in tranquil silence on the altar, because his delight is to be with the children of men to the end of time, to be their solace in distress, their strength in all the fatal weaknesses of human nature.

But what of ourselves? Are we to escape all this violence, this suffering, this death? Is there to be no sacrifice on our part in return? 'If any man will come after me, let him deny himself, take up his cross daily and follow me' No, we are not to escape! By the strength given to us in this heavenly food, we are to do violence to self, to take up our own cross, to plod painfully behind the Master, striving to follow him. Self-denial means doing violence to self, self-immolation. Just as the grain of wheat must die, so must we die to self that we may bring forth fruit in abundance. 'He that findeth his life shall lose it, and he that shall lose his life for me shall find it' (Matt. X, 39).

We must die to self before we can live to Christ. Only by the giving up of our own will can we strengthen the soul against that fatal tendency to evil that is our birth-mark, make ourselves ready to give up our own will by obedience to all lawful authority, to put others before self in kindness and charity, to be subject to God as a child to its father. We must take up our cross daily. Each day brings its own annoyances, its petty trials, the many things that go against the grain. These daily trials borne in patience are our cross; we cannot escape.

But too often we fail to recognise the cross and let it fall to the ground by our resentments, our grumbling and complaint, our lack of patience. We think we are prepared to carry a great cross for the love of God, yet we cannot bear these little trials that form our real cross. If we cannot bear the less, how shall we shoulder the greater? We deceive ourselves in thinking we have strength, whereas we are weak and pitiful under the stress of small daily tests of patience.

We must follow in the footsteps of the Master and this we do by imitating his example. One great characteristic of his life was his unfailing kindness and charity to men. He demands that if we are to be known as his followers we too must love one another, even as he has loved us. 'By this shall all men know that you are my disciples, because you have love one for another.' How often we fail in fraternal charity. It is said that pious people are harsh and critical in their judgments whereas great sinners show more charity and forbearance. Too often is this true. In spite of frequent communions, pious people are ready to blame, to criticise, to find fault, to be narrow in their judgments of others, showing a pharisaical pride in their own goodness, which may be unwitting but nevertheless is the underlying spirit of their criticisms of others. 'Thank God I am not as other men.' We must learn to crush all pride if we are to die to self, to practice self-immolation.

Judge not that you may not be judged. The path our Master trod was one of compassion for the sinner, of kindness to all in need, of sympathy with any human suffering; he was ever ready to help those in distress, to heal the sick, to cure the maimed and relieve all human distress and ailments. He has promised that the giving of a cup of cold water for his sake shall not go unrewarded 'Amen, I say to you, as long as you do it to one of these the least of my brethren, you do it to me.' He identifies himself with his brethren and we must follow him in charity to others above all else. He gave himself to bitterness and death for our sake; we must die to self for the sake of our brethren and for him who died that we might live.

The Blessed Sacrament is to show forth the death of the Lord until he come. To us it must be always a reminder of his self-immolation, of the shedding of his blood, of his death by violence in agony on the cross for love of us. It must lead us, too, to self-immolation, the death of self by the giving up of our own will, by serving others in charity, by a total subjection of self to God. That is the only true and real sacrifice that we can make, to resign ourselves totally and completely to the will of God. Thus only shall we truly live and bring our soul to its fuller life, dying to self that we may live more fully to God.

From the Blessed Sacrament we shall obtain all the strength we need to do all this and more. 'I can do all things in him who strengthens me.'

'Do this for a commemoration of me.'

XVII THE BLESSED SACRAMENT—BREAD

'I am the living bread which came down from heaven. If any man eat of this bread he shall live for ever and the bread that I will give you is my flesh for the life of the world' (Jn. VI, 51-2).

Many bewail the absence of any spiritual consolation or joy when they receive the body and blood of Jesus Christ in holy communion. They feel that something must be wrong in their communions because it all seems to be so ordinary, there is no thrill in receiving the Blessed Sacrament, there is no fervour, no spiritual ecstasy, no flood of happiness or love of God to fill the soul with joy. We may as well realise at the outset that such absence of all feeling or emotion means nothing at all; feelings are not under our control, we cannot command them as we would; spiritually these feelings are of no value whatever; we are not responsible for them since they are to a large extent outside the control of the will.

God knowing our desire to experience joy and gladness at his coming is well satisfied with our effort; he knows that it is not our fault, we cannot order feelings according to desire, we are not responsible for the absence of sensible joy and elation at his union with us. We may not feel any love for God and so are tempted to think we are unworthy. But these natural emotions belong to our physical body and depend on many varied circumstances, external as well as internal. Health, digestion, weather conditions, the attitude of others, disappointments, all affect our feelings more or less. How then can these emotions enter into our spiritual state, when they are so unstable, varying with every whim? They should not affect us spiritually at all and certainly can be no guarantee of our state of soul. Perhaps we have mistaken the meaning of holy communion, not realising that its chief purpose is to be a food, the bread of souls. In the words of scripture quoted at the beginning, the word 'bread' occurs three times, and our Lord uses that word twelve times in his promise to give us his flesh and blood; he would not so insist on this notion of 'bread' unless it had some special significance for us.

Bread is the staff of life, our chief food, the one thing of which we never tire. At almost every meal bread is taken, and nothing else can take its place for long. We get tired of most other foods if they are served too often, even of the daintiest fare, but of bread never. Yet it has but little taste; there is no particular joy or pleasure in the eating of bread. Some things, such as cake, we eat for the pleasure they give to the palate, for the enjoyment of their sweetness or flavour; but we tire of them with superabundance and want bread, even though it does give no particular thrill in the eating. At breakfast bread is usually eaten because it is the food which sustains and enables us to bear the burdens of the day, but it gives little or no pleasure beyond the satisfying of hunger and needs something with it, to make it palatable. Moreover bread sustans, but it does not do the work. We do the work, while the bread sustains; bread gives strength and endurance to carry on the labour we must accomplish.

We can apply this to the Blessed Sacrament in holy communion. Our Lord told us that he would give us 'bread'—not 'cake.' He repeats many times that this 'bread' is his flesh and since he uses the word 'bread' he intends us to understand that what bread is to the body, so the 'bread' that he will give, his flesh, is to be to the soul. It is to be the giver of strength, of vigour, to sustain us, the food of which we shall never tire, our daily bread. It is not meant to be 'cake,' to give us spiritual pleasure in receiving it for its own sake; we are not to receive because of any joy it will give or for any taste of spiritual thrill, but like the breakfast taken for the good of the body to gain the strength needed through the day to meet labour and toil, so this heavenly bread is to provide strength that will sustain us in difficulties, trials, temptations, weariness, sadness, and the continual struggle to overcome our propensities to evil, giving health and strength to the soul and enabling us to work out our salvation.

In holy communion the Blessed Sacrament does not work miracles. It will sustain us, give us strength, but we must do the work ourselves. To us, painfully toiling along the hard narrow way that leads to salvation, it will give comfort and strength. 'I can do all things in him who strengtheneth me.' So long as we make use of the strength imparted to us, we shall daily sanctify ourselves and resist temptations; we shall meet with all the various trials and crosses that fall to our lot; and if we unfortunately fail, it will lift us up again into the friendship of God. But we must not expect thrills of spiritual joy, or wonderful happiness flooding the soul with ecstasies. There would be too much danger if that were the ordinary result. We should receive for the pleasure given to us, revel in the joy obtained, and be absorbed in our own selfish happiness. It might be merely an occasion of self-gratification, instead of resulting from the desire of obtaining strength and help to deny self its gratifications.

Let us recall the first Holy Communion. It was a strange ceremony in the midst of anxieties and fears, with the Master himself beset with sadness at his approaching passion and suffering. He had warned the apostles that one of them would betray him, that Peter would thrice deny him, that all that night would be dispersed, fleeing from him in fear of their lives. It was a strange preparation for the reception of their first holy communion. They knew not what was to happen, what they were about to receive; they were not prepared for this heavenly bread. The eating of the paschal lamb being finished, Jesus took bread into his sacred hands, raised his eyes to heaven, giving thanks, blessed and broke the bread, saying: 'Take ye and eat, for this is my body.' They must have been filled with astonishment at these strange words thus spoken to them; they could hardly have had any feelings of great spiritual joy under such circumstances, hardly have understood the full meaning of our Lord's words at that moment; but this 'bread' was to give them strength to sustain them during the awful hours so soon to come upon them, when they would see their Lord and Master dragged away like a criminal from their midst to be condemned to a shameful death.

What was the result? Within a few hours all had fled in terror, all cowards at the first hint of danger. Later Peter regained sufficient courage to follow even to the court where the trial was taking place, only to meet the accusation of being one of this Man's followers by denying any knowledge of him. 'He began to curse and swear that he knew not the man.' And this in spite of having been warned that he would act so. Yet less than three hours before he had received the 'Bread of Life,' was given the strength that could have sustained him through those dire hours; but because he trusted in his own strength he failed. However, he repented bitterly of his fall and was received back into friendship with his Master. Was it not perhaps the strength given by his Holy Communion that at least brought him back so swiftly to repentance and the grace of God?

We too, in spite of our frequent communions, have failed time and again to resist temptations and fallen miserably into sin. Does not this prove how weak we are, how much we need the strength-giving bread to sustain us against that fatal weakness, our proneness to evil and the difficulty we have in avoiding sin? Let us put aside our feelings and emotions, all expectations of spiritual joy and happiness, in receiving our Lord into our souls and understand the real purpose of this most holy sacrament. True it is that we must prepare ourselves as fervently as we are able, making ourselves as worthy as may be to prepare a resting place for this most wondrous gift of the real presence of Jesus himself in our hearts. We must thank our Lord and Master for his loving condescension in giving himself to such unworthy sinners as ourselves. At the same time we must not be downcast at the absence of all spiritual joy and consolation in receiving this holy bread. That is to misunderstand its true purpose. It is not meant as a reward of goodness, as something to give us a thrill of joy or ecstasy, to touch our emotions and bring us pleasure. The Blessed Sacrament is as practical and as unemotional as ordinary bread; it has the same effect in a spiritual way as ordinary bread in a physical way. It is meant to give strength, not pleasure; to help us to struggle against our difficulties, not to please our spiritual palate with its sweetness.

True, God does at times permit us to have spiritual joy and

fervour in receiving him, but this is something added as a further favour from God and outside its true work in the soul. At best such a favour is passing and may act as an encouragement for a time; but it is not in any sense a standard by which we can judge the results of our communions. The only way to judge these results is by the greater holiness of our lives, by the lessening of the number of times we fall into sin, by a greater and more active charity to our neighbour and a fervent desire to do the will of God in all things. The absence of any spiritual joy or fervour can be totally ignored since it is not in any way under the control of our free will, by which alone all our acts are judged for merit or demerit in the sight of God.

'I am the living bread which came down from heaven—if any man eat of this bread he shall live for ever; and the bread that I will give is my flesh for the life of the world' (Jn. VI, 51-2).

XVIII THE SACRED HEART

Having created Adam and Eve, God put them in the garden of Eden and was a friend to them. Genesis tells us that into this garden came the tempter who persuaded Eve to eat of the forbidden fruit; she afterwards persuaded Adam to do likewise and their eyes were opened to evil. 'When they heard the voice of the Lord God walking in paradise at the afternoon air, Adam and his wife hid themselves from the face of the Lord God, amidst the trees of paradise.' In punishment of their grave sin, they were expelled from this lovely garden; but God loved them still in spite of their sin and he tempered the penalty by the promise of a redeemer, who would re-open heaven to man.

As the ages passed by, man drifted further from God, lost the true idea of him as a friend; and even the chosen race, protected by God, delivered from the bondage of Egypt and having numberless favours showered on them, yet thought of God as terrible and awe-inspiring whose very name must not be spoken. To them he was the God of the thunder and lightning of Sinai, who forbade things pleasurable and easy to nature. Prophets sent to remind them of the promised redeemer went unheeded, so that when in the fullness of time God, who so loved the world, sent his only Son, not alone to redeem the world from sin but to teach the true idea of God and reveal his infinite love for man, this Son was rejected. 'He came unto his own, but his own received him not.'

The incarnation was the manifestation of God's love, through the humanity of Christ. Where shall be seen such love for men as was shown by the divine man? His public life was all spent in the service of men; his first public act was to change water into wine at the marriage feast of Cana. Humanly speaking there was no need of this miracle; its only purpose was to supply a deficiency, to save embarrassment and give joy to many, but this was reason sufficient for the love of God to act so that happiness might be given and proof granted of the divine sympathy with homely pleasures. This was a beginning of miracles. 'Lord come down before that my

son die—Go thy way, thy son liveth.' Jesus meets the widow
on the way to bury her only son, her sole support; the divine
compassion is moved by her grief and the dead youth is
raised to life and given to his mother. Multitudes who followed
him had nothing to eat, therefore lest they should faint in
the way he feeds them with a few loaves and fishes. The lepers
cry after him 'Master if thou wilt, thou canst make us clean'—
'I will, be thou made clean.' The deaf, the dumb, the blind,
the lame, were thrust upon him and he healed them all. Always
he is moved by human pain and misery, never does he refuse
to grant aid. When the woman taken in sin is brought before
him to be stoned, he blames her accusers, fills them with
shame so that they slink away and then asks: 'Doth no man
condemn thee?'—'No man, Lord.'—'Neither will I condemn
thee, go and sin no more.'

Such is the love of God for the sinner; he makes her his
friend—'Now Jesus loved Martha and her sister Mary and
Lazarus.' These are simple words showing the human affection
of Jesus for friends. Thus throughout his public life, short
though it was, Jesus attracts by the beauty and wealth of
the human love in his Sacred Heart, till at the end of his ministry he gives his own flesh and blood to be the life of the souls
of men; nothing less could satisfy him than to give himself,
to remain always with men. His delight is to be with the children
of men, to share their lives and interests, to be accessible to
those in need of his comfort. To complete all, he suffers death
on the cross, the crowning act of redemption, to wipe out the
sins of the whole of mankind and give back to them the right
to be the children of God and heirs to the kingdom of heaven.
'Greater love than this no man hath, that he lay down his
life for his friends.'

Could we ever doubt the tender love of Jesus for sinners?
A love that never fails. Always we can have perfect confidence
and reliance on the unchanging infinite love of Jesus, the Son
of God. This love of Christ is not simply a human love; it is
divine, the very love of God himself, shown through the human
love of the Sacred Heart. We cannot separate the two. The
incarnation is the revealing of God's love for man through

the humanity of Jesus. Philip saith to him: 'Lord, show us the Father and it is enough.' Jesus said to him: 'Philip, he that seeth me, seeth the Father also.' Jesus identifies himself with his Father, God. 'The works which I do are not mine, but the Father's.' It was this great truth that was to be shown to us, the infinite unchanging eternal love of God for man. The heart has always been the accepted symbol of love. When we speak of a man's heart, we mean his love. The Church has chosen the Sacred Heart to symbolise the divine and human love of Jesus. But we cannot separate the love of Jesus from the love of the Father or of the Holy Ghost; it is one perfect unchangeable eternal love. The Sacred Heart is thus the symbol of God's love for man.

We are helped in this way to see in God, one who loves us with a great personal love, the height, the depth, the length and breadth of which we shall never fathom; it is too immense, too boundless for us to comprehend, a love from which all true love springs, of which our own human loves are but a faint shadow. Hence we are urged to turn our thoughts to the Sacred Heart, to learn from it the lesson of God's love for us, to understand more and more the infinite tenderness and compassion that God has for all human sorrow and suffering, the infinite pity and mercy that God shows always to the sinner, the desire of God for our true happiness throughout eternity.

We must strive to give our love in return especially in our devotion to the Sacred Heart. But devotion to the Sacred Heart must be a true devotion, not such as rests in the Sacred Heart as the end instead of the beginning.

We may not separate the heart of our Lord from what it signifies; it must always be the symbol leading to infinite love itself. From the Sacred Heart we are to learn the lesson of love, and by a greater understanding of the love of God become more and more attracted to God, giving love for love, and daily growing in the service of God. Too often are found those who kneel before a statue of the Sacred Heart in a Church, forgetful of the real living presence on the altar body, blood, soul and divinity of the risen Christ, to whom is made a perfunctory genuflection on entering and leaving but who is otherwise forgotten. Too often devotion is merely sentiment, a personal pleasure in emotional joy, the sweetness felt or brought out by some 'devotional statue' but in no wise increasing a true love for God.

How shall we test our devotion to the Sacred Heart of Jesus? How know whether our devotion is real or merely sentiment? There is only one standard: 'If you love me, keep my commandments.' Our devotion is proved for what it is worth only by the effect it has on our service of God. Are we, for instance, becoming less proud or vain? Are we growing more meek and less inclined to anger? 'Learn of me, for I am meek and humble of heart.' What we really love, we try to imitate. Do we kneel in prayer before some statue of the Sacred Heart and then going forth criticise and back-bite a neighbour? Unless we strive to imitate the virtues of Jesus, we have no real devotion. 'If you love me, keep my commandments'—'Thou shalt love thy neighbour as thyself.' This is a grave commandment of God. Any so-called devotion to the Sacred Heart that does not include an increasing love for one's neighbour is not real or true. St John writes 'If any man say he loves God and loves not his neighbour, that man is a liar.' Hence unless we strive to imitate the Sacred Heart in that ready sympathy for human sorrows and trials, we have missed the real idea of devotion to it.

'If any man will come after me, let him deny himself, take up his cross daily and follow me.' Are we becoming daily more self-denying, more unselfish, thinking of the needs or convenience of others, giving up our own will, being more obedient? Are we more patient, less irritable when things are trying and not as we would have them to be. Do we carry our daily crosses cheerfully? Life has many small trials, fatigues, burdens that daily afflict us, and such things are the crosses we must bear for the love of God. The answer to these questions will prove beyond question whether there is any worth, any reality in our devotion to the Sacred Heart.

The heart of Jesus was ever quick to respond to the needs of men, an intensely perfect human love, springing from divine love. The human love of the eternal word of God is inseparably united to the divine person; in him we see revealed all the beauty, the immensity of God's love for men. It is impossible to sound the depths of the divinity, impossible to comprehend the love of a God who sought a feeble human nature to express an infinite love in terms of human things; yet we find nothing to exemplify God's love so satisfying as that chosen by the eternal Father himself—a human heart, the Sacred Heart of Jesus, true God and true man.

How much has God done for each one of us personally? Everything in life has come to us through the infinite love of God, and though there are matters that we do not understand, yet we know by faith that all is for the best. He upholds us through life, gives us numberless graces, is patient and understanding when we fall, draws us back to himself by repentance, and rewards each good act, however small it may be, thus showing day by day the immutability of God's infinite love. How gladly we should suffer all things for God. But human nature is weak and cowardly hence the need of trying to understand the love of God and to learn of it by the study of the Sacred Heart—greater love than this no man hath.

XIV THE HOLY GHOST

Real devotion to the Holy Ghost is rare, possibly because of ignorance of his work in our souls. Few have more than a vague idea of the intimate relationship between the soul and the Holy Ghost and because of this lack of knowledge there is but little personal love of him; his work is so hidden as to be hardly recognised. The Holy Ghost is love personified, God's love for himself and of us. To a certain extent the idea of God the Father, the Creator, is understood; the idea of God the Son, Redeemer, God made Man, is familiar to us; we grasp the idea of the love of the Sacred Heart for men and accept with gratitude the mystery of the Blessed Sacrament. But the Holy Ghost, known only by revelation and accepted purely by faith, seems perhaps less real, to have less contact with us, and to be less concerned with our welfare. No greater mistake could be made. Since the love of God is indivisible, God's love for himself and for us is one and the same love, a love personified in the Holy Ghost. Through the Holy Ghost were we created by the Father and redeemed by the Son. All true human love is a faint reflection of the Holy Ghost, nay more it is his gift to us. God loves through and in the Holy Ghost with love infinite and unchanging, whether we are in a state of grace or in sin; the change caused by sin is not in God, but in us; we have ceased to love God, but he still loves us. By sin we place a barrier between the soul and God—as the sun, though hidden by a thick cloud, continues to give out light and heat, so the love of God is poured out for us unchanging. Having put the barrier of sin between God and our soul, we cannot remove it ourselves but the Holy Ghost comes to aid us by offering the grace of repentance, which being accepted the obstacle is removed, and we are once more friends of God.

The Holy Ghost has a twofold mission on earth, both external and internal. The external mission is concerned with the Church of which the Holy Ghost is the soul, vivifying, teaching, and guiding, somewhat as the soul in the human body. This mission began on the day of Pentecost. Our Lord enjoined

89

on his disciples that they should remain in Jerusalem until the Paraclete should come; he would teach them all things, strengthen their faith, enable them with fortitude to spread the gospel to the world. The Holy Ghost descended on them under the visible sign of parted tongues of fire, and has since remained with the Church, guiding her and keeping her from all error in her teaching of the gospel. In any grave matter the Church always implores the guidance of the Holy Spirit. There is the lovely Mass of the Holy Ghost which precedes any important work. Often is heard the prayer: 'Come, o Holy Spirit, fill the hearts of thy faithful and kindle in them the fire of thy love.' Holy Church well knows the need of help and guidance in all things which the Holy Ghost alone is so able to give.

The internal mission is a more personal one of which many have little idea. Our Lord has told us: 'No man can say the Lord Jesus, but by the Holy Ghost.' We are utterly weak and helpless to do anything of ourselves for our salvation; unaided we are incapable of any supernatural act; we depend in all this upon the working in us of the Holy Spirit. This work consists in the sanctification of the individual soul through the sacraments, graces, gifts, fruits, infused virtues, and inspirations by which the Holy Ghost gently and imperceptibly moves our free will towards choosing what is good for our salvation. 'Know you not that you are temples of God and that the Holy Spirit dwelleth in you?' God is everywhere, but in the souls of the just he exists in a special manner as friend with friend; that is the indwelling of the Holy Ghost.

At baptism the Holy Ghost takes possession of the soul; in confirmation, this possession is increased, strengthening our faith and fortitude, and throughout life our sanctification continues, so that whatever good we do is brought about by the power of the Holy Ghost.

As St Paul reminds us: 'The charity of God is poured forth in our hearts by the Holy Ghost, who is given to us.' Not alone is charity poured forth in our hearts, but faith and hope too, with the four cardinal virtues from which all others grow. Moreover by actual graces we are moved to act in resisting temptations or performing acts of virtue. The Holy Ghost bestows on us his seven gifts: (1) *Knowledge*, to see and know God in his creation; (2) *Understanding*, to perfect the mind that it may penetrate the truths of faith; (3) *Wisdom*, to see all things in their highest cause i.e. God himself; (4) *Counsel*, to perfect the intelligence, that it may properly decide what concerns God and salvation, and to enlighten the conscience; (5) *Fortitude*, to perfect the will so that it may endure trials in patience; (6) *Piety*, to perfect the emotions of love, joy, and desire in our lower nature, so that they find their greatest satisfaction in God; (7) *Fear of the Lord*, to perfect the emotions of fear and desperation in that same lower nature and so to keep us from all sin.

These gifts lead us to follow the teachings of Christ, to find our joy in the beatitudes and obey his precepts.

From this activity of the Holy Ghost in the soul are produced the twelve fruits by which we understand the acts of a soul in grace springing from the infused gifts. Some of these perfect the soul itself. (a) *Charity*, which makes love active within us; (b) *Joy*, which makes the soul glad and enjoy the peace of a good conscience serving God in a cheerful spirit; (c) *Peace*, which keeps the soul undisturbed by the annoyances and disappointments met with in life; (d) *Patience*, to teach us resignation to the will of God when we are afflicted by evils; (e) *Long-suffering*, to help the soul to endure delay in answer to prayer or other matters.

Others fruits concern our neighbour: (a) *Goodness*, which is willingness to serve others and succour them in distress or any need; (b) *Kindness* to serve others by word and deed in graciousness and kindliness of manner; (c) *Mildness*, to ensure the absence of any resentment, ill-will or anger towards others; (d) *Faith* or fidelity, which denotes loyalty to engagements and duty, freedom from falsehood, deceit or guile, straight-forwardness in all our dealings. The remaining fruits regulate personal actions: (a) *Modesty*, or moderation and reserve in speech dress or manner; (b) *Continency*, which implies resistance to the allurements of sexual desire; and (c) *Chastity*, which aims at eliminating the desires of the flesh in accordance with the law of God.

In all these different ways the Holy Ghost is directing and influencing our thoughts, words and actions at all times and we, on our part, must co-operate with the graces thus offered. How great is the dignity conferred on man by this indwelling of the Holy Ghost. How zealous we should be to keep this presence of our guest, how eager to work with him for our own good. We cannot fathom the wonder of his work in sanctifying and drawing us to God through the sweetness he imparts in his infinite love for sinful man.

The beautiful sequence in the Mass of the Holy Ghost, said at Pentecost, reveals the effects of this indwelling by the titles it applies to him. He is called 'The Comforter, consoling us in the sorrows and vicissitudes of life, the Father of the Poor, Giver of Gifts, Light of our Hearts, Coolness in Heat, Solace in Woe'. The sequence continues: 'If thou take thy grace away, nothing good in us will stay,' showing our utter helplessness to do any good of ourselves without his help. He is the one who heals our wounds, renews our strength, moistens the dryness of our hearts, melts our frozen hearts with love, warms that which is cold, guides our faltering steps, bends our stubborn wills to grace. No tongue can tell of this infinitely tender love which is poured out upon us. All good in us comes from and through him; every inspiration is his gift to us; each temptation is mastered and overcome solely by his aid. Without him we are incapable of furthering our salvation; with him aiding us we can do all things.

Truly we ought to recognise all that the Holy Spirit does for us and for our salvation, the dangers from which we are protected, the many actual graces and inspirations which we so frequently spurn and fail to use for our soul, the holy desires of doing more and more for God, the gradual improvement of our spiritual life, brought about so gently and freely by the abiding love of the Holy Ghost for men.

Is it that we do not recognise his influence because we have thought that all these things were done by our own unaided efforts? Is it that we do not realise our own utter helplessness, the impossibility of doing any good of ourselves except by the power of the Holy Ghost? If that is why we have so little love for the Holy Ghost, then we are sadly deceiving ourselves and laying ourselves open to failure through trusting in our own efforts.

Let us give all the honour where it is due, to the Holy Ghost. Never shall we fathom the depth, the wonder of this love, never be able to give sufficient love in return. If we ponder and consider all that the Holy Ghost means to us, surely some spark of devotion will kindle in our hearts, some small flame of love and gratitude burst forth from our cold hearts in return for all that is done by him, a small flame that, aided by his love, will become a blazing furnace of love for God. He is depicted in art by the symbols of a dove or a parted tongue of flame; he is the spirit of true peace, that peace given by God which the world cannot give; he is the spirit of true love, burning within the heart. If we would learn what the Holy Ghost means then let us ponder on the meaning of love, for God is love and love is the Holy Ghost.

'Send forth thy spirit and they shall be created.'

'And thou shalt renew the face of the earth.'

XX LIFE—ITS MEANING

To many life is a great puzzle. Difficult indeed is it to understand how all the trivial episodes, accidents, worries of life,
jumbled together as they are, can be part of a great design
planned by God in his creation. Life consists mainly of joys
and sorrows, work, play, eating, sleeping, meeting various
people, some likeable others repellent, mingling in our lives,
helping or hindering; some go through most of life with
us, others drop out. What does it all mean? What has this to
do with salvation? How do all these events make sense in
God's plan?

Shall we try to imagine life as a design in embroidery? The
canvas is stretched on its frame, the needle, the vari-coloured
silks prepared, all is ready for the work to commence. We are
to work together; but you work from underneath, I work from
above forming the design known to me alone. I pass the needle
through drawing with it a blue silk thread; you push it back
again. Many times this is repeated, the colour changing errati-
cally to you, yellow, green, red, black, white, purple; to you
all comes in a bewildering succession, forming nothing but
a confused jumble of coloured threads crossing and re-crossing.
It would not be surprising if wearied of all this meaningless confusion you impatiently broke the thread. The work would
be hindered, the thread have to be joined again because of
your petulance. The occupation is so uninteresting to you
because so meaningless, yet somehow you keep on, perhaps
wondering the while how these confused threads can possibly
form any design, until, the work completed, you see it in all its
beauty of colour and form. That is life.

We are working out a design with God, who alone knows
the pattern and how each one fits into the scheme of creation,
with his special task which he alone can personally accomplish.
When God gave us life he intended each individual to fit as
a component part into the whole complex scheme, though
each would remain ignorant to a great extent, working from
the wrong side yet vital to the complete success of the whole.
God, as it were, sends each thread for us to return to him;

so to us the design is a meaningless jumble, the puzzle of life! This design can be considered in a twofold way: (a) each life in itself; (b) each life in relation to others. Let us examine the first. We may find yellow thread coming through representing the ordinary days, monotonous in their sameness; we get up, go to work, come home again, eat, play, sleep; day after day, week after week it goes on, with Sunday providing a slight variant of religious duties. It does not seem to mean much in the scheme of creation. The colour changes, a white thread of spiritual joy, a green thread of earthly enjoyment, a black thread of sorrow and loss, a purple thread of sickness or disappointments, a scarlet thread of victory over temptation, a blue thread of some unselfish act of kindness, still all jumbled together in apparent chaos. Growing weary, perhaps, we try to make something of our own design and break the thread by sin. We must wait for God to repair that thread by calling us to repentance, and so begin again our task. Then comes the revelation. Life's task is done, and fearfully we wait the verdict of our Judge. Unwilling to use the chosen colour, have we spoilt our task preferring our own choice as happier, more understandable? Have we ruined the design of God? Give an account of thy stewardship! We see the design, a basket of choice flowers. Now we see the meaning of the drab monotonous days transformed into golden roses, and all the incidents of life that seemed so trivial forming in variety of colour the beauty of the whole: 'Well done good and faithful servant!' Some mayhap will gaze on a ruined work caused by their own wilful choice of self, a mass of broken threads, useless chaos forming nothing: 'Depart from me ye cursed,' God lost to them for ever, because they would not work with him.

Though each life works out its own special task or part in the scheme, yet it does not stand alone; it contacts other lives that fit in with the plan, each being but a tiny part of the great whole, joining and blending to form the design. We influence others, are influenced in turn by them, for good or evil. Our parents train and guide us from our earliest days until we grow out of their care and influence, starting out on our own career; or perhaps death takes them from us and we know the sorrow of loss; their work is done. At school our teachers help to form our character; we are watched over by our priests, trained in the way of truth, given the sacraments and our footsteps turned to God. We meet playmates, friends, work-mates, each one playing his part in the plan. We meet some we like, others we dislike; some get on our nerves, or do us an injury, some few we love and find happiness, help, and comfort in their friendship. Like different threads interwoven they join up our personal task with the whole scheme. By their presence or loss we meet with joy or sorrow, but it remains always a confused mass of meetings, incidents, accidents, that we cannot understand, for which there seems to be no reason. Yet all this is forming life, is in some way helping or marring our task, leading us on to salvation or eternal damnation according as we accept the changing threads and use them all for God's purpose, or refuse to work with God and try to shape all to our own will. So we find that people come and go, mingle with our own life for a time and then depart, and in some way all this is forming and working out God's plan. Not till the end shall we know the meaning of it all, then we shall see how our tiny basket of flowers, our own personal task, fits harmoniously into the great tapestry of creation.

If we try to see life in this way, it will become less of a puzzle, more understandable, so long as we are content to leave in God's care the ultimate working out of his scheme. As the ages pass the loom of time is slowly weaving the great design of God. Each single life, one among the millions of others down the ages, is a tiny but essential part of the whole, each act in that single life building up what no other may do, having an unknown worth in God's sight, each day adding a little to the complete design. It may help us to understand a little how the various incidents in our own life, in the progress of the world at large, fit into each other and have a place in a scheme so divine that we cannot have anything but the faintest idea of its immensity and scope. So prosperity in this land, famine in another, droughts, abundance, storms and calms, riches and poverty, catastrophies, earthquakes, and all that goes to make up life in this planet, the lame, the blind, the dumb, the sick, the healthy, cripples and deformed, and the whole variety of human kind, have all a definite place in the scheme of God, foreseen and planned in his creative act so mysterious and hidden as far as we are concerned, but so necessary in the working out of God's masterpiece.

God brings good out of evil, causes the fruits of virtue to spring from pain and sorrow, balances all happenings in some way for the good of the whole. Even the great turmoil of wars, as we have experienced them during the present century, plays a definite part, perhaps purging the world in some mysterious way of its evils caused by the passions and ambitions, the selfishness and arrogance of individual men or nations. War brings out many hidden virtues and astonishing capabilities in human nature, in spite of all the turmoil, suffering and privation caused. God brings good out of evil! If we can bring ourselves to accept the truth of this, it should reconcile us to the differing incidents that make up life, teach us resignation to God's all-loving will. If we look back on the years passed we find that life levels itself out and, taking it as a whole, joy and pain balance each other when viewed in the perspective of time, for time heals all. What seemed to overwhelm us when it happened gradually fades to insignificance; what we thought never to survive has passed to the limbo of forgotten things. Stricken down by sorrow, with God's help we rose again and went our way, since always God sends strength to endure whatsoever he permits to happen in our lives. Always our Father is watching over us, caring for our welfare, and in his love we can go forward unafraid in complete trust, fearless of the future since all is in the hand of God. Could we but see that each event is of value in God's sight, in his plan, that all the time he is working with us, sustaining and helping us to carry the burdens which fall to our lot, then we could face with courage whatever may befall and co-operate with God, in the knowledge that never shall we be tried beyond our strength but shall be given grace to endure for him whatever he deems good in our regard.

Take courage then and work with God and for God. Always,

in all places, God is with us, giving us his grace by which to carry through the design he intends in our personal life. If we try to see some design in each thread of life, in no matter how dim a way, to believe that there is a definite plan in the mind of God which will bring all to our greater good, then we shall courageously bear whatever toil, grief or sorrow falls to us, make the most of our station in life, the conditions under which we live and work, and be satisfied that such is the will of God. Then we shall no longer envy those who have greater possessions, more opportunities than come to us, being content to leave all to God, knowing that he will turn all to the advantage of our soul so long as we are faithful to our trust and try to work out in patience his scheme of life for us in his great plan, thus earning for our soul the reward of good and faithful service. 'Because thou hast been faithful over few things, I will place thee over many things. Enter thou into the joy of the Lord.'

XXI   GRACE

Unaided by God, man can do nothing to save his soul, but God has promised all the help needful for salvation and this gift of God is called 'grace.' There is nothing so important to man as this grace of God; it is the life of the soul, given in Baptism, strengthened in confirmation, fed by the Holy Eucharist, restored by penance; each sacrament is a channel by which grace is given for some special purpose in the soul's life. By it we are made children of God, heirs to heaven, friends of God and brethren of Jesus. It is a great mystery indeed, but there is no doubt of its necessity to us. Its name simply means a ' free gift' of God, a favour to which we have no shadow of right or claim, a token of God's loving care of us and his desire that we should be holy and live a supernatural life. Since it is supernatural it has a value far surpassing any natural gift.

Grace has a double purpose, distinct in character and operation; one purpose is to sanctify, to make holy, and is called sanctifying grace or saint-making grace; the other, called actual grace, is concerned with particular actions or conditions of life.

Sanctifying grace is an abiding quality which gives holiness and beauty to the soul, caused by the indwelling of the Holy Spirit, who begins and perfects friendship between God and man. St Mary Magdalen de Pazzi says: 'If a man in a state of grace knew how pleasing his soul was to God, he would die of excess of joy.' In Blosius we read: 'If the beauty of a soul in grace could be seen, mankind would be transported with wonder and delight.'

In his 2nd epistle St Peter writes: 'By whom (Jesus Christ) he hath given us most great and precious promises; that by these you may be made partakers of the divine nature.' What a wonderful thought! In some mysterious way we partake of the very nature of God himself; no wonder then that the soul becomes pleasing and beautiful to God.

This effect of grace may be shown by a homely example. Take a length of old rusty iron, a dull unlovely thing, and

99

plunge it into fire. Soon it glows red, gradually increasing in brightness as it takes into itself more of the nature of fire, until it gives out light and heat from itself. It will get white-hot and become soft so that it can be formed into any shape, simply because it has received some quality from the fire itself. So with the soul, the first influence of grace at baptism changes the soul into something of beauty which gradually increases as the soul grows more holy, until it becomes wholly under the influence of the Holy Spirit and can be shaped into whatever form of holiness God desires such a soul to achieve. Such is the effect of grace in the soul.

But take once more the lovely glowing red-hot iron, plunge it into water and what happens? Instantly it loses all the nature of the fire, its heat and light, and becomes again the dull, unlovely bar of rusty iron it was before. So the soul by choosing to commit mortal sin at once loses all its participation in the divine nature, becomes loathsome in God's sight and fit only for the company of devils so long as it remain unrepentant. Now it must be given this free gift of God, the grace of repentance, it cannot obtain or claim it for itself, but is wholly dependent on the mercy of God to call it back to himself. See, then, how terrible an evil is sin; how great the risk a sinner takes in choosing to cast off this divine quality imparted to it whereby instead of being a friend he becomes an enemy of God, doomed to lose him for all eternity unless God in his infinite mercy recalls the soul to himself by grace.

The following effects are brought about in the soul by the Holy Spirit under the influence of grace.

1 The soul is purified from sin. Sin and grace are incompatible, totally opposed to each other; they cannot exist side by side, since mortal sin means the exclusion of grace. Grace, however, does not at once cure the hurt caused in our nature by original sin; hence in spite of grace we are still prone to evil; the flesh lusteth against the spirit always throughout life.

2 We become the 'Temples of God.' 'Know you not that you are the temples of God by the indwelling of the Holy Spirit?' St Thomas Aquinas writes: 'By the action of the Holy Spirit we are transformed into gods.' St Maximinus

says: 'The Godhead is conferred on us with grace.' St Basil writes: 'As iron glows when heated by fire, so man is changed by the Holy Spirit into the Godhead.' How great indeed is the dignity of the human soul thus participating in the divine nature by grace; how foolish to run the risk of losing grace for the sake of a few moments of sinful pleasure.

3 We become the friends of God. Man by creation is God's slave; sin makes him God's enemy; by grace both servitude and enmity are changed into a true friendship which is a mystical union between God and the soul. Friendship implies mutual love and esteem, an exchange of service; it brings about a certain equality, raising the inferior to a higher plane. All this is effected in the soul by grace.

4 We become 'the sons of God and heirs to the kingdom of heaven.' Grace is God's adoption of his children; and if sons, heirs also. Hence we cry 'Abba, Father;' and truly God is the Father of all in a state of grace. St Cyprian tells us: 'To be numbered among the sons of God is the highest nobility.' Let us then value above all things this precious gift.

Such is the effect of saint-making grace; without it we are dead; with it we live to God; it is our surety of eternal happiness in heaven.

The more we participate in the divine nature, the holier we are; and we increase this participation by meritorious acts of virtue. But by his own power man cannot merit; natural acts need to become supernatural in order to merit and this change can be wrought only by God. 'No man can say the Lord Jesus but by the Holy Ghost.' Man needs a further help from God in the form of 'actual graces' to enable him to merit an increase of holiness. In each meritorious act God enters by his grace in moving the will towards good and enables man to do the good act whatever it may be. This is simply a transient influence, leaving the will perfectly free to act or not act; God never compels action, nor interferes with freedom of choice. Thus suppose we are tempted to do evil (this will be presented to us as something apparently good, but a false good), God at once gives an actual grace exposing the fraud and showing the true good for the soul, and he gives the strength to reject evil and choose good without taking away any freedom. If we accept this help and reject the temptation, then God will count this as merit to us, though we have done no more than our strict duty to God as his creature, and sanctifying grace will be increased giving a greater participation in the divine nature even though we remain unconscious of this. In the same way we are influenced to do virtuous acts of all kinds by the Holy Spirit, all of which gain merit and increase of grace if we co-operate.

Many varied channels bring to us these transient graces through which the Holy Spirit influences the will towards good. Sermons, books, illness, the death of others, good example noticed, religious pictures, advice of parents or friends—all are used as tools by the Holy Ghost to influence the will to good : ' the Holy Spirit breatheth where he will.'

The hermit, St Anthony, was moved by hearing a sermon on the 'rich young man' in the gospel; St Ignatius, by reading the lives of the saints ; St Francis Borgia was affected by seeing the dead body of Queen Isabella ; St Norbert, by seeing a death caused by lightning. All these might have exclaimed with St Cyprian: 'When the Holy Ghost came into my heart, he changed me into another man.'

Always we are left perfectly free to co-operate with, or reject, grace when it is offered to us. The whole value of our good acts before God lies in the fact that they are our own free choice without any compulsion. He wants our willing service as his friends. When we co-operate with grace, then further graces are offered; resistance to grace, though not sinful, yet entails a loss of that and other graces offered and our obstinacy must be answered for to God. The servant who received five talents and gained another five was commended, but the unprofitable servant who was given one talent and buried it lost even that which he had: 'The unprofitable servant cast ye out into the exterior darkness . . . there shall be weeping.'

Graces are not equally distributed: 'The Holy Spirit breatheth where he will.' All men are given sufficient graces for salvation, but some are given more than others and of them God demands more. Moreover the influence of actual graces is not continuous but passing, offered for the need when it arises. God is prodigal with his grace, but we must guard against any presumption. A man might be tempted to sin and yield to it thinking to repent and confess later to gain pardon. To repent is a grace given by God, but since we cannot claim grace as a right, for it is a free gift, God is in no way bound to grant it and should he withhold that grace we cannot repent. We run a grave risk whenever we commit sin. We have been warned that 'God is not mocked' and it is mockery to presume that we shall be given any grace to repent from sin freely chosen by the will.

Nothing can equal the importance of God's grace, whether it be to make us pleasing in his sight by sanctifying us, or actual grace helping us to increase in holiness. It is our most precious possession to be faithfully guarded under all circumstances. Unceasingly we should pray that we may be always in a state of grace and friendship with God, that we may always faithfully co-operate with God in our sanctification.

St Paul wrote of himself: 'There was given me a sting of the flesh, an angel of Satan to buffet me. For which thing thrice I asked the Lord that it might depart from me and he said: My grace is sufficient for thee, for power is made perfect in infirmity.' Again he wrote 'By the grace of God I am what I am, in me his grace has not been void.' And again 'I can do all things in him who strengtheneth me.'

XXII PRAYER

Prayer is a vitally necessary duty appointed by God as the means of obtaining all our needs; but it is not a duty that comes easily to us. By prayer we are brought into touch with God, raising ourselves from mundane affairs into a supernatural atmosphere. God knows all our needs before we ask, better even than we know them ourselves; he does not need informing of them; but prayer makes us aware of our utter dependence on God for all, reminds us of his great goodness to us. A definite promise has been given: 'Ask and you shall receive.' But it is also a command to make use of prayer to obtain any favours or necessities. God, who is faithful to his promises, will listen to our petitions and grant an answer to prayer.

Some may say that they have prayed but in vain, thus appearing to imply that God has not kept his promise. They blame God instead of looking into themselves for the failure to obtain their requests. St James says: 'You ask and receive not because you ask amiss.' Our prayer is wanting in some essential quality; we do not ask in the right way for our prayer to be acceptable to God and made efficacious.

We hardly need to insist on attention in prayer; its need is too obvious. Without attention, prayer is an insult: 'This people honoureth me with their lips, but their heart is far from me.' In talking to others we give attention to what we are saying if only from courtesy; we do not always give the same to God, but allow our attention to wander. Of course we cannot avoid distractions creeping in, but when these are wilfully permitted to occupy our attention during prayer, then they are a grave discourtesy to God.

There are other necessary conditions to fruitful prayer:
(1) What is asked for must be of benefit to the soul, or at least not adverse to salvation, and of that we cannot always judge; we do not know all that is good or harmful to our soul.

God, all-knowing and understanding, may foresee evil results in the granting of our petition in the way we wish it. The mother of the sons of Zebedee came to our Lord with the prayer: 'Say, Lord, that my two sons may sit, the one on thy right hand, and the other on thy left hand, when thou comest into thy kingdom.' Our Lord answered: 'You know not what you ask.' She was hoping to get good political posts for her sons in an earthly kingdom, utterly ignorant of the real meaning of the 'kingdom' of which our Lord spoke. So too we often ask for things of which we do not understand all the possible consequences to ourselves.

If a child, attracted by the glitter of a sharp knife, cries to have it to play with it, would a mother give it to the little one? Neither will God give to us the sharp knives we ask for which may cut our soul off from salvation. We know not what we ask! A sick person may plead to be restored to health; it seems a reasonable and good request. But maybe God foresees that restoration to health will bring about forgetfulness of religion and of himself, entailing eternal punishment; hence that petition is not granted in the form asked, and seems wasted as far as the sick person is concerned. But in reality the prayer is answered in a far better way such as, for example, by the gift of patience or resignation to suffering, which is more beneficial to the soul.

We must always ask in a spirit of resignation to God's will, leaving him to judge of the suitability of our request. 'Not my will, but thine be done' must always be the spirit of prayer. Jesus prayed: 'Father, if it be possible, let this chalice pass from me.' What would have happened to us if that petition had been granted? But Jesus added: 'Yet not my will, but thine be done.' Then an angel descended to give him the strength to endure for our sakes the terrible anguish of the passion and death on the cross; that was the answer to his prayer. So with us; we may not get what we ask in the way we want it, but our prayer is not in vain since something of greater value is given to the soul.

Again, when prayer seems to remain unanswered, we may find that all desire for what we wanted passes away and some other thing that gives more satisfaction has taken its place. That is the answer to our prayer and the way in which God has granted our request. Hence when we pray it should always be with the determination of leaving to God the decision as to whether it is good for us to have such a request granted, or to give us some other more suitable gift. It is ignorance which makes us resent the refusal of exactly the thing we desire.

(2) Confidence, tested by perseverance, is also essential to prayer. God did not promise to grant what we ask at any special time. Some have so little confidence that, not receiving immediately, they give up hope and pray no more. St James says: 'Let him ask in faith, nothing wavering. For he that wavereth is like a wave of the sea which is moved and carried by the wind. Therefore let not that man think he shall receive anything of the Lord.' Without faith and confidence, prayer is barren. 'Amen, if any man say to this mountain, Be thou removed and cast into the sea and shall not stagger in his faith, it shall be done for him.' Do we pray with that confidence and faith which removes mountains? Many wish to settle the time and manner of having their request granted; they tell God what he ought to do rather than seek humbly the favour they need. Not getting what they ask when they have decided that they want it, they cease to pray, failing in that perseverance which is the test of real faith and confidence.

St Luke tells us: 'We always ought to pray and not to faint.' Thus our Lord tells the story of the man who, needing bread, knocks on the door of a friend and asks for three loaves. The friend, having retired to bed, refuses to be disturbed to give what is needful. The man continues knocking so that the friend is forced for the sake of peace to get up and give what is needed. Persistence is rewarded. When St Augustine was steeped in heresy, his mother prayed for years for his conversion. One would have thought such a request worthy of an immediate answer, but God tested the confidence of this mother first and then granted her petition a hundredfold.

We must be prepared to be tried and tested, to be kept waiting till God sees fit to give what we ask. 'The kingdom of heaven suffereth violence and the violent bear it away.' Unless we persevere in our prayer we are doomed to disappointment. God has the right to demand faith and confidence, to test us by our perseverance, and to grant our petition when and where and in the manner he chooses, which will always be to our best advantage.

(3)   Humility is also essential as befits one who asks a favour. 'I will speak with my God, whereas I am but dust and ashes.' We must be aware of our nothingness in the sight of God, of our utter dependence on his goodness, of the immense difference between us who ask and God who is to grant. We must realise our unworthiness, our insignificance, and God's infinite condescension in listening to a creature as sinful and wilful as man. 'The prayer of him that humbleth himself shall pierce the clouds.' St James says: 'God resisteth the proud and giveth grace to the humble.' The centurion asking that his servant might be healed was truly humble: 'Lord, I am not worthy that thou shouldst enter under my roof; say only the word and my servant shall be healed.' There is both humility and confidence shown in his petition, humility, because he realised his unworthiness, confidence since he believed it sufficient for our Lord merely to speak the word.

The publican because of his humility in prayer was justified; the pride of the pharisee in prayer caused his condemnation.

(4)   We must be at peace with all our brethren. 'God listens not to one who hath anything against his brother.' If we pray with bitterness against some other or with unforgiveness of another poisoning our heart, God will not hearken. 'If when thou comest to offer thy gift, thou rememberest that thy brother hath anything against thee, leave there thy gift and go first and be reconciled to thy brother.' How can we hope to be heard in prayer unless we have charity towards all men?

Such are the essential qualities which all prayer must have if we are to be assured of a favourable hearing. Prayer is not just a matter of asking for something; it must be endowed with the disposition that a suppliant should possess before God. We are not forbidden to ask for temporal favours; the promise does not specify any definite object. Our Lord said: 'Whatsoever you ask the Father in my name, he will give it to you.' There are no restrictions; we may ask for anything which seems good and desirable to us, and which will not hinder our salvation. All failure in prayer comes from our dispositions and not from any unfaithfulness on the part of God to his promise. We can be absolutely sure of God; he is always infinitely faithful. We, however, are often wanting in the essential qualities of prayer and it is our want of proper dispositions that causes failure and disappointment in prayer. We must pray with true resignation to the will of God, who knows all things and gives only what is good to us. Our faith and confidence are to be real and solid, proving their worth by perseverance, not fainting by the way, but able to remove mountains. God will grant the favour in his own time, not when we wish it, as too often we expect, being wanting in humility and patience. Being but dust and ashes it is fitting that we should realise our nothingness in the sight of God and his infinite condescension in listening to sinners.

'Ask and you shall receive'—'Whatsoever you ask the Father in my name it shall be given to you'—'The kingdom of heaven suffereth violence and the violent bear it away.'

XXIII DIFFICULTY OF PRAYER

Prayer, though one of the chief duties of religion, does not come easily to us. Being the basis of religion, our own personal attitude towards God, some conscious effort is needed to gain union with God in prayer. But this will not come of itself; free will must be exercised. True indeed it is that God knows all our needs, all our desires, before we pray; but this does not make prayer unnecessary. God respects the freedom of our will; he never forces his gifts on us; therefore prayer is necessary in order to produce in us a proper attitude to God, to change the mind and heart, to prepare us to receive, to realise our utter dependence on God for all things. No parent can give to a child unless that child is willing to co-operate; a man may be the wisest in the world, but he cannot give his knowledge to the child who does not evince the proper attitude; there must be a desire to learn; knowledge cannot be forced on a child. So unless we subject the will to God we cannot gain union with God, nor can he give us what we need when we are not receptive. Prayer puts us in the proper attitude of subjection of will to God, of readiness to receive gifts, and is a necessary act of religion.

Prayer is by no means easy to us and entails a struggle with our natural propensities. At times it is easy because we happen to be in the mood and God feels near; at other times it is the very opposite, we feel completely out of touch with the affairs of the spirit. Such feelings count for little in spiritual matters, being beyond our control, and not subject to our will; we cannot order our feelings as we wish. That ease in prayer to-day may be the effect of well-being; that difficulty to-morrow due to some physical ailment such as indigestion or moodiness; such feelings can be disregarded as of no account. God values the effort made to gain union with him in spite of natural difficulties which so hamper the efforts of the soul in its desire to be subject to God.

Prayer is difficult to us from its very nature; it is supernatural i.e. beyond the power of nature; we are natural, i.e. bound down to natural objects. To pray is to lift ourselves from the natural into the supernatural, which is obviously beyond our own natural powers and needs the help of God. Take a fish out of water; it gasps for air, flounders about making intense efforts to get back to its natural element, and is most uncomfortable out of the water. In prayer a man is something of 'a fish out of water,' in spite of the effects of grace, and tends to slip back into his natural element. One of the great difficulties in prayer arises out of this strenuous effort to live in the supernatural order which is strange to us, the continual struggle to avoid slipping back to the natural.

Hence arise what we call 'distractions' in prayer which are simply the slipping back into the natural. We begin our prayer with the best of intentions only to find that we are thinking of business, of anxieties, of pleasures, or other interests; a fresh start is made with the same result. This is very disturbing but not sinful. We cannot leave such things outside, as we can a dog or an umbrella; our daily interests are always with us and will not be denied but drag us back to earth in spite of our intentions. This is but the release of natural activities which occur without any conscious act on our part. Not till we become aware of them and then deliberately pursue them do we have a 'wilful' and therefore 'sinful' distraction in prayer.

We must guard against discouragement; we must be patient with our nature, persevering in spite of difficulty in the effort to keep in touch with God. Discouragement is the devil's ally and the worst enemy of the spirit. Once we are discouraged, the devil finds it easy to persuade us to give up the effort of prayer; hence we must go on trying in the face of the difficulty to keep in touch with God, fighting against our natural propensity, the difficulty of existing in a supernatural environment. Let us realise at once that prayer is difficult and with God's help persevere.

But perhaps we can do more; we can turn these very distractions into prayer. Something is weighing on the mind and will not be denied; tell God all about it; nothing is too trivial for his love to notice; he wants to share in our daily cares and interests: 'Come to me all ye that labour and are burdened.' If we visit a friend we do not run away from him saying that we are too worried to talk with him; rather should we find that having discussed the matter with our friend we felt so much the better for it. Is not God the best of all friends to whom we can unburden our minds and from whom gain strength?

Do we make prayer more difficult because we do not talk to God as friend to friend? That is the essence of prayer: 'God spoke to Moses face to face as a man is wont to speak with his friend.' That is real prayer. The disciples begged: 'Lord teach us how to pray.' That was a perfect prayer which obtained an immediate answer. They were talking ' as friend to friend.' Is our prayer like that? There should be nothing unnatural in the words we use; too often prayer is not natural in the words we speak, is too impersonal in the sense that we try to be something we are not and soon tire. Look at it from the personal standpoint: 'I must talk with God in my own words, not acting or aping another, trying to speak above myself. I must be natural. A friend is not impressed by my high-flown talk; he would merely be amused; so I am natural with him. God knows me better that any friend, so it is useless to pose. I must be "myself."' We must realise that fact and be natural in the words used. Some people are emotional and can use the language of ecstasy; others are practical and such language is merely a pose. What suits one will not fit another. Ready-made clothes may fit one man, but not all; neither will ready-made prayers fit all. We must be honest in prayer and not say what we do not mean. Why say ' O God, take me to thyself' when really we want to remain on earth?

Perhaps some would be better without prayer-books except for official prayers. When we write to a friend we do not get 'examples for letters' and choose what seems to suit the occasion; we sit down and let our thoughts flow out in our own words; the letter is 'personal.' A copied letter would be stilted and unsuitable. So, in many ways, a prayer-book is merely a model, not *our* prayer. A certain great saint prayed: 'O thou stream from the life-giving fountain, thou fragrance and sweetness of divine delight, I prostrate myself in my indigence and misery in the presence of thine overflowing fulness.' Does poetic language of this kind appeal to you? If not, do not use it. But in contrast take this official prayer of the Church: 'Grant we beseech thee, Almighty God, that we who justly suffer for our sins may be relieved by the consolation of thy grace. Through Jesus Christ our Lord.' A few simple, easily understood words. Has this prayer more appeal? It will depend on temperament, for our prayer must suit us, otherwise it becomes unnatural and burdensome. How simple the publican's prayer: 'O God, be merciful to me, a sinner.'

Prayer must be personal and express what we really mean to say. We must pray in the method that suits. It must be 'I,' not some one else.

If it is found unduly irksome, do not try to pray for long periods. Talk to your friend as long as you wish, then keep silent. God speaks to us in the silence of our hearts, but often we give him little chance to speak. God does not want us to read to him at length out of a book; he wants to hear all about our interests and needs, to share our personal lives. He does not want us to be talking all the time; friends can be quite happy together in silence. In the Sermon on the Mount our Lord said: 'When you pray speak not much as the heathens. For they think that in their much speaking they may be heard. Be not like them, for your heavenly Father knoweth what is needful for you before you ask him.' He then gives us that lovely prayer 'Our Father' in plain simple words full of deep theology and calling for profound thought to fathom all its meaning and beauty. Usually in prayer we try to do all the talking and do not give God the opportunity to speak to us. There is no need to keep up a continual flow of words; he is our friend, so let us sometimes be silent with him.

It may be that we could more easily keep in touch with God by means of frequent short ejaculations throughout the day, rather than by trying to spend some long time in praying and then, thinking our duty done, forget about God. It is easy to call God to mind at intervals during the day, to call on his holy name, to ask for mercy and forgiveness, to beg a favour, to thank him for his kindness. Just as the thought of a friend will often come into the mind, so if we really look on God as a friend, we cannot but help thinking of him at intervals; that is real prayer. We might so easily say: 'Thank God for this lovely day.' 'What a beautiful garden. If flowers are so beautiful, what must God be?' The thought of God is prayer, and it does not need deep spirituality to raise our mind to the thought of God and so to pray to him. The more we accustom ourselves to this frequent thought of God, the more habitual it will become in us, the more we shall pray and increase in God's grace, growing nearer to him day by day.

We should each find some method of prayer to suit our temperament and keep us in continual union with God. We are not all alike; where one can spend an hour in prayer, another would become intensely wearied by it, and for such a one, short periods of prayer, even ejaculations only, would suit better. All have to struggle against distractions, the slipping back to the natural element; but these can be made the subject of prayer, if not too frivolous. Pray in the language that you use normally, instead of aping another and being unnatural, or posing. God does not want us to read to him, but to speak as friend to friend, and at times not to speak at all but to keep silent with him that he may speak to us himself in the silence of our heart. Prayer is union with God. No matter how we attain it, so long as the union is achieved, prayer is doing its work in our soul.

'I will speak with my God, whereas I am but dust and ashes.'

XXIV DEVOTION

When people say they have a special devotion to some saint or mystery it too often means nothing more than a sentimental feeling towards the object that is attractive without any knowledge of what devotion truly means.

Devotion may be defined as 'a setting apart,' 'a zealous application of the powers to a certain object.' That is what devotion means—the setting apart of our spiritual nature to the love and service of God, a zealous application of our powers to the accomplishment of God's will. That sensible joy occasionally felt in serving God is not devotion in the true sense, though it may be the outcome of devotion; devotion does not consist merely in 'feelings' of attraction or satisfaction in holy objects.

Man's resemblance to God lies in the intellect and will, therefore all our religious attitude to God lies in these two powers. We know God by intelligence; we serve him by will through love. These two powers control all the service of our being. Whatever we possess in common with brute creation may be ruled out as being of no consequence. Emotions or feelings are merely physical things not under our control; yet many try to make religion simply a thing of feeling and emotion, thinking this to be devotion, whereas religion is scarcely a matter of emotion at all. True there is a sensible devotion, that feeling of joy in serving God, but this is not essential to devotion at all; it is at most simply an adjunct.

Devotion is also taken to mean those acts of religion which we perform towards some special saint or mystery; hence we speak of devotion to the Sacred Heart, to our Lady, to St Therese or some other saint that appeals to us, according as we feel drawn to making some special effort in their regard. The test of the reality of such devotion is the effect it has on our love and service of God himself. It must lead us to him, or there is something wanting in it, it is unreal.

Devotion means the habitual disposition to give oneself promptly to God, a readiness to serve him at all times. It consists in a fervent love of God, springing from knowledge of him and submission of the will to him in all things. It is not a passing phase but the lasting endeavour to serve faithfully. Every other kind of devotion is the offspring of this setting apart of self to perseverance in the service of God. The sensible feeling of joy or consolation felt in this service is unessential; it does not merit of itself, but it may be a valuable help from God and a foretaste of the possibilities of true spiritual happiness, leading us to despise the attractions of the world and turn more fully to God. Such feelings are usually transient, beyond our control entirely, however much we may desire to feel joy in serving God; hence we cannot judge of devotion by such passing emotions. They can in fact be dangerous by making us presumptuous, impatient, even disobedient. Their real worth is to foster obedience, to make us truly humble, to urge us to a stricter fulfilment of duty.

There is a temptation for some to shirk duty so as to spend more time in 'devotion.' This is of course contrary to true devotion. The love of God and of our neighbour go hand-in-hand; they cannot be separated. As love for God increases, so must love of our neighbour become greater; by this we may test the reality of our devotion. True devotion to any object, whatever it may be, must lead to a greater love for God and our neighbour, or it is failing in its chief purpose.

How shall we obtain a true devotion?

(1) We must remove the obstacles to devotion.

(a) Perhaps we seek earthly consolations and pleasures which are inconsistent with true devotion. 'No man can serve two masters,' God and the world are in continual opposition. The more worldly pleasure is sought, the less inclination there is towards God; that is inevitable. Pleasure and devotion; the carnal and spiritual; these are definitely opposed to each other. If we seek the one, we must despise the other, since both claim our whole service and we cannot serve two masters. God claims all our love and service; so does the world. We must choose to which we shall give our allegiance. So often we make the mistake of trying to fulfil the two claims and fail.

This does not mean the cutting out of all innocent pleasure,

115

but it does mean a moderate use of it as a means of restoring our flagging energy. Experience proves that the more we turn to worldly pleasure the less we seek the service of God, the less we frequent the sacraments, the less time we give to visiting the church. 'Where thy treasure is, there is thy heart also.' There is so often the attraction of pleasure as against the going to confession; the attraction of the fireside or cards at home as against going out in the cold to evening service on Sunday. How often do we succumb to the worldly and set aside the spiritual good of the soul?

(b) Many are too anxious about temporal affairs. We must work for a living and through that means, too, advance towards salvation, but there is a command that we work not for the things that perish. Too much time is given to acquiring worldly possessions rather than seeking spiritual needs; we are too occupied in making ourselves comfortable, in preparing for old age, in accumulating unnecessary trifles, but leaving too little time for spiritual needs to be gained. 'Be not solicitous what you shall eat or what you shall drink or wherewith you shall be clothed, your heavenly Father knoweth that you have need of these things.' Do we give credit to God for such knowledge? Does not our anxiety about temporal things show a want of trust in God? It is because of this want of trust that we devote so much of our time to temporal needs, to the neglect of our spiritual needs. 'Seek ye first the kingdom of God and these things shall be added unto you.'

(c) Curiosity about the affairs of the world is a hindrance to devotion. How anxious we are to know all that is happening, to hear all the news. We can discuss all the affairs of the world but we cannot give a simple explanation to those who ask of the truths of religion, of what we believe. Of what value to the soul is all this knowledge of the affairs of the world, when we are ignorant of the truths of the spirit? Why do we not show at least a similar eagerness to know about God and talk about him to those who will listen? Knowledge of the world's affairs cannot teach us to know God, yet that is our chief duty in life, for God made us to know him.

(2) What are the positive means of gaining true devotion?

(a)   The consideration of God's infinite goodness towards us, his loving care for our daily needs. We take all for granted as though we had a perfect right to all things; the sun shines, the rain falls, the earth yields its fruits, we are fed and clothed. How often do we give a thought to the giver of all good things in thanks for his care of our needs? We fall into sin and expect forgiveness; we have showered on us graces that we neglect; we show ingratitude to God. The consciousness of defects, our want of love and service should make us desire to be more fervent. We are weak and helpless, incapable of any good by our own effort without God's grace. Such thoughts as these should spur us on to a truer service.

(b)   The frequent thought of the presence of God. We know that God is everywhere, that nothing can be hidden from him, but does it mean anything to us? Could we but get the habit of adverting to this all-present idea of God, it would make a notable difference in our lives. A daily offering of self to God to work for him and not merely for the things that perish, this would lead us to a truer devotion. Prayer is always a powerful aid to devotion; the effort towards union with God keeps him always before our mind, reminds us of all that we owe to him in love and service.

We must try to get a true idea of devotion, that setting apart of self to the service of God. It is no vague sentimental feeling towards some pious object. It is pathetic, and even nauseating at times, to see what is done in the name of devotion. Devotion does not consist in protracted prayers before some statue, nor in extraordinary actions, in burning candles at some shrine, putting flowers before a statue. It does not consist in austerities, penances, hair-shirts and such like. It is not a feeling of being good and holy, of feeling happy in 'devotional services' in church. Devotion is practical in all states of life, is consistent with all kinds of work, is an attitude of the soul to God.

Each of us should be full of devotion because we ought to be 'devoted' to the service of God at all times, in all places, ready to submit our will to his. We must realise that true devotion consists in knowing God by the intelligence, loving him with the whole will, and through this knowledge and love giving him our whole-hearted service; nothing else can be true devotion. All other things, feelings of joy, consolations, and such like, may be the fruits of devotion but are quite unnecessary and unessential and their absence proves nothing at all. In the beginning of our real turning to God there may be great joy and consolation; it may soon pass never to return. But devotion is unending perseverance in serving God and our neighbour through knowledge and love.

To know, to love, and to serve God is the essence of all devotion, the setting apart of our whole being, body and soul, in complete subjection to the holy will of God.

XXV SUFFERING

The problem of suffering is always a puzzle to man, who finds it most difficult to reconcile pain and suffering with the infinite love and goodness of God. It was no part of the design of creation that pain and hardships should be the lot of man; God intended all his creatures to be happy, but the free-will of man upset God's plan by disobedience in claiming to be independent of God. Sin is the cause of pain, and man must pay the penalty which results from his choice of evil. Pain or suffering includes all that goes against the grain, physical pain, mental anguish, disappointments, humiliations, poverty, the struggle between the flesh and the spirit, sadness at seeing others enjoy what one would like for oneself, the difficulty of keeping the law of God and such-like disabilities, all of which are the penalty of sin and so must be accepted as inevitable in this vale of tears. It was man that made 'this vale of tears,' not God. Hence suffering in some form is the lot of all human beings and must be endured and life must be adjusted so that suffering is made profitable to man's spiritual state.

There are many false ideas about suffering. There are those who think that the christian way of life glorifies suffering for its own sake; but that is a wrong conception. The christian ideal is to use suffering as a means of virtue, to turn evil into good, to accept pain as an atonement offered by the mystical body in union with the sufferings of Christ, its head. Even our Lord did not choose suffering for its own sake. He avoided it when he could so do without impairing his mission on earth. 'They took up stones therefore to cast at him. But Jesus hid himself and went out of the temple.' (John VIII, 59). Again in the Agony in the Garden, his human nature revolted against the pain and suffering of the passion: 'Father, if it be possible, let this chalice pass from me.' He did not seek suffering for suffering's sake but he accepted it because of the future good to be gained. Thus St Paul writes to the Hebrews (XII, 2). 'Jesus . . . who having joy set before him, endured the cross.' This passage is often misunderstood to mean that a choice between joy or pain is set before Jesus; that is not so. It means that to obtain the future joy of eternal happiness for the mystical body he accepted the present suffering of the passion. He had no purpose except 'to do the will of my Father who is in heaven.' Since the decree of God entailed all the sufferings of the passion and death on the cross in order that atonement for sin be made, Jesus accepted these sufferings because it was the will of God; he did not choose suffering for its own sake, his human nature cried out against it.

Suffering is not good in itself; it is indifferent. The good or evil in suffering lies in the attitude of mind towards it. It may be either a blessing or a curse; it may ennoble man's nature or stultify it. Take the example of a hermit and a prisoner. Both live in the narrow confines of a small cell, but the hermit is contented and happy whereas the prisoner repines against the loss of liberty; the hermit through his love for God has all he needs, but the prisoner feels deprived of everything without his freedom. Another example is found in those who were crucified with our Lord. Both suffer the same torments, but one accepts his state as a just punishment for his misdeeds and obtains a promise of future bliss; the other rails against his state and curses Christ, making his state worse than before.

It is the attitude of mind towards suffering that makes it good or evil. We are not asked to seek suffering for its own sake, but to accept it as the inevitable consequence of sin and to endure it out of love for God. Thus suffering is turned into spiritual good by uniting it with the sufferings of Christ, whereby we, as members of his mystical body, suffer in union with the head and share in his atonement for the sins of mankind.

As to the true mind of the Church, which is accused of glorifying pain as something good in itself, it may happen that individual preachers may overstep the mark and seem to glorify pain for its own sake, but they are proved to be in error by objective facts. Witness the number of institutions served by religious intended solely to alleviate human suffering, the efforts of the Church to better the condition of the working classes, the dispensations granted from even the small amount

120

of mortification imposed as penance. Christians are not forbidden to better their state, to enjoy lawful amusements or benefits, to seek remedies from pain. The Church does not glorify suffering for its own sake; she does not worship pain; but she worships God by love and the acceptance of his will even when that entails suffering. Knowing that suffering is the inevitable result of sin and must be endured, the Church strives to teach man how to adjust his attitude of mind so that by the right acceptance of his disabilities he can gain spiritual profit and salvation for his soul.

Another false idea is that suffering is a punishment sent by God for personal sin. 'What have I done to deserve this pain?' one will ask. It seems unjust to be made to suffer without knowing why; the injustice rankles in the mind, causing bitterness of heart and resentment against pain. But God is not unjust; he does not punish by sending suffering that is undeserved. Pain may be the result of personal sin, but then it follows often as the ordinary result of our want of prudence. We may suffer intense anxiety of mind because of the evil we have done. That is our own fault; it is not God who afflicts us. We may suffer physical pain through want of care; we cannot blame God if we are crippled for life by rushing carelessly across a busy street. That comes from want of prudence and we are ourselves entirely to blame. Nature exacts its own penalties for imprudence.

'What cannot be cured must be endured,' but not in despair nor with a pagan stoicism; rather by accepting suffering as the inevitable lot of man and turning it to benefit for the soul. There is no doubt that suffering can, if used rightly, ennoble man's nature. Ruskin writes: 'The man who has passed thro' life without the chastening discipline of bodily pain has missed one of the best parts of existence. To suffer is one of the noblest prerogatives of human nature. Without suffering life would be robbed of half its zest and the thought of death would drive us to despair.'

As gold is tried by fire and refined, so man's nature is purified and refined by suffering borne in patience for the love of God. It makes one more gentle, tolerant and sympathetic;

it teaches thought for others, understanding and unselfishness. Hence it increases virtue and spiritualises a man's nature. How can a man really sympathise with another, i,e. suffer with him, unless he has first suffered himself? One who has never felt the pain of toothache can have no idea of the suffering it can cause, or one who has never been ill cannot feel patience with the sick. But when one has first experienced suffering in oneself, then one is able to understand and sympathise with another in pain. Suffering broadens a man's outlook, makes him compassionate and eager to help other sufferers. It will teach him patience, resignation to God's will and real charity.

At times suffering is the only thing that will bring back a soul to God. It proves how empty and unsatisfying are the deceitful promises of the world, the futility of seeking any lasting happiness in pleasure or the ceaseless search for new excitements. Suffering convinces a man that his true and lasting happiness can be found only in the service of God and in submission to the will of God, the one purpose for which man was created and in which alone any real happiness can be found. Man has lost his way, but suffering can bring him back to the right and only path to human happiness and the true purpose of life.

This christian way of life, then, does not glorify suffering for its own sake nor does it seek pain as a good, but it does recognise the inevitableness of suffering and tries to utilise it for the good of the soul. 'Christ suffered leaving us an example that we should follow in his steps.' We profess to follow Christ, but shrink from anything that entails sacrifice of self. We prefer the consolation of God to the God of consolation. God has promised that we shall not be tried beyond endurance. He permits us to use the many joys created for our benefit. Life is not all sorrow; it has its meed of happiness to counterbalance sorrows, but true joy can be found only in the wholehearted acceptance of God's will. The christian must be submissive to God in all, he must be faithful in everything, and the suffering entailed by this fidelity must be accepted if we follow Christ. Jesus had no morbid love of pain for its own sake, for poverty, hardship and such like; he simply accepted them as inevitable in his human career as decreed by his heavenly Father. The key to his whole life is this: 'I came to do the will of him that sent me.'

The christian must be Christ-like in his acceptance of whatever may be his lot, giving faithful service and showing submission to God's will whether it be the cause of joy or of suffering. There is no need to seek suffering; it is sure to come. We have but to accept it and use it to ennoble our human nature. We may pray that the 'chalice of suffering may pass from us,' yet it must be in the spirit of Christ which can add: 'Not my will but thine be done.'

XXVI CONSCIENCE

'Without laws, the human race would be no better than wild beasts of prey' wrote a heathen sage. Of laws the first is the natural law which is the fundamental rule or standard of human acts, imprinted on the heart of each human being even though he knows not God. Each man has an intuitive notion of right and wrong, which decides for him the morality of his acts, teaches him the important requirements, homage to God, respect for one's own life, the rights of others, etc. In addition to this natural law there are the ten Commandments, or the revealed law which is an amplification of the natural law. Further there are ecclesiastical law, or the commandments of the Church, and civil law, or the law of the land which binds those subject to it under obedience so long as nothing contrary to divine law is contained therein.

From knowledge of the law arises conscience, i.e. an act of judgement deciding the legality or otherwise of an action. Conscience is a most important factor in our spiritual life since it is the deciding faculty in questions of right and wrong. Each human being is endowed with this faculty to guide him in discerning law and applying it to any specific act. It is not a virtue, a habit, but a decision or judgement of the practical reason about a certain act as to whether it is or is not in accordance with the law of God.

We are never allowed to act in a way contrary to this decision of conscience. St Paul writes: 'All that is not of faith (i.e. according to conscience or "in good faith") is sinful.' Suppose that, by mistake, I think to-day to be a Friday, on which day the eating of meat is forbidden, whereas in fact it is Thursday, and I eat meat, thereby acting against my conscience. In that case I sin in so doing, because I have consented to what conscience tells me is unlawful at that time.

Conscience is directed by knowledge of the law and is the application of such knowledge here and now to some particular act; the consequent decision regulates our moral conduct. Obviously conscience is of the gravest importance, hence we should understand its working as far as we are able. We shall be judged by the measure of our compliance with its dictates. Granted that we have a true conscience, it is an infallible guide to all acts. It has been called 'the voice of God' but is in fact 'an act of the practical reason deciding what is to be done, or not to be done, here and now.'

Conscience may be 'antecedent' or 'subsequent.' Antecedent conscience decides the lawfulness or otherwise of what is proposed before we do it. We are bound to follow this decision unless we have grave reason for thinking that we may have a false conscience.' If we go against this decision, we sin. Subsequent conscience is the peace or disquiet of mind following the act. We have either a 'good' or a 'bad' conscience in passing judgement on what we have done. A good conscience gives peace and joy to the soul; a bad one makes us ill at ease and embitters the soul, so that it torments us until we repent of the evil done. It can drive us to despair, as it did Judas; or to repentance, as it did Peter.

Conscience is of different kinds also; one may have a true conscience or a doubtful conscience, even a false conscience. The true conscience judges in conformity with the law of God; the doubtful hesitates or fears to decide; the false is out of harmony with divine law. It is a principle that we are never allowed to act on a doubtful conscience; we may not give ourselves the benefit of the doubt in things moral, but must decide one way or the other. If possible we must seek advice to settle the matter and remove all doubt; if the matter is urgent, we are permitted to do what seems most reasonable at the moment and seek advice later; in other words we must make a decision before we may act. If a choice must be made between two evils, what appears to be the less evil must be chosen. If two duties of obligation conflict, we must decide which has the greater claim, e.g. the choice between the obligation of hearing Mass or the necessity of attending to a sick person; we must decide which is the more urgent claim, and act accordingly.

A false conscience is a very different matter. If through ignorance of the law which is no fault of our own conscience misleads us, we are still bound to follow it. If we are convinced

125

that to-day there is an obligation to hear Mass, we are bound to do so, even though in fact there is no obligation; otherwise we disobey conscience and sin in consequence. But if a person of normal intelligence is culpably ignorant, i.e. ignorant through his own fault, or wishes not to know the law as an excuse to evade it, if he neglects ordinary diligence to learn what he ought to know, then he has a false conscience, and each time such a conscience is followed sin is committed.

A lax conscience, sometimes cloaked under the name of broadmindedness, is one that easily condones evil because of bad habits, passion, or for similar reasons; it fails to detect evil in what pleases, or excuses itself on the plea that 'God will understand.' In time such a conscience may cease to act either in warning or blaming. It becomes a dead conscience.

The scrupulous conscience is a disease of the mind causing a foolish fear of sin rather than a sane judgement of reason. St Francis de Sales says that it has its source in pride, though it may also be due to nervous derangement or other physical causes. Like a timid horse that shies at shadows, endangering its rider, such a conscience imagines sin where none exists; it is liable to cause disobedience and stubbornness. People afflicted in such a manner must distrust their own judgement in conscience matters and rely implicitly on the advice of their confessor, giving him complete obedience in his directions as the only cure for such an illness of mind. Signs of a scrupulous conscience are to be recognised in too much anxiety about past confessions, in profuse and irrelevant explanations of the circumstances of an action, in want of obedience to the confessor's advice—or in seeking advice from several confessors on the same matter through want of trust or disagreement with the decision given. The cause of such a state may be temperament, hidden pride, nervous disposition or taking too much notice of what is said by others who are in no way qualified to decide in matters of conscience.

Since conscience is of such vital importance to the soul, we must strive to study the divine law, by perfect sincerity with self, by fervent prayer, by fighting the lower impulses of nature and by obedience to the decisions of our confessor in any matter. We cannot be too earnest in the desire to know what should be known; too many allow themselves to be influenced by others who have not sufficient knowledge themselves to teach what is right or wrong or to give advice on matters of conscience. They can only guide us by their own conscience and we have no evidence that their own conscience is a true one. The directing of conscience is a very delicate matter and in any doubt the advice of the priest should always be asked; it is his business to direct consciences to the truth; he is fully qualified by study of the law to instruct others. If we are sick, we do not go to the butcher or the baker to find out what is wrong; we go to a doctor qualified to diagnose what ails us and to give us the proper remedy. Similarly in all matters of conscience we ought to go to the properly qualified 'soul-doctor,' the priest.

Further, we must not be misled by 'mass conscience.' One often hears the easy judgement 'It is all right: everyone does it.' But is that a sound piece of reasoning? Materials are at times taken from the factory by workers who say it is all right because everyone does it. But does the employer know and approve of the custom? If he objects to stuff being taken, then it is stealing in spite of the fact that all do it. Many wrongs do not make a right. Prejudice is also misleading. We must not allow the prejudices of others to influence conscience. Prejudice is the ill-formed judgement of the mind made without sufficient knowledge or reason or without due consideration. It deems wrong what is right, and right what is wrong. It is no standard by which to judge the law. Some people, for instance, maintain that it is a sin to receive Holy Communion without previous confession the night before; they are ignorant of the Church's ruling on this point. They are guided by their prejudice which is no standard for true decisions.

Each must follow his own conscience, not another's; he will be judged by his own conscience. One may have a lax conscience, another a false, or a scrupulous conscience; we cannot accept their advice. In all cases of any doubt the only safe course is to ask the advice of a priest who by his study and knowledge of the law and of human responsibilities is alone capable of advising in matters of conscience. His advice is based on his knowledge of the law and its application; that of others is based on the promptings of their own conscience which may be true, but may also be lax, scrupulous or false. How can we place any reliance on others who probably know little more than we ourselves know and who are not able to direct themselves properly in many cases? If we cannot settle our own doubts, how can we be sure that another is giving correct advice without any personal prejudice, unless we are satisfied as to his qualifications? We must not play the fool in so delicate a matter on which so much depends in our spiritual life. St Paul writes (II Corinthians IV): 'To me it is a small thing to be judged by you or by man's day; but neither do I judge myself. For I am not conscious to myself of anything, yet I am not hereby justified, but he that judgeth is the Lord.' He cares not what judgements are passed on him by man because his own conscience is clear and at peace; that is sufficient; God alone can judge him. If we act in accordance with the dictates of our own conscience, if we act 'in good faith,' then we shall be at peace with God in our own mind, knowing that we have done our best. It matters not what others may do or judge. We act by our own conscience, not by another's.

XXVII TEMPTATION

We read in the Epistle of St James: (I, 12) 'Blessed is the man that endureth temptations; for when he hath been proved he shall receive the crown of life which God hath promised to them that love him.' It is the lot of man to be tempted; life on earth is a warfare, so that from the dawn of reason, when the child first knows the difference between good and evil, until the moment of death he is liable to temptation. As children we found it hard to be good, easy to be naughty; that was our early experience of temptation. Growing older we met new temptations. The more we experience life, the more temptations beset us. Throughout life this continues without cessation; no one is exempt, no age, no time, no place, no state of life is free; at home, at work, in church or cloister, in solitude or in company, temptations afflict us. People in the world, married or single, cloistered monks and nuns, priest and bishop, hermits, saints and sinners, have all to endure temptation. Even Jesus himself was tempted: 'Jesus was led by the spirit into the desert to be tempted by the devil.' From this we know that temptation is not sin; we need not be scared by its onset; it cannot force us to sin. By God's grace we can overcome all temptations, no matter how grave they be.

What is temptation? It is a trial of fitness for eternal life. It may be defined as a persuasion or suggestion, coming from within ourselves or from some external source, to do what we know to be contrary to the law of God. The source from within is called 'the flesh': that from without either the 'world' or the 'devil'; hence at baptism we renounce the devil with all his works, the world with all its pomps, the flesh with all its temptations. The devil makes use of the world and the flesh to tempt us; seldom if ever do we perceive his presence for he is too cunning. Did we sense the presence of his cloven hoof when an alluring vista opened before us, we should be wary and suspicious of danger. When there is no indication of the devil at work it is difficult to see how some little self-indulgence may lead to sin.

Let us examine his method in the temptation of Jesus. The devil does not begin by suggesting definite evil; he is too wise. Jesus was hungry after fasting ahd a suggestion came that he should turn stones into bread to satisfy his hunger. There does not seem any wrong here, just a yielding to a natural desire for food. But Jesus knew that to yield in such a way, that is by the working of the suggested miracle, would be an inordinate use of divine power. Therefore he rejected the temptation. The next suggestion is to cast himself down from the pinnacle of the temple, the devil reminding him 'He hath given his angels charge over thee, lest thou dash thy foot against a stone.' Our Lord could have done it, of course. But for what reason? It could only have been for ostentation, self-advertisement, pride of power or vanity. Again the devil's suggestion was scorned. Then came the worst temptation, to fall down and adore Satan to gain world domination, to spread the gospel by force rather than by humility. Just as Alexander the Great or Julius Caesar had conquered, just as Napoleon, and in our day Hitler, had attempted to gain the world by force and almost succeeded, so too the devil offered our Lord an easy way to gain the world by force and power. The devil at last showed himself in his true colours and was finally bidden 'Begone, Satan.'

So the devil works on us, and woe to us if we listen to his first suggestions, however innocent they appear. A slight yielding to the flesh such as a little over-indulgence in nice food, the comfort of a soft bed, such things are not intrinsically wrong; but to yield brings about the first weakening of our defences, the spinning of the fine threads that will eventually become ropes to drag us down into sin. We do not suspect the influence of the devil in these slight matters, but it is thus he gets us accustomed to giving in to self in small ways, weakening our will to resist and deadening our conscience until sin no longer scares us.

St Teresa tells us that after the fervour of her early years she fell away little by little through reading romantic novels which led her to take pride in her personal appearance, to the use of scents and jewellery, to a fondness for dress, an eagerness to make an impression on others, till she fell into dangerous sin. Probably she greatly exaggerated the gravity of her fall, but she shows the danger of these slight threads which lead away from piety and fervour to end in sin. The devil will even foster virtue until it becomes excess. The reasonable prudence and wise frugality of Judas grew into ungovernable avarice leading to the betrayal of his master. It makes it all so much more difficult that these impulses seem to rise spontaneously within oneself; we never suspect the hidden Satan lurking near.

The 'flesh' is a powerful enemy making us prone to evil; by it we mean not only sin against chastity but all evil desires rising within from our corrupt nature, anger, gluttony, pride, selfishness, sloth, vanity and such. We can never run away from self, nor from the continual lust of the flesh against the spirit. The world demands that we be in the latest fashion at all cost; we are offered pleasure at the expense of duty, inducing us to frequent amusement to the neglect of the sacraments and the spiritual needs of the soul. Power and wealth are offered by fraudulent means; we are enticed to give up religion for power, to join forbidden societies to further our ambition to get on, to marry in the registry office to save trouble—the world is very plausible in its suggestions as to what is good for us. The flesh and the world, used by the devil as his tools, form a terrible combination against the soul and without the grace of God we would be quite powerless to resist. How foolish we are when we deliberately rush into dangerous occasions of being tempted to sin which we could easily avoid.

Temptations often worry people, who fear they have sinned because of the suggestions to evil which they have experienced. Let us analyse temptation and see how it works. There are three steps in its progress: first a suggestion that a certain thing or act is very desirable and would result in our gaining happiness; direct evil is never presented but always an apparent good which deceives us until we perceive the underlying evil and sin. Next we experience pleasure or attraction in what is suggested. Finally there is the persuasion of the will to consent to the acceptance and performance of the act necessary to attain the desired end.

We must note that we are always cheated into thinking some sinful object to be good for us, and therein lies the danger! Take a simple example. A boy sees a tree loaded with ripe apples in some garden. First it occurs to him that it would be a treat to have one of those apples, and he could easily take one without being caught. Next he realises the pleasure he would gain; the apples look very desirable. Finally he knows he may not take one without stealing, but then makes his decision. Either he decides to take an apple; the will has consented to enjoy the forbidden fruit and he commits sin by so doing. Or he decides to heed the voice of conscience telling him that it is wrong to steal and will not consent to this evil. Thus he avoids sin, and gains merit through resisting the temptation to sin.

This simple example can be applied to all temptation. A mistake is made in confusing the pleasure or attraction felt with the consent to do evil. A temptation may come repeatedly, each time we feel the attraction offered; but until the will consents there is no sin. The boy could not help but wish for the apple; he wanted one badly; but he refused his consent to evil and so did not sin. Were there no attraction, no apparent good offered as an inducement, there would be no temptation to sin. That is the very essence of temptation, the attraction to an apparent good.

Since the consent of the free will is implied in formal sin, neither internal nor external causes can force us to sin. Only the free choice of the will can bring about sin; hence the difference between temptation and sin. The rebellion of the passions, the inducements of the world, the suggestions of the devil are no more than temptations; until the will consents freely to evil there is no sin, but rather merit in resisting these enemies of the soul. They are powerless to force consent, though we need God's grace to strengthen the will and help it to resist.

In the presence of temptation fully realised, it is not lawful to remain indifferent, i.e. neither assenting nor dissenting, since this exposes us without just cause to the danger of being overcome. In other words we must not dally with temptation but immediately reject it as soon as perceived. The resistance of the will may be implicit or explicit: displeasure at the presence of temptation is implicit resistance; the resolve not to give in is explicit. Again it may be internal or external; displeasure at an unchaste thought is internal; doing some work to divert the attention from the unchaste thought is external.

How are we to overcome temptations? 'Watch and pray,' our Lord tells us. We must be always suspicious, expecting it and ready to resist as soon as aware of it, not relying on our strength but on God by asking in prayer for grace to resist. We should remain calm and undisturbed under the influence of temptation. A stone in the hand can be flung away with force, or merely dropped. Temptation is best dropped, not flung away. We can do this by a change of occupation; temptation which comes only in solitude can be overcome by seeking company in which we cannot give way; temptation caused by the company we are in must be overcome by leaving such company.

Idleness is a fruitful source of temptation, for the devil finds work for empty hands, and it will not be good work! Cheerfulness banishes many temptations such as sadness and brooding over injuries, as well as jealousy, hatred, uncharitable thoughts, desire for revenge, which all need the soil of resentment and sadness in which to thrive. If temptations persist for long periods, mention them in confession; the devil hates being exposed and thus we are rid of him. Do not fear any temptation, but trust in God. 'God is faithful who will not suffer you to be tempted above that which you are able but will make also with temptation issue that you may be able to bear it' (1 Cor. X. 13).

XXVIII SIN

What is sin? Sin is a mystery not to be understood until we know God himself in all his purity. Sin is disobedience, rebellion against God and is found in any thought, word, deed, or omission against God's law. This conveys but little to us of its horrible malignity. Sin is too spiritual, too infinite, to be understood; yet we talk glibly about big or little sins, evaluating this or that sin in our own estimate as though we knew the evil of it. God alone can understand sin in all its vileness. There is no 'small sin;' every sin carries an infinite guilt more awful than physical evil. To us it seems unbelievable that all the physical evil suffered by men is less evil than one 'small lie.' Yet this is so since physical evil, pain, torment, suffering, are finite, limited in extent, whereas a lie has infinite guilt as an offence against God, who is truth itself. Sin is rebellion, a refusal to serve, directed against God as its object. Every sin is disobedience towards God.

Sin is so grave because it takes its guilt, not from the quality of the one sinning, nor from the quality of the act itself, but from the infinite perfection of the one against whom it is committed. Take an example: I meet a boy in the street and slap his cheek; I may be fined lightly for a simple assault. I meet the King, riding in state, and I slap his cheek. At once there is an outcry! Insult offered to his Majesty! I should be cast into prison, in olden days condemned to death. Why the difference? The one guilty is the same, the act is the same; but the difference is 'the cheek slapped,' the person against whom the crime is committed and this decides the 'guilt.' Sin is a 'slap on the cheek' given to God, from whom it takes an infinite value, meriting infinite punishment, needing infinite atonement.

Sin may be mortal or venial. Mortal sin implies total aversion from God. Venial sin does not imply such aversion, so is more easily forgiven. It is wrong, nevertheless, to speak of it as merely 'a little sin.' It is an offence against the infinite God and so has an infinite guilt. Mortal sin entails three distinct things: (a) the matter, what is done, must in itself be grave; (b) it must be known to be grave; (c) there must be full consent of the will to this known grave evil. It is a deliberate refusal to serve God than which there can be no greater crime. Such sin rejects the right of the creator to demand obedience from his creatures; it is the choice of the devil and hell in preference to God and heaven. So grave is the guilt of mortal sin that the very weakness of human nature excuses the sinner before God because of our proneness to evil, our want of thought, the violence of temptation and passion, our want of knowledge, hesitation in giving full consent, all of which lessen the guilt of our actions by obstructing the freedom of the will in its choice. God excuses because 'we know not what we do.' We cannot commit mortal sin by accident, nor be unaware of it. Few would deliberately and freely choose hell. By mortal sin we turn away from God, rebel against his will, choose self rather than God, prefer hell to heaven; for God does not condemn the sinner to hell; he chooses it himself. There cannot be too great a horror of sin; we cannot detest even venial sin sufficiently; for, though it does not have the terrible consequences of mortal sin, yet it weakens resistance to evil and disposes the will to consent more easily to grave mortal sin.

False values are given to various types of sin according to our ideas. All sins are not equal in guilt, since our Lord says: 'He that hath delivered me to thee hath the greater sin' (Jn. XIX, 11). But our estimation of sin is often erroneous. Many consider that sins of the flesh, chiefly unchastity, are the worse sins; some think them the only grave sin. But the Church has always taught that spiritual sins of their very nature are more grave than the sins of the flesh. St Thomas Aquinas writes: 'Carnal sins, such as impurity, are not so grave as spiritual sins, e.g. pride. Hatred of God is the worst sin of all, and sins against our neighbour are worse than others.' Another theologian, Billuart, writes: 'Take heed of this: not a few who wish to be spiritual despise with pharisaical pride those who fall into the sins of the flesh and thereby commit the worse sins of pride and detraction.'

The English mystic, Hilton, writes: 'He that riseth against the feeling of fleshly or carnal sins more than against pride,

135

covetousness, or envy (which all seem less evil because more spiritual), is blind because he seeth not his uncleanness in God's sight. I will not excuse those who fall into the delights of impurity or gluttony as if they had not sinned, but my desire is that thou esteem all sins according as they are; the greater to be the greater, as spiritual sins of pride; the lesser to be the lesser, as are carnal sins of impurity.' Similarly Fr Bede Jarrett, O.P.: 'Impurity is not the only sin, nor the worst form of sin. We may easily get into the way of being obsessed by this one form of evil and forget that it is merely one of the many enemies with which we are at war. Indeed the Catholic Church has always taught that though all sin is evil, spiritual sins are on the whole worse than carnal sins; that pride, for example, is more deadly and despair more destructive than the sins of the flesh.'

Carnal sin is usually thought to be the worst type of sin because of the natural shame caused by such sin. Many who condemn others for impurity are guilty of a more grievous sin because of sinful pride which causes no shame to be felt since it is spiritual and there is no natural reaction. We are too prone to judge evil by the feeling produced in us by such sin, though such feelings are no standard by which to judge of guilt. Too many very grave sins are lightly regarded because we do not consider the innate evil of the act itself. Thus calumny and detraction are too easily condoned; we call them by names that sound less evil such as uncharitable talk, backbiting, or talebearing, all of which are calumny or detraction bearing an obligation of restitution ere they can be forgiven. We pride ourselves, unconsciously perhaps, on not giving way to a certain type of sin, when in fact we have no inclination towards it, no temptation or maybe no opportunity to commit it. There is no merit in that! We flatter ourselves, thanking God we are 'not as other men,' because we do not the same things, having no desire for them. But we have other weaknesses, perhaps worse, though not recognised as such. Far be it from us who do not understand the temptations of others, to condemn any man. We are all weak in some way, all disobey God in some thing, all sin in some form or other. Every sin is disobedience against God and the guilt of each sin is assessed not by the type of act, but by the amount of aversion from God in the will. How can we judge whether one man has been more averted from God by a sin of impurity than another by a sin of pride? We do not understand sin as God does; he alone is capable of judging between sin and sin; he alone knows to what extent his Majesty has been insulted. Yet we miserable sinners in our pride glibly condemn one for grievous sin while we excuse our own faults, considering them but small. We talk easily of this sin being greater than that sin, but know nothing at all of the mystery of sin, its guilt or its consequences.

One of the reasons is because certain sins make us feel ashamed of having given way. Carnal sins cause a natural sense of shame. This is not necessarily true sorrow, but at least it does make us aware that we have been guilty of sin. Spiritual sin, though of its own nature more grievous than carnal sin, has usually no effect of shame whatever; hence we judge it to be of less account. We are also affected by the 'world's estimate' of what is right and wrong, forgetting that the world condones any evil that is convenient or hidden, but condemns the unfortunate who are found out. God judges us by our own conscience, by the aversion of our will from him, and these it is quite impossible for us to compare in one another. There is a definite command: 'Judge not, and you shall not be judged.' How often we sin by being disobedient to this command, perhaps sinning more grievously thereby than that other whose sin we presume to judge and condemn.

To gain a greater appreciation of what sin means, let us ponder on the sufferings, the passion and death of Christ caused by sin. Man cannot atone adequately for even the least venial sin, infinite as it is in its guilt, since he is finite, limited in his capacity to atone. God alone can offer adequate atonement for sin, because he alone is infinite. Hence God became man to give an infinite value to all he did as man and to offer an infinite atonement for sin by his utter obedience and subjection to God: 'obedient even to the death of the cross.' Sin, a rebellion of infinite guilt against God, was atoned for only by its opposite, the utter subjection to God of the human

137

nature of Christ. Sin—infinite rebellion; Christ's obedience unto death—utter subjection to God, worthy to atone for all the disobedience, the refusal of subjection, in the sins of men.

No evil can compare with sin, the greatest of all evils. Though we are not able fully to understand the guilt of sin, yet by considering all that it entailed in the sacrifice of Atonement we may gain some idea of the awful horror of it in the sight of God. Let us remember the proneness to evil in human nature, its fatal weakness under temptation, and strive to overcome this weakness by a horror of sin and by self-denial in what we think the least of sins. By the grace of God we can overcome all our tendencies to evil. And though we may fall through human weakness, we can at least withhold full and deliberate consent of the will to grievous sin by God's grace. We must cultivate a sense of evil in venial sin, so that we may realise more the awful horror of mortal sin by which man flouts the majesty of God and chooses to serve the devil, preferring hell to heaven by his own choice.

'Father, forgive us, we know not what we do.'

XXIX INDULGENCES

The word 'indulgence' is perhaps an unfortunate word since it is open to misconstruction. For many non-Catholics it stands for self-gratification; they have no conception of its meaning as used by the Church or of its purpose in relation to sin. It is really a 'remission' or pardon of the punishment due to sin after its guilt has been forgiven. Many say they do not trouble to gain indulgences, thus exhibiting a lamentable ignorance of the meaning and value of this mercy given to us.

Each sin, in addition to its guilt, has a just punishment or penalty attached to it, known only to God, but one which must be satisfied to the uttermost farthing; it is a debt which must be paid either in this world or in the next. In the sacrament of Penance, generally termed 'Confession,' though the guilt of the sin is completely wiped out, the penalty still remains except for the portion paid off in the penance imposed by the priest. (In the case of mortal sin this punishment is reduced from eternal to temporal). That remainder must be paid either in this life or hereafter. God counts much from us in the way of satisfaction from our acceptance of sickness, poverty, adversity and voluntary penances, all of which help to reduce the debt. We cannot, however, know whether we have paid all that is owed; and since we sin almost daily in some way, the probability is that we never do pay off all our debt, unless we use the means offered by the Church.

To St Peter was entrusted the 'power of the keys.' A key is used to open a locked door. Two things lock the gates of heaven against us—sin and the penalty due to sin. The Church has power to loose both: 'Whatsoever thou shalt loose upon earth, shall be loosed also in heaven.' The Church has power to forgive and to remit penalties due to sin; the first by the sacrament of penance; the second by means of indulgences. The penalty for sin is thereby not simply cancelled out; but what is wanting to our own satisfaction is given to us from the treasury of the infinite merits of Christ and the added merits of the saints. This treasury can never be exhausted and will always exceed the penalties due for sin committed through the ages. By the communion of saints all have a share in these merits, which are applied to those in need when they do what is required. No one is exempt from the payment of his debt for sin, since whatever is needed is granted from this infinite store of merit by which payment is made.

In the early days of the Church, rigorous public penances were imposed on sinners. These were commuted at times into lesser ones, or totally remitted, by a sincere repentance or the intercession of a martyr. In later times these public penances were abolished, and the sinner paid his debt by means of almsgiving, crusades, or pilgrimages. In recent times this pardon of penalty is granted in a simpler way, namely by prayer, the sacraments, and good works. Thus we are persuaded to pay off our debt of sin during life on earth, rather than leave all to be satisfied after death. The ancient rule of discipline is still the standard or measure by which the debt is to be settled and its application in the matter of indulgences should be properly understood.

An indulgence may be either a total or a partial remission of the penalty, according to the decision of the Church. It is laid down that the recipient be in a state of grace and perform whatever good works are stated to be the conditions for gaining an indulgence, and no other good works can be substituted. It is similar to an amnesty granted by a king which may be a mitigation of the sentence or a free pardon. A man condemned to death may have the sentence commuted to a number of years in prison, or receive a free pardon. Here is a simple example to illustrate how an indulgence brings about this pardon. Suppose some one left an enormous treasure to help those burdened with debt. I am appointed to take charge of its distribution and to determine the conditions under which a debtor may benefit. One comes and says: 'I have a £1,000 debt. Will you help me to pay it off?' I might reply: 'If you will take this letter to the post, I will give you £200 towards payment of the debt.' That would be a 'partial indulgence.' What is done is out of all proportion to what is gained; hence it is an 'indulgence.' Another may come saying: 'I owe £25,000. Help me to pay it off.' I reply: 'Go to the library and copy out the article on debts from the encyclopedia and I will give you the total amount.' That would be a plenary indulgence or a total payment of the whole debt. But in either case payment would depend on the conditions being properly fulfilled. I might say: 'Since you have done it so imperfectly you shall have only a portion, instead of the whole.' In other words all the conditions affect the pardon offered.

In like manner the Church disburses the treasure of merits won by Christ and the saints, giving us, under definite conditions to be fulfilled, a remittance of penalty; and this is accepted by God as though we had actually paid off such penalties by our own penances, so long as we fulfil the conditions to the best of our ability. Many prayers may be found to which such indulgences either partial or plenary are attached.

After some little prayer in a book, we may see in brackets *100 days*, which means that each time this prayer is said we may gain an indulgence of 100 days. What does that signify? Some will say that it means 100 days less in purgatory. But there are no days in purgatory! It has, in fact, nothing to do with purgatory immediately. What it does mean is that the same effect is produced as if we ourselves had performed 100 days of public penance such as was done in the early days of the Church. The penitent stood at the door of the Church clothed in sackcloth with ashes on his head in public token of penance, or some other such penance was imposed on him. By saying a prayer indulgenced with 100 days, we could pay off just so much penalty for sin as though we had stood at the church door publicly carrying out the penance imposed by the Church. How much value this has in the sight of God is known only to him.

To repeat, then, indulgences are partial or plenary. The first remits only a portion of the debt; the second pays off the whole so that we are completely freed from any debt of penalty to God at that moment. Certain conditions are imposed. It is always necessary to be in a state of grace, since we cannot possibly pay off any debt if we are at enmity with God; we must be in the friendship of God to be capable of any good or meritorious works. A dead member of Christ's Mystical

Body cannot share in any benefit to be obtained from the merits of Christ. In addition to our being in grace, whatever other conditions are stated for gaining the indulgence must be duly performed to the best of our ability. For a plenary indulgence these are naturally more onerous than for a partial indulgence, and almost always include confession of sins, the receiving of Holy Communion, prayer for the Pope's intentions and some other good work in addition.

At the hour of death a plenary indulgence may be gained by those who, having received the sacraments and invoked the Holy Name, if they are capable of so doing, receive the Papal Blessing which most priests have the faculty of giving. What a tremendous mercy is thus shown to the dying. The effect of this special indulgence at the moment of death is to wipe out completely the whole debt or penalty due to all sins committed in life, so that the soul may wing its flight immediately into the vision of God without any waiting in the cleansing flames of purgatory. Thus does Mother Church provide for her children the means of paying off all penalty for sin, and the power to enter immediately into their reward of eternal happiness. What a tremendous mercy is thus shown to sinners. How we ought to pray daily that we may be able to benefit by such mercy, that we may be saved from an unprovided death.

Many indulgences may be applied to the souls in purgatory so long as it is so declared by the Church. Thus do we carry out our obligations entailed by 'the Communion of Saints' through the gaining of the indulgences permitted and paying off the penalties on behalf of those souls who are cleansed from the effects of sin, and hastening their entry into the glory of heaven. Think what it means to a suffering soul when some kind friend takes over its debt and by gaining a plenary pardon immediately releases such a one from pain and waiting so that it goes at once into heaven. Let us therefore be diligent in gaining and applying a plenary indulgence to some soul in purgatory.

Thus does Mother Church, ever mindful of the needs of her children, provide a simple and easy means of paying off the great debt of penalty incurred by sin. God is infinitely merciful, but he is also infinitely just. Here on earth, his mercy permits us to obtain pardon of sin and its penalty by simple means that are out of all proportion to our guilt and deserts. Once we pass through the portals of death his infinite justice must be completely satisfied and this demands that we pay back to the uttermost farthing. Here on earth we can, by some small inconvenience or self-denial, pay off much of our debt, even all of it so that we have nothing due for payment after death and so escape all the pain and waiting of purgatory. Should we not be extremely foolish to neglect the simple means offered to us of thus paying our debts to God?

Let us do good whilst there is yet time, for we know not the hour or the day. Death comes like a thief in the night. We may be caught unprepared by his visit, if we neglect the opportunities whilst life is still ours and we can work good for our souls. One day we shall be called upon to render a strict account, to pay to the uttermost farthing. Let us try to pay off as much as we can while we have yet time to do so. 'Whatsoever thou shalt loose upon earth, shall be loosed also in heaven.' The unjust servant shall be cast out till he pay off the whole debt.

XXX MORTIFICATION

How we dread the word 'mortification'! It suggests terrifying penances, hair-shirts, plank-beds and other extraordinary hardships practised by some saint. Mark the work 'extra-ordinary.' Such penances are not for 'ordinary' people like ourselves, but for those called by God to be out of the ordinary through the help of special graces. Yet penance in some form or other we must do, since we are bound to mortify the flesh and its desires. What does mortification really mean? In a spiritual sense it may be defined as the act of subduing the passions and appetites of our lower nature by fasting or sever-ities inflicted on the body, the act of subordinating all natural impulses to the influence of the Holy Spirit. In a natural sense it may denote being humiliated by circumstances, de-pressed by disappointments or vexations; but these are not penances in the strict sense, though they may be turned into true mortification by our method of acceptance.

Mortification essentially consists in self-denial : 'If any man will come after me, let him deny himself.' Self-denial means saying 'NO' to self, which for most people is a difficult thing to do. By sin our willpower was weakened; we became prone to evil, finding it easier to give in to the desires of the flesh than to resist them. Because of sin the soul lost its domination over the flesh, so that 'the flesh lusteth against the spirit.' The chief work of mortification is to strengthen the will power and heal the wounds caused by sin. By denying self what is lawful, the will is strengthened to resist what is unlawful, and some measure of atonement is made. Therefore penance is imposed as a strict duty. Thus the Lenten and other fasts imposed by the Church consist in refraining from a certain amount of food, otherwise lawful, so denying to us the pleasure of satisfying hunger completely. Too often these grave obligations of fasting are dismissed as impracticable because of hardship or incon-venience, before any attempt has been made to find out if they are really so.

It is difficult to understand how anyone can settle in con-science so grave an obligation in so casual a manner. Certainly some are excused by the nature of the work they must do, or for other good reasons; but this does not free them entirely from all obligation of doing penance of another sort. We are bound to deny self, and that is the essence of penance. We need so much to be strengthened against temptations that only by denying lawful things to ourselves can we hope to be strong enough to deny the unlawful also.

Some pride themselves on their strength of will, but too often it is shown only in denying something to others rather than to themselves. In reality such people are simply stubborn and actually weak-willed, since they are not able to say 'NO' to self. Let us test ourselves by the following questions:

Do I always stick to my own opinions and insist on having my own way?

Can I admit to being in the wrong, or that I have made a mistake?

Can I give in gracefully to the wish of the majority?

The answers to such questions as these will soon prove whether we can say 'NO' to self or whether we are self-willed.

Mortification is necessary for all. The wounds of nature demand an effort to strengthen the will against its propensity to evil; the more we indulge our natural desires the stronger and more insistent they become in demanding satisfaction, the more difficult to resist in their appeal. However, it is not necessary to undertake special hardships or penances beyond those imposed under obligation by the Church. Life itself provides a variety of opportunities for mortification that we cannot escape. The pity of it is that we endure without much or any spiritual profit much that might be mortification, because of the wrong attitude we adopt towards these various vexations. We can make a virtue of necessity by accepting in a spirit of patience and humility the daily trials forced upon us. Take any ordinary day in life. Probably we must get up earlier than we wish, we should like to stay in bed much longer. It is not easy to rise promptly; it demands self-denial. How do we react? Do we come down peevish and disagreeable, upsetting others by our grumbling and irritation? If this is our reaction, then we have lost the chance of mortifying ourselves, instead of turning the necessity to spiritual profit by accepting it with patience. We have to go to work, oftentimes hard and disagreeable, to work with others who get on our nerves, to take orders given in a curt manner, and endure many other similar vexations that can be very irritating. What is our attitude to such things? They can all become occasions of true mortification if accepted in a proper spirit. Obedience to others, which is the submission of our own will to that of another, can be a very real and difficult penance. Too often we become impatient and disgruntled, resent the orders given to us and miss the chance of being spiritually mortified under adversity.

Life is full of such opportunities: we make silly mistakes, are humiliated by others, meet with disappointments, hear slurs cast or disparaging remarks made about us; accidents make us ludicrous and cause laughter and ridicule at our expense. These things are certainly humiliating to our pride and self-conceit, but do we turn them to spiritual worth by a humble and contrite spirit in accepting them as mortifications? If they simply cause us to become disagreeable and to complain, there is no penance; they are lost to us entirely when they might have been real crosses borne for the love of God, real penances accepted in a spirit of self-denial, some atonement for the sins we have committed.

We are told to perform the three good works: Prayer, Fasting and Almsdeeds. These can all form some kind of mortification for us.

By fasting we mean here self-denial in any form, the giving up of one's own desires and inclinations. We are forced to this at times by circumstances, yet profit little because we accept grudgingly, with resentment and complaints about the hardness of our lot.

Prayer might find a larger place in our lives and provide penance at the same time. For instance we might give up an evening's pleasure so that we may go to Benediction. How many give up the Sunday evening to selfish comfort rather than go out to the evening service? It may be cold and wet; it is so much pleasanter to sit reading by the fireside, or playing cards with friends. The weather is so often an excuse to avoid going to church, but it would not prevent us from going out to the cinema or to a dance. It is difficult to give up pleasure and comfort to go to church, hard to mortify our desires, to say 'NO' to self! To give up our comforts can be a real mortification.

Alms-giving does not necessarily mean giving money away. The best alms is to give happiness to others. Any kind action done for the love of God and our neighbour, any small service especially if it means self-denial, is acceptable to God as mortification. Our Lord went about doing good, never sparing himself. We, on the contrary, find doing good to others to be too much trouble and to cause too much inconvenience to ourselves. We could make a point of doing at least one kind act a day to help another, as a mortification. We could do much more to ease the burdens of others, to bring happiness or solace, and if this entails denying self and putting ourselves to some inconvenience so much the better, it will mortify us all the more.

There is no need to undertake extraordinary penances life provides its own opportunities of mortifying self. We do not know that our Lady or St Joseph ever did any special kind of penance, but they did accept the many trials and sufferings of life, grief, hardship, poverty, hard work, and such like, in a spirit of resignation to the will of God. The early disciples do not seem to have done extraordinary penances, but we may note that St Paul writes: 'I chastise the flesh to bring it into subjection . . . lest perhaps I become a castaway.' If St Paul felt the need of 'chastising the flesh,' how much more we who do so little to atone for all the number of times we give way to our evil inclinations. We must chastise the flesh by denying to it the satisfaction it demands, even in what is lawful, that we may strengthen ourselves to refuse all that is unlawful and to thrust down the inclinations and desires of unlawful passion, by denying the pleasure of lawful desires at times. We must learn how to say 'NO' to self.

To resume therefore, we cannot escape mortifications, even

though we do not seek them. Life will provide many opportunities of self-denial; let us see to it that these unavoidable
vexations are all turned to profit for the soul by accepting
them in a spirit of penance and humiliation for our many sins
and as a means of strengthening our will-power against our
proneness to evil. If we would realise that hardship, sickness,
poverty, disappointments, vexations, inconveniences, even the
monotony of life, can all be spiritually useful and made profitable by a spirit of humble acceptance and mortification and
for the love of God, we should be carrying out our obligation
of doing penance lest we perish.

It is all a matter of will-power pitted against the fatal attractions of sin in which we prove so weak and easily overcome.
Only by denying self what is lawful, or accepting what we
cannot escape as a means of self denial, can we become strong
in our resistance to what is unlawful, strong to resist the many
temptations that beset us from the flesh, the world and the
devil. We must atone for sin by true repentance and by penance
joined to the sufferings of our Lord, that they may become an
atonement for our many sins.

'Unless ye do penance, ye shall all likewise perish.'

XXXI THE BEATITUDES

Human affairs are regulated by laws to produce order so that work, education, recreation, social life in general fit into an orderly scheme. In the spiritual affairs of the soul there would often seem to be no such order; progress seems to be made haphazardly as the soul strives after God in a vague and uncertain manner. Yet the fundamental principles have been clearly set forth by our Lord in the eight beatitudes which are a set of definite steps. These are not a series of more or less unconnected statements; they form a scheme of definite progress in spiritual matters. Let us examine the beatitudes so that the scheme may be understood.

1 BLESSED ARE THE POOR IN SPIRIT. This is the fundamental principle on which the spiritual life is built. It is the answer to the claim made by the world to our allegiance. The first step is to detach ourselves from that claim, to spurn the allurements offered by the world. God claims the whole of our allegiance; so does the world also; but we cannot serve God and mammon. To attach ourselves to God we must first detach ourselves from the world, put away desire for power or riches, learn to disdain luxury, pleasures and comfort which easily lead to forgetfulness of God. We are not forbidden to own property, to enjoy innocent pleasures, to have comfort in reason. It is the attitude of the mind towards worldly affairs which is important. Our attitude must be one of detachment, and everything must be used as a means of progressing spiritually. The heart must not be fixed on what is offered by the world: 'Where thy treasure is, there is thy heart also.' Thus disappointments, loss of worldly goods or position, should not disturb us but are to be accepted as God's will. The rich man deals with his wealth as God's steward; the poor man accepts poverty without repining as God's will. Some go further and renounce all ownership by voluntary poverty. To strive for heaven entails the renunciation of worldly treasures. The choice is between heaven and the world, eternal certain happiness in exchange for uncertain temporal happiness. 'Seek ye first the kingdom of God,' then all else falls into its own place,

is valued at its correct worth; whatever else is needed shall be added to you by God's promise for trusting in him. This first step being taken, having won to some measure of detachment, we are ready to go on.

2 BLESSED ARE THE MEEK. The world esteems not meekness, mistaking it for cowardice. It would have us advertise self, stand up for our rights, put self-advancement before all else. But Jesus says: 'Learn of me, for I am meek and humble of heart.' To the world, meekness suggests being faint-hearted lack of spirit, timidity; it knows nothing of victory over self, of the struggle to put self in the background, of denying self the allurements so attractive to fallen nature. Hence before we can be meek we must have learnt how to despise the world, to be poor in spirit, to be detached from earthly treasures. Gentleness, a retiring disposition, may be the effect either of cowardice or of great moral strength. True meekness is the result of the terrific struggle of the soul to detach itself from the world, a quiet gentleness acquired by a trial of strength, the result of victory over self in the continual struggle. A moral coward could never achieve true meekness; only the hero proven in combat can claim it. Though our Lord was meek and gentle, he could yet be angry when the glory of his Father demanded it. Jesus was angry when he cast out the buyers and sellers who desecrated his Father's house. We too must be ready to have a holy anger for the rights of God, to have courage to withstand the enemies of religion. Meekness is victory over self, holding the passion of anger in check, giving way to others for their good, being gentle and considerate in dealing with our neighbour as charity demands.

3 BLESSED ARE THEY THAT MOURN FOR THEY SHALL BE COMFORTED. To be poor in spirit and to be meek entail a continual struggle against powerful forces, against the tendency to relax and give in to the unceasing pressure of the world. To persevere in this struggle means suffering. Victory cannot be won without painful effort and sorrow. Others may enjoy the many delights offered by the world; but we may not, realising that we cannot serve God and mammon. Hence we must oft-times mourn and weep in this vale of tears while others rejoice;

we groan and are in travail of spirit because the way is long and hard, our weak nature always pleading for satisfaction in the pleasures so attractively offered.

Yet does St Paul write: 'Brethren, I reckon the sufferings of this time are not be compared with the glory to come.' That is to be our comfort; there is no comparison between what we suffer by giving up an uncertain joy and the perfect happiness of eternity we shall win thereby. Our Lord has promised to be our comfort: 'Come to me, all ye that labour and are burdened and I will refresh you.' He does not desert us and leave us to struggle on alone. He will give us a foretaste of happiness if we are faithful; if we take our burden to him he will comfort us.

Thus far we have been getting rid of the obstacles and preparing the way which is now open for progress and intense activity of soul.

4 BLESSED ARE THEY THAT HUNGER AND THIRST AFTER JUSTICE. Justice consists in giving all that is due to God and to our neighbour. All that we have comes from God, so justice means giving all to God, longing for him, desiring to be holy, to love God more and more, to be more closely united to him. To serve God and our neighbour always is the justice that we must pursue with all our being. We must hunger and thirst after it so that we may possess God: 'As the hart pants after the fountains of water, so does my soul pant after thee.' This means intense activity of soul moved by the desire for God, who alone can satisfy the soul's craving for happiness. In him alone can happiness be found; all else is delusion and vanity. To strive after justice is to try to imitate our master in all things and one of his outstanding qualities is that of mercy. So we come to the beatitude of mercy.

5 BLESSED ARE THE MERCIFUL FOR THEY SHALL OBTAIN MERCY. The Lord is patient and full of mercy. How we need the mercy of God, we with so many sins for which we crave mercy, whose only hope is in repentance. 'God desires not the death of the sinner but that he be converted and live.' We can rely on the mercy of God; but he has made it a condition of his

mercy that we also show mercy to others. The essence of mercy is forgiveness of injuries: 'Forgive us our debts as we forgive our debtors.' Only by being merciful ourselves can we ever hope for God's mercy. The unforgiving servant was cast out into the exterior darkness and 'so shall my heavenly Father do to you, if you forgive not every one from your hearts.' That is the contract: forgive and you shall be forgiven; mercy is for those only who show mercy. To err is human, to forgive divine; so do we imitate the mercy of God when we forgive others. Our sins forgiven we can rise to higher degrees of sanctity.

6 BLESSED ARE THE CLEAN OF HEART FOR THEY SHALL SEE GOD. Purity of heart means more than expiation and reparation for sin; it means horror of even the least sin, of any wilful resistance to the grace of God. How often have friendships with others drawn us away from the resolutions we have made. To strengthen our weakness and to succeed against the influence of human affections we must turn our hearts to our Lord; 'He that loveth father or mother more than me is not worthy of me.' To see God is the reward of this cleanness of heart. We must strive to see God even in this life, to see in the divine person, who alone can still the longings of the human heart, all that we need. Human friends have their place in our lives, but they must be loved in God and for God, so that they never gain too great an influence over us. This cleanness of heart prepares us on earth for the full vision of God in heaven, the reward of all our hopes. The vision of God gives perfect peace; only those who have the way of perfect peace can show this way to others. Hence the clean of heart have a work to do that they alone can do perfectly.

7 BLESSED ARE THE PEACEMAKERS FOR THEY SHALL BE CALLED THE CHILDREN OF GOD. Our hearts know so little of peace. Troubled and afraid from the dawn of reason until death, we can know no real happiness unless there is a deep abiding peace. 'My peace I give unto you.' Such peace can be found only in the absence of all sin, in the perfect friendship of God. This peace which is given to us must flow out to all men: 'As much as in you, be at peace with all men.' This does not mean peace at any price, but such peace as is in accor-

dance with the law of God. We cannot be at peace with those who would lead us from God into the ways of the world. But we must keep the peace by denial of self, and giving way to others rather than insisting on what we think to be our rights.

The last beatitude is the summing up of them all:

8 BLESSED ARE THEY THAT SUFFER PERSECUTION FOR JUSTICE SAKE, FOR THEIRS IS THE KINGDOM OF HEAVEN. We have to face a lifelong conflict, the struggle between inclination and conscience. The heart torn between its wayward inclinations and the warnings of conscience, between worldly attractions and the ideals of the spirit, knows no peace for there is no final victory except in death. Peace is offered by the world at the price of surrender to its mastery, but conscience warns that such a course will bring no peace at all. To be true to conscience means a lifetime of unending persecution, a veritable martyrdom, from the world, from corrupt nature and from the devil. We are heartened in the struggle by the encouragement of our divine leader who comforts and revives us in the long persecution: 'Blessed are they that suffer persecution for justice sake,' for the sake of truth and holiness and the love for God, ' for theirs is the kingdom of heaven.'

Thus step by step we progress in holiness. First we rid ourselves of all that impedes our way to God, even though we mourn because of the sacrifices made. Having opened the pathway to God, we begin an intense activity of soul that leads us more and more to God as we grow more sanctified, trusting in the grace of God to draw us yet more closely to his service.

'Be ye faithful unto death, and I will give you a crown of life.'

XXXII MOTIVES

We read in the first Book of Kings that Heli, the high Priest, speaking to his sons, asks them: 'Why do ye these things?' He was seeking the motives of their actions. It would be well if we asked ourselves that same query: 'Why do we these things?' That word 'WHY' is most important. Though we may not advert to it, it does enter into every act, is the deciding factor often as to the goodness or evil of what is done, and will also tell us much about our own character in general. The answer to that 'WHY' gives us the motive for doing a thing and this is what God considers most in our actions; it is a deciding factor in what we do, making it good, bad, or indifferent.

What is meant by a motive? It is the purpose or reason by which we are moved to act; it is the intention we have in our mind for doing some certain thing, even though we do not actually advert to this intention in any specific way. We are familiar with the idea of motive power; thus in the steam-engine steam is the motive power which though hidden is the actual cause of movement; in a watch the main spring is the motive power on which the usefulness of the watch depends. In our actions it is the intention that moves us to action and gives that action its true quality.

This motive is most important in God's sight. He looks not at the results but at our intention. Success or failure, as judged by our standards, counts very little with him.

In any act of ours three aspects can be distinguished: (a) what is done: (b) the means of doing it; and (c) the reason or motive for doing it. Unless the thing done or the means adopted are intrinsically evil, the merit or demerit of the act depends almost entirely on the last aspect, the motive; and even the morality of an action in which the thing done or the means adopted are bad may be modified by the motive, as, for instance, where there is inculpable ignorance. Though all these three aspects of any action have a bearing on its morality, it is obvious, therefore, that the last one, the motive, is the one that demands our particular attention.

In some cases the thing done is indifferent; by that we mean that it has no moral quality, either good or bad, and does not affect our spiritual life of itself. But in practice there is almost always a motive which colours otherwise indifferent actions. Thus walking is an indifferent action in itself; but almost invariably we have some purpose or intention in our walking which is thereby made good or bad in some degree. Even our eating and drinking, whatever we do, may be done (as St Paul reminds us) for the glory of God.

There is a common opinion (falsely attributed to the Jesuits) that the end justifies the means. But that opinion is certainly contrary to Catholic teaching, if not indeed to common sense. If I steal in order to get money to give to the poor, after the legendary fashion of Robin Hood, I break a commandment of God and do an injustice to my fellow-man.

But we are especially concerned here with those actions, good or indifferent in themselves, which get their real morality from our intention in performing them. Let us therefore take a simple example and observe how intention affects moral value. I pay a visit to the church. The thing done is obviously good in itself. I go there on foot or by bus, a matter of indifference in itself. My motive, however, may be one of many. I may want to examine the architecture or look at some work of art. I may desire to visit the Blessed Sacrament out of love for our Lord. Or again I may go that others may see me and admire my clothes or think me devout. The first motive makes my action one of no apparent spiritual good, though it is not morally wrong. The second motive obviously makes the action not merely good but of great spiritual value. Whereas the third kind of motive, being one of vanity or pride or hypocrisy, turns what should be a good deed into a notably sinful one; it becomes indeed merely an act of vanity or pride or hypocrisy.

Thus we see that, since the object itself and the means of achieving it were both lawful and even good, the deciding factor of the morality of such an act was wholly centred in my intention or motive, which could bring about three very different results.

So in every act the motive tends to make or mar what is achieved. Our whole character is influenced by our common motives; as our motives are noble or mean, selfish or generous, charitable or uncharitable, so will our character be; for our actions are the cause of our habits, and our habits make our character. Many a noble work is ruined by the meanness or selfishness of our motives, but noble motives will produce nobility of character in us. If, therefore, we wish to have an insight into our character we should study our usual motives, which will indicate much about ourselves that perhaps we have little realised. Nevertheless motives are secret, hidden things; hence we may not judge any person's action unless and until his motive is disclosed.

The commonest and most powerful of motives is self-love. Many of our actions are aimed at obtaining some personal advantage, such as pleasure, happiness or comfort. Love of another is also a powerful motive which can overcome self-love. It is said: 'If a man give all for love, he shall count it as nothing.' It is even powerful enough to make a man lay down his life for his friends. Other strong motives are pride, hatred, jealousy, love of pleasure, avarice, ambition—all forms of self-love, all despicable in the sight of God yet all too common in their evil work of turning good into evil.

It would be well indeed, therefore, for us to consider seriously this question of motives, to ask ourselves 'Why do we do this or that?' Day after day, we go to work—WHY? Is it merely to earn our wages? Why do we seek the company of friends? Is it just for what we can get out of them for ourselves? Do we act out of vanity, doing things in the hope of flattery or praise? Such questions each alone can answer for himself since motives are secret, shamefully hidden from others, sometimes even not admitted by ourselves.

Our Lord might be said to have had one great motive, his desire to do the will of his Father. Our Lady likewise had a single perfect motive: 'Be it done unto me according to thy word,' the acceptance of the will of God in all. Could we not be actuated by some such noble spiritual motive? What a difference it would make to the least of our acts if we did them because it was the will of God. To aim to do all for his glory would spiritualise all our deeds and give them infinite worth. If we work daily merely for earthly gain, what good does it bring to the soul? We gain no merit, but we lose an opportunity of furthering our salvation. Suppose we offered our work to God, did it because it is his will that we should labour in that special way and did it to the best of our ability, then it would become at once a prayer with a moral value to the soul and would ennoble our work whatever it may be. 'Why stand ye here all the day idle?' That is what many are doing in spite of seeming to work hard, because they gain no merit; they work for the things that perish, which we are told not to do.

The idea of the morning offering is to turn every activity of life into prayer of benefit to the soul in increasing grace and merit. How easy it is to say: 'My God I offer thee all I do this day for thy honour and glory,' and by that offering and intention sanctify each deed the day long. The effect of such an intention persists though we may not advert to it, so long as we try honestly to do our best. Our days would not then be 'idle' but full of fruit for the soul. In themselves these things seem poor and useless gifts to God, but since we are his children he values the intention of giving him glory even in these small things and blesses all we do, accepting these things as our offerings to him, a token of our love. We can only offer what he has given; we have nothing else. Just as a mother treasures the useless little gifts (which she probably paid for) from her child, so God treasures each little act done for him as a love-token. 'Whether you eat or drink or whatsoever else you do, do all for the glory of God.' *There* is the motive that can transmute all our actions into spiritual gold, that ennobles all our work, our play, or whatever we do, lifts our whole lives to a supernatural plane and lays up treasure in heaven. Away with all mean, debasing motives; we cannot offer to God what is done through pride, jealousy, vanity, or self-love. He judges our success or failure not by what we actually achieve but by what we purpose to do; the result is as nothing compared with our intention. It is worth while then to look into our motive in all we do, examine closely the mainspring of our actions. If we are honest with ourselves we shall stand revealed for what we are, either noble, generous and spiritual, or mean, selfish and vain. Noble motives will ennoble our character; mean and ignoble motives will demean our whole life. If we act chiefly from self-interest we cannot be anything but selfish but if we act for the glory of God we shall become generous and great-souled.

Nothing is too small, too insignificant to offer to God, nothing too ordinary. Such as we are he made us, loves us, cares for us as his children, and all we do concerns him. If we offer all for his glory, no matter how poor such offerings may be, they become of great value to God as tokens of our love for him. We are here on earth to work out our salvation, and we shall be judged more by our motives than our achievements.

'Whether you eat or drink, or whatsoever else you do, do all for the GLORY OF GOD.'

XXXIII IDEALS

We sometimes hear of a man called an 'idealist' and considered to be a freak full of unpractical ideas, a visionary who wants more than he can hope to obtain. Dissatisfied with things as they are, he wants improvements, better conditions and higher standards, but others blame him for not leaving well alone. Nevertheless the idealist, unless he is merely a dreamer, will get things done in the end. Though he may never achieve his complete ideal, he will yet effect far more than one who is content to remain in the common rut. The reason of this is that the idealist has an object in view, something to strive for even if he fail in the attempt, but the man who is content with things as they are has no incentive to spur him on.

Mother Church is a great believer in ideals; she continually puts before us the example of the true idealists, men and women who lived on earth, fought the good fight, and won the crown of eternal glory, and an important purpose of these examples is to give us an ideal to strive for, an ideal which men and women like us achieved, to encourage us also to become heroes of the faith. Our divine Lord might be called an idealist, but he achieved to perfection all his ideals, the chief of which was 'to do the will of my Father, who is in heaven.' He also realised the need and the value of ideals for us, to raise up our efforts from the common level by having something definite to aim at. Thus he invited us to 'follow' him, that is imitate him in all things, be as much like him as possible.

To be of any real value an ideal must be placed high; we might say it ought to be almost unattainable to be of any real worth, certainly something not easily achieved, since once we attain an ideal we are satisfied and cease all effort. The pharisees acted thus: they had a very low ideal of religion which consisted in the mere outward observance of the letter of the law, but inwardly they were 'whited sepulchres' full of rottenness.

If we are content with things as they are, or with low standards that have no power to raise us up, we may very easily be no better than the pharisees themselves.

It is a weakness of human nature to fall short of any ideal;

but the higher the ideal, the further we shall climb in all probability. Let us take an example: two men set out to climb the mountain peaks. One chooses a peak of 1,000 feet, but the other aims at one of 5,000 feet. If both fail, it is almost certain that the one who chose the higher peak will achieve a greater altitude than the other. Even should the first achieve his 1,000 feet, thus gaining his objective, and the other fail at half way, the latter will be considerably higher than the one who succeeded in his ambition. Moreover the one who did not gain his object will be unsatisfied and will make another attempt ; but the other having achieved his aim will perhaps be content to rest on his meagre laurels.

So with us, unless our ideal is placed high we may too easily achieve it and be satisfied with our endeavour. To climb high we need the incentive which a low ideal can never provide. Without that incentive we shall be content with a low standard of holiness. There are those, however, who have high ideals, but for others, not for themselves. A young maid dreams of the husband she wants, some man who will fulfil her ideal; a young man sets an ideal for the woman he would take to wife. Many seek the ideal friend who will be all that a friend should be. But what of an ideal for themselves? Too often we demand a certain standard in others, and feel aggrieved when they fail to attain to the standard set, but we do not set a like ideal for ourselves. What right have we to set ideals for others, to demand a certain standard of conduct from them, unless we are prepared to set the pace ourselves? Does the young woman seeking an ideal husband also strive herself to be an ideal wife? In seeking an ideal friend, do we try to live up to the standard demanded in another? It is unfair to demand perfection in another, and yet remain content to be as we are, imperfect and unworthy. Why demand from another what we are unwilling to achieve in ourselves? We demand much, yet give so little.

Life can be made much happier by having such ideals as enable us to see things through the eyes of our Lord. See that beggar, wretched, dirty, ragged and unkempt. Do we see anything beyond his unwashed and grimy exterior? Do we realise that underneath there is a soul that God loves infinitely, one whom he died to save? 'Amen I say to you, as long as you did it to one of these my least brethren, you did it to me.' Do we see God in the poor? That grimy unkempt man may have a cleaner soul than ours; he may be less sinful, more God-loving in spite of his disadvantages. This beggar is one of God's children, made for eternal happiness equally with us; he is just as precious in God's sight, our equal in humanity before God. There is the idealism of Christ. He would have us look beyond the outward appearance and in the poorest of the poor behold himelf. Even the sordid aspects of life can be viewed differently, each task be something done for God.

An ideal spurs us on, gives us something to strive for, urges us to high achievement. Our natural tendency is to be 'of the earth, earthy,' to work for low human standards, to judge success or failure by the world's estimate. We ought to aim at higher motives, the spiritual should be our first consideration and all else be subordinated to that.

Beware of seeking human praise : 'Amen . . . you have already received your reward.' Knowing man's needs, our divine teacher set forth the highest possible ideals. He set one that we dare not have chosen for ourselves: 'Be you perfect, as also your heavenly Father is perfect.' The infinite perfection of God himself is set as the ideal, the standard that we must strive to achieve. No ideal could be higher, nor yet as seemingly impossible as this. But it is more than an ideal; it is a command 'Be ye perfect!' It must be possible or God would not command it of us, would not set it as the standard to be achieved. True, of ourselves we are helpless, but as St Paul says: 'I can do all things in him who strengtheneth me.' With the help of God it is possible; though we may not attain to it in this life, yet with God's help we may go far, if we really do strive after it, certainly much further than if we were content with anything less. Many of our Lord's commands are in the nature of ideals. Love thy neighbour as thyself; there is an ideal standard of love. ' Learn of me for I am meek and humble of heart.' 'Take up thy cross daily and follow me.' 'Pray always.' But we are often times too occupied in making ourselves comfortable in this life to strive after the ideals set before us that we may make certain of eternal salvation.

How perfectly our Lord achieved his own ideal in the minutest particulars. On the cross he could say: 'It is finished,' it is achieved, the ideal has been attained, that high ideal of utter and complete subjection and obedience to his heavenly Father.

Our blessed Lady, his mother, had a similar ideal: 'Be it done unto me according to thy.word.' Because she too did not fall short of it she has been called 'our fallen nature's solitary boast.'

In words often repeated we set ourselves the same ideal. 'Thy will be done on earth as it is in heaven,' we say. But what effort do we make to carry out the sentiments there expressed? St Joseph might well serve us as a model, ready as he ever was to give instant obedience without question or dallying with preparations. He had complete trust in God; we do not trust God absolutely but delay in obedience so that we may prepare for what we may fear in the future. Our Lord tells us: 'Be not solicitous for what you shall eat or what you shall drink or wherewith you shall be clothed, for your heavenly Father knoweth that you have need of these things. Seek ye first the kingdom of God and all these shall be added to you.' Have perfect trust in God and leave all to his loving care. Here is another ideal that can lead us on to great spiritual heights. Trust in God as a child trusts its parents.

Let us have high ideals; only thus can we raise ourselves above the common plane. Many ideals have been set before us by the teachings of our Lord. Choose any one of them, then strive to attain to the goal set. Many have gone before us who have achieved the heights of sanctity because they aimed at these ideals. We are commanded to seek perfection thus; we have no choice but to obey. Unless, though, we see these commands as leading to the ideals of sanctity, instead of being mere burdens laid on us that we unwillingly try to obey as little as we can, we shall never climb far. To have them as ideals to strive after is wonderful, something to attain by prayer and the help of God. Better to fail striving to climb the heights, than be content to grovel in the valley beneath.

'Be you perfect as also your heavenly Father is perfect.'

XXXIV THOUGHTS

In endowing man with the faculty of thought, God gave him a great gift which can be, and unfortunately too often is, misused. The power of thinking raises man above the level of brute creation: animals cannot think, man can. This power gives to man, or should give him, dominion over material things; he can puzzle out ways and means, contrive expediencies to overcome difficulties and to supply his needs, invent new things for utility or pleasure or the saving of toil; he can master the sea, the land, and the air, turning the latent powers of nature to his own advantage. But it is only by deliberate thought, concentrated in ideas, that he achieves these effects.

There is another kind of so-called thought, however, which must now be considered, which should more accurately be called imagination. It is concerned with those imaginings that rise in the mind when it is not occupied in concentration on some definite idea. Much work is purely mechanical, leaving the mind free to wander in imagination. Such things as knitting, digging, walking in the lanes, watching a machine do not need any concentrated thought, but the mind is busy with ideas or allowed to wander amongst day-dreams. Much of our day may leave the mind free from the need of real, practical thought. What do we think about at such times? The matters which entertain us at such times may be an indication of character and have a greater influence in forming character than we credit.

The mind might well be likened to a garden where thoughts grow like flowers and weeds. A garden should be a thing of beauty. Let us thank God for a garden. Man was put into a lovely garden when created; it was to be his natural sphere of action. Flowers of various kinds flourish in a garden, roses, lilies, carnations, violets and a host of others. They glow with colour, scent the air, give joy to the beholder in a riot of loveliness, and speak of the beauty of God himself. This does not happen by chance. As we gaze we realise that a gardener must tend with interest and care with watchful eye, choosing what shall grow or what be cast out. Here and there a weed may creep in, but as soon as it is noticed it will be uprooted and cast out. Only unremitting care can keep a garden a thing of beauty. Alas! there is another kind of garden round an empty dwelling, once possibly a thing of beauty, now derelict and uncared for with no lovely flowers but only weeds, fungus, nettles, thistles, matted growths smothering all beauty—the garden that has no watchful eye to tend it.

Flowers have long been made symbols of human qualities; so a rose means love, a lily suggests purity, violets speak of modesty and carnations of friendship, while rosemary is for remembrance. The same symbolism can well be applied to weeds; nettles are for spite, thistles for bad-temper, smothering growths for selfishness and fungus for impurity.

This symbolism can help our present consideration. A person's mind is like a garden entrusted to him by God, to be cared for and tended so that it may be a thing of beauty in the sight of God. Thoughts are the flowers that grow therein. Each is the appointed gardener of his mind and on him depends what shall flower in his own mind. He must see that nothing but what is beautiful grows in it, that no weed takes root to spoil it. God does not interfere, except with the help of grace offered; each is responsible for the cultivation of his own mind. The mind can be filled with flowers of thought, of happy memories, kindness, help to be given. There may grow the lily of purity, the rose of true love, the carnation of friendship, the violet of humility, the daisy of modesty and other virtues. If this garden is to be kept beautiful it will need very close attention, watchfulness that no weed takes fast root. Into every mind evil thoughts intrude, just as in every garden weeds will appear; it is the curse of nature through sin. But as a watchful gardener uproots the noxious weed as soon as it is noticed, so must the evil thought be cast out as soon as it is perceived for what it is. What sort of mind has a man who allows any and every thought that enters to entertain him, to take root and be indulged? Like the garden of horror that untended, uncared for, harbours only noxious weeds, so the mind of the man who indulges his imagination in evil things, in uncharitable thoughts like nettles, in angry thoughts like thistles ready to wound, in impure thoughts like foul fungal growths, in selfishness smothering all good aspirations, in all those hateful growths that soil the mind intended by God to be a thing of beauty. Truly a horror in God's sight is this untended, uncared for, unwatched mind full of evil imaginations.

Only God can read our secret thoughts; yet an indication of our character may be provided by the expression of our thoughts, whereby we allow others to peer into the garden of our mind. If a person frequently speaks in an uncharitable manner or of impurities or is always complaining, if he speak of revenge, of jealousy, or displays his selfishness, does not this indicate the general state of his mind, show what trend his thoughts usually take, give us a glimpse into his garden of weeds? If a man speaks uncharitably it is an indication that he thinks uncharitably; he has let the nettles grow. If he delights in unchaste talk his mind must be full of foul fungus. Whether we like it or not, unconsciously we expose our garden to the view of others by our words, and allow them to see what we cultivate, the flowers of virtue, or the weeds of vice.

Thoughts can influence character. One sometimes meets with the individual who is disgruntled with life, vindictive, narrow-minded, given to back-biting and criticism of an unkindly nature, the type of person who, having lived too long alone and missed hoped-for joys in life, has nursed a grievance against fate, and brooded over it until the whole character has become warped and narrow in outlook. Such thoughts entertained in the lonely hours producing the weeds of bitterness, unkindness, criticism, and jealousy of the joys of others, have given us the acid spinster and crusty bachelor who unloving and unloved go their lonely way shunned by all. Had they trained their minds towards kindness and charity in spite of life's disappointments, they would have been lovable in old age, with many friends. Thus do these evil thoughts influence the character forming it for better or worse according as the garden of the mind is tended or not. Take heed, therefore, that only kind and charitable thoughts are encouraged to remain; be aware that brooding over past ills and resentment against fate warp and destroy the whole character; that evil thoughts cause degeneration of mind and spirit. Character is not entirely fixed and unchangeable; it is coloured by the habits of our thought. If thoughts are charitable, then speech and outlook will be the same and the character will develop and grow unselfish. Brooding over injuries, fancied or real, will warp the spirit; any sort of evil entertained in thought will make us similarly evil. This is not the work of a day or a week; lovely gardens are not produced over night, but are the result of years of unremitting care and attention: so too is a beautiful mind the results of years of training and unremitting watchfulness.

In some gardens we may find a glass-house where flowers of a delicate and tender nature, used to a warm and more genial climate, can flourish sheltered from the cold winds and frosts that the outer garden knows. The air must be kept at the proper heat to suit these choice blooms of another clime lest they wilt and die. There might well be a glass-house in the garden of the mind. In this could thrive the spiritual flowers in a supernatural atmosphere, the thoughts of God and holy things. These need to be sheltered from the cold blasts of the world, from earthly delights, from the distracting influences of life, from self-indulgence, all liable to blight these spiritual blooms. An even greater care and watchfulness is needed to cultivate the thoughts of God and his perfections, which do not come naturally to us but must be sought after, as a traveller seeks after the rare orchid in the tropical forest. We need more help and grace from God, but that will surely be given if we strive to keep our wayward thoughts fixed on him and all that belongs to him.

We must realise too, that all sin begins in the mind: the thought of evil is the first temptation always, and if this were uprooted like a noxious weed the moment it is perceived, there would be no sin. Thought always comes first, then follow from it speech and action, or sloth may cause some duty to be neglected. Much effort is needed indeed, aided by the grace of God without which we are helpless. Hence prayer must play its part in the work of cultivation; we must ask God to help us to create a clean mind and heart that it may be fit for him to gaze on. Not in a week, nor even a year, will the desired result be attained. It will suffice as the years pass by, if the mind grows more beautiful with age. By the law of nature, a neglected garden will revert to weeds, and all beauty be crushed out; so too by this same law will the neglected mind degenerate and become vice-ridden because of human proneness to evil. We must seek the grace of God in prayer, and by tireless effort train the mind to love thoughts of virtue and cast out all that is unlovely. Beautiful as a lovely garden is, the mind of man can be infinitely more lovely if trained to think only of what is good and virtuous. Then looking down upon our mind God may see 'a garden that is a thing of beauty and a joy for ever.'

XXXV MOODS AND FEELINGS

We are all subject to 'moods' or 'feelings' which are as changeable as the weather; now we are glad, now sad; happy and cheerful, soon irritable and gloomy; at times serious, then frivolous; now content, then discontented. Whence come all these changes within us? Often the cause is physical; now we enjoy good health, later on we get 'liverish,' suffer from indigestion or some other derangement of health. Weather can make us depressed or cheerful. Temperament plays its part; a sanguine temperament produces vitality, energy and irritability, the choleric one is hasty, the melancholic is given to brooding and sadness, the nervous is subject to swift changes of mood. All these varied temperaments influence feelings and emotions, produce moods that affect our outlook on life, and our attitude to things is oftentimes governed by our mood. What now amuses may later seem merely silly; this present interest becomes boring; a book we are reading with pleasure loses all interest because of a change in mood. All things have a bright and a dark side, a right aspect and a wrong aspect, according to the way we view them, itself due to the mood we reflect.

There is a principle in philosophy that whatever is received is modified (we might say 'moodified') by the mode or mood of its reception. Some look always on the dark side; they are the pessimists. Others see the bright side; these are the optimists. So much depends on the mood of the moment. This tendency may be partly inherited, partly acquired. In its most pronounced form it is the result of nature and habit and determines one's point of view. Two people may go out into the same garden. One returns gloomy and depressed saying the garden is horrid, every rose has a thorn, every bee has a sting, the apples are worm-eaten, and life is so wretched. The other comes in radiating smiles and happiness avowing the garden is so lovely, the roses have such a sweet smell, the bees are all busy gathering honey, the apples look tempting and it it is jolly to be alive. It is largely a question of point of view, of what one is moved to look for.

Unfortunately our gloomy moods readily affect others. Our cheerful moods can do the same, though it is often the gloom in us that affects others most easily. Because we are sad, we spoil another's joy; our pessimism destroys the optimism in another. If we indulge our gloomy moods, we shall find that we are shunned as 'a wet blanket.' Unfortunately we cannot choose our moods, we cannot produce feelings to order, nor can we always control them entirely; but we can, and must, prevent them from controlling us. It contributes to mental and boldily health to try to look always at the bright side, to live in the sun rather than in the shadow. To people who indulge their fits of the 'blues' everything seems wrong. To give in thus is to yield to a tyrant who casts an obstinate spell over his victims. We must fight against it.

Moods are catching and affect those with whom we come into contact. Smiles and frowns, joy and gloom, are all infectious, so for the sake of charity we must cultivate a happy disposition by refusing to be controlled by any opposite tendencies, lest we steal away, instead of adding to, the joy of others.

We know from our own experience that people have this kind of influence over others. There are those in whose company we lose our light-heartedness and become depressed, others whose cheerful spirit exorcises the gloomy forebodings that may have occupied our minds. We must realise that just as others affect us, so we affect them; we can turn their sadness into joy, or their joy into gloom. We are bound, therefore, in justice to ourselves and in charity to others to fight against our moods of despondency, refuse at least to be controlled by them, and spread happiness and joy around us by the joyousness of our own outlook.

So much for moods in ordinary human dealings. But what of their affect on our spiritual life? Many people judge the state of their soul by the mood they are in, make their religion a thing of moods and feelings rather than of solid piety and real love for God. We are affected to a greater extent than we perhaps realise because we pay too much attention to feelings, judge our spiritual state by emotions that are merely physical, whereas these have not the slightest affect on our spiritual life, unless we make the mistake of yielding to them. Do we, for instance, cease to pray because we are 'not in the mood for prayer'? What has our attitude to God got to do with the mood caused maybe by bodily indisposition? Many imagine that God is pleased, not by the effort they make in spite of difficulties to get into contact with him, but by how they 'feel' in praying to him. They think they are saints when they 'feel' good; sinners if they feel otherwise. Probably the very opposite is true. Spiritual writers tell us that the further we 'feel' from God, the nearer he may often be to us. We are distressed because we do not experience a wave of sweet emotion when we receive Holy Communion, as we perhaps imagine others must do. Not moved by any thrill of devotion, we think that God is not pleased with us. Yet, could we but see into his loving heart, we should find that he is very well pleased with the efforts we continue to make in spite of the lack of any such untrustworthy emotions.

As we have already remarked, we have little or no control over our feelings, and because of this they are valueless to us in the spiritual life. We are helped therein only by what we will, not by what we feel. If today we feel an access of joy in prayer, the nearness of God's almost physical presence, it may simply be basically due to the fact that we had a good dinner and that digestion is normal. We must be matter-of-fact about these things. If tomorrow we cannot pray, do not feel in the mood for it and are tempted to think that God has deserted us, let us similarly look for the cause of the present mood. It may prove to be some trivial bodily disorder. That may sound a little cynical; but it is, in fact, nothing else than the simple truth. Such moods of exaltation and depression are produced in us by these and similar unimpressive agents, whether they be within us or outside us. A wet day or a disappointment can play havoc with our feelings of devotion. But the fact that we do not feel any sweetness in Holy Communion or that we do not feel sorry for our sins does not indicate that our Holy Communion has not been pleasing to our Lord and of inestimable value to our soul, nor that our sorrow for sin is not deep and sincere. Our prayer is not intended to provide us with a thrill of emotion; it is an effort towards union with God; it is the raising of the mind and heart, the intellect and the will, to God. If our acts of religion brought their own delight of sensible emotion, there might be a grave danger of seeking them for the pleasure we found in them rather than for the glory that should thus be given to God. 'Amen I say to you, you have had your reward.'

There is indeed a joy that comes to those who try to serve God. Sometimes, though not often, a sense of spiritual sweetness is given by God; more often, however, it is a joy deep in the soul that flows from love of God and the effort to do his will in spite of all difficulties, changeable moods and natural disinclination to do what is hard. God values all efforts to overcome self, and self includes the domination of moods and feelings. In both our natural and our supernatural life we must fight against self and its moods or they will dominate us in the end, more particularly such as are depressing, saddening and gloomy. We are more easily inclined to sadness than to joy; joy is no trouble to us, except to keep it, but sadness soon takes hold of us, and we in turn are apt to infect others. That is not charitable, because by the law of charity we are bound to further the well-being of our neighbours. Even self-interest should persuade us to cultivate cheerfulness and joy, since thereby we win the comfort of companionship with others, whereas by allowing our morbid feelings to overcome us we lose our friends. But what is far more important, our spiritual life also demands control of moods, since these easily tempt us to slackness in our spiritual duties, to misjudgement of the state of our soul, and maybe lead us into sin, especially sins against charity by backbiting and jealousy. Gloom and baseless sadness are fruitful causes of sin, whereas joy and gladness will save us many a temptation and sin.

XXXVI LITTLE THINGS

It is written in holy scripture that 'he that contemneth small things shall fall by little and little.' Life is composed mostly of small things—acts, thoughts, words, desires—which, though apparently small, are the things to be judged hereafter. Most things begin in a small way; the mighty oak began as an acorn; the huge building is but many stones placed together; life is a succession of small deeds, good or bad. It is but seldom that a really big thing happens to us, but any one of the small daily happenings may be the beginning of some great thing. St Teresa tells us that she was fond of small vanities and because of them she was shown a place prepared for her in hell. She changed her mode of life! Many are fond of small vanities, of such things as lip-stick, powder, dress. Where will these lead?

We think of venial sin as small and often are careless about it in consequence. The old adage bids us 'take care of the pence and the pounds will take care of themselves.' So in the spiritual life; if we are careful of the small imperfections we need have no fear of mortal sin. No man becomes a criminal suddenly, except in very rare cases; he begins in a small way. A thief starts by petty pilfering, goes on to robbery and possibly, to escape being caught, to murder. Deliberate venial sin spoils our lives, prevents the grace of God from doing its work in the soul, weakens resistance to evil, and paves the way to mortal sin. In the same way small good deeds prepare the way and influence the whole of life; small acts of self-denial prepare for greater ones; small good deeds increase grace in the soul which thereby grows stronger, more eager to serve God. Our Lord speaks of many small things: a cup of water given for his sake; the widow's mite greater than other offerings; the grain of mustard seed; the lost groat; the leaven and so on.

To God nothing is so small that it has no value; all is done with infinite care. Let us learn from nature! We may be admiring some glorious vista of lake and mountain bathed in sunshine, we are lost in the wonder of God's creative power, when a tiny gnat buzzing round us causes irritation and with a stroke we crush it out of existence without a thought. Men can make lakes and mountains, but a living gnat is beyond all power of man to produce. It is a marvellous organism created by God with infinite care, not too small for the power of God to bring into existence, living, enjoying its life, doing the work intended by God, but to us merely a nuisance to be destroyed. Does not this tiny living thing portray God's power even more than the eternal hills? That purple glow on the hillside is but thousands of tiny flowers; the green carpet of the fields is composed of millions of blades of grass; the welcome shade beneath the tree is formed by millions of small leaves; the miles of beach by the sea are but countless grains of sand; all tiny insignificant things that we cannot do without. The life of man is the steady succession of millions of seconds, each one of a definite value in God's sight. Life is not made up of great isolated deeds, of great sacrifices, but of tiny things in which smiles, kindnesses to others in little things, small duties generously performed, are asked of us, each one of value and building up what we call life.

The hidden life of our Lord is our real model. He ran errands for his mother, played with other children, learnt to use tools, attended the synagogue, and when old enough worked at the bench making things for use, like any working man. That is our normal life also, doing the ordinary tasks that each day brings, and doing them to the best of our ability. Despise not the little things. A poet has written: 'God has made millions of leaves for forest shade; smallest stars that glory bring; God employeth everything. Then the little thou has done; little battles thou hast won; little masteries achieved; little wants with care relieved; little words with love expressed; little wrongs at once confessed; little favours kindly done; little toils thou didst not shun; little graces meekly worn; little slights with patience borne; those shall crown thy pillowed head, holy light upon thee shed; those are the treasures that shall rise far beyond the smiling skies.' That is what God asks of us, what will make life a success in his eyes.

Many will say that they want to do something worthwhile

173

for God, and are always waiting, waiting for something they think worthwhile, and missing all the daily opportunities of doing things for God because such things seem too small to be of value.

That work by which we earn our daily bread; that little kindly deed done for another; that small self-denial—that is what God wants of us. If we cannot do these small things for him, how shall we do the greater if it should appear? If God wants great things from us, they will be offered; if they do not come, then God does not need them of us. One thing is certain, he does not want us to stand all the day idle because we imagine that there is nothing big enough to be worthwhile doing. Many think they would like to die for God, but few are willing to live for him the ordinary humdrum life. Yet which is the harder? It is tedious and difficult to go on day after day, doing little things well, but it is those little things that are building up life. As the grains of sand form the beach, as the tiny leaves clothe the trees, so little acts, too often despised and ignored, are building our lives and are the means of salvation—or damnation—for us.

Let us consider some small insignificant things, too often ignored by many. Punctuality is a tiny item, but it can affect others a great deal and we are often careless about it or its effects. Many are careless about being in time for appointments; though it is irritating to others to be kept waiting about, wasting time idly. It vexes people, makes them impatient, and we are responsible for these imperfections in others when it is our failure that causes them. It is not a small thing that affects another's spiritual state. To busy men, time means money; we should not waste their time by being unpunctual; it may mean other more important engagements become impossible. We must be punctual to catch a train; it will not wait our convenience, and we are left stranded if we are not in time. Hence we get to the station in time. Why treat another with scant courtesy when he is kind enough to give us some of his time? A priest is a busy man with a lot of engagements. If he is kept waiting on our convenience, it means that others must be put off, maybe the sick are kept waiting or those needing confession kept longer because of our dalliance. At public gatherings, some think it the 'thing' to arrive late and inconvenience others who must be disturbed to let the late-comer to his seat. It shows a want of courtesy, and courtesy is one of the attributes of the true follower of our blessed Lord. A gentleman is one who has thought for others. To be late for Mass is disrespectful to God. If a sermon is in progress, the latecomer distracts the preacher, causes him to lose his continuity of thought; it disturbs his hearers and they lose the lesson that is being taught. Usually it is thoughtlessness that causes unpunctuality; it may seem a little thing, but it can greatly affect our charity to others.

Politeness is another small thing, but like oil in a machine it makes life run smoothly. It may be only the outcome of social good manners, but it is in truth an aspect of charity. Little kindnesses shown to others in difficulty are the essence of politeness; to give up a seat to a lame person or one bur-dened with a child, to help the blind across the road, these are little things, but helpful to others: 'Amen I say to you, as long as you do it to one of these my least brethren, you do it to me.' Some people are noisy in their manner, talk loudly, rush about the house, bang doors or throw things about, full of their own importance, fussing and bustling about as though there were no others to be considered, nothing so important as their own tasks. Such conduct can be most irritating to those who love quiet and repose, to those whose work demands that no distractions shall be thrust upon them. There is suffi-cient unavoidable noise in the world without our adding to it. We have a duty, small perhaps in our estimation, of recognising the rights of other people, of curbing self in those matters that may be a source of annoyance to others, of consideration of our neighbours' needs and convenience.

Consideration and restraint in these small matters affecting others is a duty of charity which we must observe and which they have a right to expect from us. Nothing is too small to consider especially when it involves others, and we have no right to cause irritation and impatience to be shown because of our want of consideration. Despise not the little things of life; they are important. Every minute is of value in which something can be done for the glory of God, even if it be merely to keep quiet for the sake of others, to give a smile and a kindly word in season, to be helpful and considerate, to be punctual.

We must not wait idly for some big thing to come along that appears worth doing for God; let us get on with the small things and thereby prepare for the bigger. We never know but what some small deed may be the beginning of some great achievement; by missing it we may let slip an opportunity never to be regained. Life is made up, not of great sacrifices or duties, but of little things. If we can look back upon the day and find that we have done some small act of self-denial to help another, said one word that gave encouragement or eased a smart, then we can count that day as being of some worth. But if we can trace nothing that has helped or cheered another along his way, then that day is lost for ever. There is an old doggerel which runs: 'For want of a nail the shoe was lost, for want of a shoe the horse was lost, for want of a horse the rider was lost.' No one would consider a nail to be a big thing, but though so small it was of vital necessity to the rider. So it may be with a tiny item that we despise. Any small thing may be the beginning, the cause, of something far greater with lasting effects. It may be the beginning of salvation or—which God forbid—the beginning of damnation. 'He that contemneth small things, shall fall by little and little.'

XXXVII WORK

'In the sweat of thy face shalt thou eat bread.' Such was
the curse that fell on Adam and his descendants because of
sin. The necessity of work is laid down in holy scripture. Our
Lord says: 'There are six days wherein you ought to work.'
St Paul writes: 'If any man will not work, neither let him eat.'
Obviously work is something more than a curse; it is a duty
imposed for a definite reason. What exactly do we mean by
work? It is the opposite to idleness; it does not necessarily
mean earning a living, doing a job for payment. It really
means 'occupation' as distinct from idleness. Not all need to
earn a living. Some are independent of wages, having a sufficient
income from other sources, but they must have occupation of
some kind even if only playing games. One man's play is
another man's work, e.g. driving a car or taking photographs.

Work is no disgrace whether it be done to earn a living or
to avoid idleness, neither can the most humble work be deemed
unbefitting the dignity of man. Our Lord was himself a true
working man; he was taught a trade by St Joseph, worked
as a carpenter at a bench, labouring with his hands, using
tools to make articles of daily use; he no doubt received payment for his work, with which he helped to keep the household
in necessities. After the death of St Joseph, he was the sole
bread-winner for his mother and himself. Hence work has
been sanctified and given a dignity of its own. If he who was
God did not disdain to work with his hands and follow a trade,
shall we think it beneath our dignity to work? The ordinary
working-man is following in the footsteps of Jesus by labouring. Moreover it matters not what the work is, no matter
how degrading or menial it may be considered by men. In God's
sight all work has its own value and dignity provided it is
done to the best of a man's ability. The man who sweeps the
gutters, empties the dust-bins or cleanses the drains, is doing
in God's estimation work at least as worthy as that done by
the manager of a great business concern; it may well be far
more worthy. The fact that he gains less profit has nothing to
do with the dignity of his work. The men who look after the

welfare of a great city by tending to its sanitary needs are doing a work of great social value as necessary as the work of a doctor, for prevention is better than cure; whereas a man dabbling in the buying and selling of stocks and shares for his own private gain is doing work of no social value. Yet the world despises the poor, but necessary, scavenger, and fawns on the wealthy stockbroker who may perhaps be the ruin of many through his shady dealings. Certainly in the sight of God the work which benefits the many will be of a higher value than the work done for merely personal gain, no matter how men may consider it.

What gives real value to work, however, is its capability of furthering holiness and salvation; for work is not done merely for its own sake; it has a definite relationship to our service of God. All work must be referred to God in some way if it is to benefit the soul and sanctify it. When Jesus bade St Peter launch out into the deep and let down the nets, St Peter answered: 'Lord we have laboured all the night and taken nothing, but at thy word I will let down the net.' The result was a huge catch of fish. When they laboured all night for themselves, they took nothing; when they worked for God and with God, they made tremendous profit. If we work merely for monetary gain or self-satisfaction, we are idle so far as the soul is concerned, all our labour is profitless; God must come into our work, we must work with him and for him. To many their labour is spiritually profitless because they work, not from a right motive of giving glory to God, but for a selfish motive in which God has no part. Hence spiritually they are idle, the soul is gaining nothing. There can be no object in the divine commandment to work unless it profits the soul and furthers sanctification and salvation.

Many try to divide life into two compartments, spiritual and material, to keep them separate and apart as though running parallel without any connection. Thus going to Church, avoiding sin, praying, receiving the sacraments, these things belong to the spiritual life; whereas work, meals, sleep, amusements belong to the material. This shows a complete misunderstanding of life and its purpose. We cannot separate the spiritual and material; both must interweave, intermingle, to form one whole, just as the body and the soul form one composite being. The material must be spiritualized, the natural become supernatural.

Our Lord bids us 'pray always.' How can we do this unless work is prayer? The great St Antoninus, O.P. said: 'To work is to pray.' How can this be? Whatever is offered to God is spiritualized and turned into prayer, hence the ' morning offering' to God of all we do. By this offering we have the intention of doing all for God and thus it becomes prayer; moreover this intention persists so long as it is not retracted. Whatever we offer to God becomes his property, we do it for him and so he enters into it, sanctifies it, and uses it to pour grace out upon the soul; thus it becomes meritorious and profitable to the soul.

This, however, entails certain obligations on us as to the manner in which we work. In the book of Deuteronomy we read: 'Thou shalt not sacrifice to the Lord thy God a sheep or an ox wherein there is any blemish or any fault; for that is an abomination to the Lord.' Only the best is fit to be offered to God in sacrifice. A sacrifice is an offering to God; hence if our work is to be offered to him, we cannot offer anything but the best of which we are capable, we cannot offer work that is faulty or badly done.

We could hardly imagine St Joseph doing shoddy work, or teaching the Child to fake faulty material or work to be sold to another, nor could we think of him accepting payment for work badly done or made with poor materials. He would always give of his best. So we, if we offer our work to God, must give of our best also. Those on piece work are often tempted to hurry the work to get more pay, but hurried work may be faulty, faults be covered to pass the foreman (they will not pass God), and the buyer suffer through bad work. That is not justice: it is fraud, and cannot be offered to God. Dare we offer for sale work known to be faulty and have no qualms of conscience about it? Do we say 'It is business' and let it go at that? To cheat others is none of our 'business,' nor dare we offer to God a thing that is thus blemished. If we work for a fixed wage, there is danger of wasting time which is not ours. We are inclined to slack off, to take things easily, since it makes no difference to our material earnings. But what of our spiritual earnings? Our employer has a right to the time for which he pays us to do work for him; if we filch time from him we are not giving the just due and our work is blemished, not fit to offer to God.

Work can bring into play various virtues and teach us good habits. Usually our work entails obedience to a superior, which is a virtue pleasing to God. St Peter bids us (I. Peter II, 18): 'Servants be subject to your masters with all fear, not only to the good and gentle, but also to the froward. For this is thanksworthy.' So often we resent being ordered to do things though we are forced to obey; but such resentment deprives us of spiritual gain. Work can lead us to be humble if we take orders in the proper spirit. Forbearance and patience come into play in dealing with fellow-workers, especially those whom we dislike. It can teach us to be kindly and helpful to others in difficulty, to be meek and docile when shown how to do a job. All this is good for our spiritual advancement, an occasion of winning grace and merit through the ordinary labours of the day. Even those who do not work for any master, may turn all their daily tasks to spiritual good by working for God and doing everything as well as possible for his sake.

It is just common sense to turn work into a means of sanctification. It adds nothing to our labour, except to do whatever it is as well as we possibly can; it is doing exactly the same thing, but for higher motives and spiritual profit. We must try to get a different outlook on work, which is often regarded merely as a curse. Too many consider work merely as a means of livelihood as though it were alien to true life. Few can see the connection between work and personal sanctification. The holy family is the best answer. It is strange that Jesus, who was God, spent the greater part of his life as an ordinary working-man, labouring with his hands. With his foster-father he was a working-man in the truest sense, striving to earn his bread in the sweat of his face, thereby sanctifying all work and turning it into a blessing for mankind. He shows the true dignity of labour. His mother Mary was busy about the menial tasks of the household, cooking, cleaning, washing, mending. She, who was 'full of grace,' daily increased in grace by the menial tasks of house-keeping.

Since our Lord spent so many years in this hidden life of work, it must surely be to teach us the lesson of true human life, the humdrum working life that the majority must lead. His public life was out of the ordinary, and very brief at that. It was not the normal life of the normal man. Hence his hidden life is the example, the model that befits the greater number, and that was a life of work well done.

These considerations ought to give us a new idea of the dignity of work, to give us an incentive to turn work to spiritual gain. 'Work not for the meat that perisheth.' Work is not just a means of getting wages, it is the means by which we sanctify our daily life; it plays an important part saving our souls. It is not a necessary evil, but a fruitful source of grace and blessing. The greater part of life must be spent in work; that is God's ordinance. Hence it must play a major part as a means of merit in sanctifying the whole of life. 'To work is to pray!' Do not treat work as something outside the spiritual life, but use it as a means of furthering the good of the soul. Offer all to God, and so turn all into prayer. Work well, play well, sleep well, but do all for God that it may be raised to a supernatural plane.

'All whatsoever you do in word or in work, do all for the honour and glory of God.'

XXXVIII   WORLDLINESS

St John writes in his first epistle: 'Love not the world, nor the things which are in the world. If any man love the world, the charity of the Father is not in him.' When we received the sacrament of baptism, we promised to 'renounce the world and all its pomps' as one of the great enemies of the soul, drawing us away from the service of God. The danger lies in that it offers so many attractions which seem to promise happiness and, though many of these attractions are not in themselves actually sinful, yet they do cause us to fix our desires on them to the detriment of the soul, making it lax and tepid in the service of God. Many of the world's tenets are definitely sinful but they offer some specious argument giving the appearance of being good and beneficial to mankind. Love of the world and its attractions is one of the greatest evils of modern times, evil because of the unrest, the desire for excitement, the wish to satisfy any impulse, be it right or wrong.

There is great need for us to be on our guard about what is read or heard; the daily press, books and pamphlets are presenting evil under the guise of good, using new terms for old. Thus what was before termed 'discipline' has now become 'self-repression' and said to be an evil thing. Moderns teach that the natural instincts should not be repressed since this causes a 'complex' which will be a hindrance in the struggle for existence. Thus by a specious excuse they advocate giving free rein to all natural impulses, good or evil. They would restrain correction of children in glaring faults lest they suffer from repression and so grow 'nervy.'

Even Catholics become infected with these new-fangled ideas, deceived by the false reasoning, and wonder why the Church is so 'old fashioned.' Because of economic difficulties, the result of modern civilization, advice is tendered to married people to restrict the size of the family by sweeping away all moral restrictions in the use of marital rights. Reproduction is prevented by illicit and artificial means contrary to natural law, so that the pleasures of the flesh may be enjoyed without restriction. These unnatural evils are presented as being 'good' for human beings, and many are foolish enough to be misled by such false arguments. In spite of all the warnings given by the Church, these ideas gain ground among the faithful (or rather the unfaithful!) who feel that the Church lags behind modern progress, failing to see that modern 'progress' is simply encouraging the baser appetites and passions of the flesh. As the guardian of the word of God the Church cannot call 'right' that which is sinful: 'Heaven and earth shall pass away, but my word shall not pass!' Those who listen to the teachings of the world are forgetful of their solemn promise made 'to renounce the world.'

Apart from things definitely sinful, the world offers many attractions innocent in themselves when moderately used, which have the power to, and in effect do, make us irreligious, careless in God's service, preferring the amusements and excitements of pleasure to the demands of religion, to the benefits of the sacraments and the life of prayer. We are told to be 'in the world, but not of it,' in other words to use lawful things for their intended purpose, but not as an 'end' to be sought for their own sake; to use recreations as a means of 're-creating' our flagging energies, as a stepping stone to God, not as the chief things in life. We are but 'strangers and pilgrims' journeying to our real home, we have not here a lasting city; it is not fitting to remain by the wayside absorbed in things that are not our real end. On a journey, though we may admire the scenery in passing, we do not tarry because of the attractions by the way and forget the purpose of our travel or our destination; such attractions merely help to pass the time. So we are but on a journey through the life of this world, and it is not meet that we should settle down to enjoy transient pleasures, forgetful of the real purpose of life. Our thoughts should always be turned to God, our last end. We are not forbidden to use the innocent attractions offered, but to place our hope of happiness in them is futile and contrary to the purpose of life, which is to serve God and advance in holiness.

The chief attractions offered consist in riches, honours and pleasures; the bait is happiness. But it is a happiness that is deceptive and unsatisfying. Because of the innate desire for happiness, we are too easily deluded into thinking it can be found among the pleasures of the world. In God alone can we ever find real satisfying happiness. The happiness offered by the world inevitably ends in disillusion and weariness of spirit; the world never fulfils its promise because it is incapable of so doing. Yet in spite of our experience we do not grow any the wiser, still allow ourselves to be deluded, still believe in the frauds offered.

It may be said that this is a pessimistic view of life. But no; it is the simple truth which experience dearly bought should prove. It was meant to be so by God, that we might turn always to him who alone can satisfy the craving of the human soul for perfect happiness.

Riches! Was any man ever satisfied with what he had? Ever truly happy in his many possessions? Wealth brings worry and anxiety in its train, fear of loss, multiplication of needs as possessions increase, more is desired to keep pace until the possessor is no better off in the end, and the bogy of loss is always present. Those having sufficient to gratify every whim become so satiated with pleasure, having all that money can buy (except too often the simple things of life) that they become bored and dissatisfied with all, finding joy in none. Those who have but little are often envious of the rich, desire riches with which to gratify imagined wants, embittering their lives with discontent. If we have such desires we are worldly and religion will have no savour. Are riches worth the loss of spiritual good? Jesus gave us the secret of happiness where possessions are concerned: 'Blessed are the poor in spirit,' happy are they who have the right attitude of mind to all worldly possessions and lay up treasures in heaven.

Honours! What are they worth? When a man dies all worldly honour ceases for him and is utterly useless and worthless; as a river once known by name loses its identity on reaching the sea and ceases to exist, so the honours of the world. Yet men seek these honours so eagerly! Akin to honour is the desire always to be in the latest fashion lest we lose caste among acquaintances, to be up-to-date in dress, full of outward show, anxious lest others get ahead. Some strive to be leaders of fashion, more daring in style than others, less modest even. 'Be not solicitous wherewith you shall be clothed.' Of what avail will the latest fashion be when we are called before our Judge to give an account of our service? This does not imply that we should be 'dowdy' or careless about dress, but we ought to be simple in our tastes, satisfied with ordinary decency and modest raiment, valuing more the raiment of grace in the soul.

Pleasures! Do we make pleasure the main object in life? Dances, cinemas, theatres and such-like excitements? The youth of to-day have an unhealthy craving for excitement. Work is something to be endured until they can rush off to the pictures or a dance; cinema stars are their heroes and heroines, known by name and appearance, talked about as supermen and aped in their mannerisms. But the saints of God are unknown, have no appeal, are not mentioned and still less imitated. Pleasure is the only appeal they know, the home has no entertainment, they have no self-reliance for occupation or recreation, the creative instinct has no meaning to them. Seldom do they visit the church, only when compelled by obligation and at times not even then on the plea of being too tired—worn out rather by the search after pleasures. Bitter experience will teach them that all pleasures grow stale and insipid by too frequent repetition; they will be bored and empty with nothing left to fill the void. They lounge listlessly, not knowing what to do with themselves when the usual excitements are not available. They will not be convinced of the truth, yet it is a law of nature that all things grow stale if enjoyed too often; nor will they admit that they are worldly.

Amusements are permissible as a change from routine and weariness, but if they become the chief object in life we must pay with unhappiness and disillusionment. Then perhaps we turn to God, to devotions, but find no sweetness therein, no consolations; therefore we think religion has failed us, whereas it is we ourselves who have failed religion. We gave it no chance in the past, yet now expect it to comfort and heal the bruised spirit. We are like people recovering from sickness who must pass through a period of slow convalescence ere we can find delight in devotion and the service of God.

We are strangers and pilgrims in this vale of tears, hence we cannot expect the road to be all happiness and delights. If we tarry by the way forgetting the real purpose of life in passing joys, we lose all desire for spiritual advancement. Our Lord warned us: 'Now you are sad, but your sorrow shall be turned into joy.' Life is made of joy and sorrow, and both have a purpose. Sadness makes us realise that we have not here a lasting home; joy helps us to plod along the road. True happiness is to be found only in spiritual things. Earthly joys pass leaving naught but regret. Spiritual sweetness fades but leaves no emptiness of soul; it fades lest we become too content with life on earth, but its passing makes us yearn for the true lasting happiness of heaven.

Let us not attempt the impossible! Jesus has told us: 'You CANNOT serve God and mammon.' It must be either the one or the other, but not both. God and the world are utterly opposed and we must choose the one or the other. The choice has already been made at baptism: 'I renounce the world and all its pomps.' Have we been faithful to the promise made? Let us beware of worldliness; it is insidious, deceitful, clutching hold of us ere we are aware of it. The more worldly we are the less spiritual. Be in the world but not of it!

XXXIX EXAMPLE

Our Lord said to his disciples: 'You shall give testimony of me.' They were to bear witness to the truths he had taught to explain all the lessons they had learnt and lead others to a knowledge of the true way in which life was to be lived and God worshipped. This is the meaning of giving testimony. Not only were Christ's apostles to witness to truth, but also all those who followed his teaching and theirs through all time. It means, therefore, that we are included among the givers of testimony.

How shall this be done? Are we to go out and preach the gospel, to stand in the market place, the workshop or the field and proclaim the truths of faith? It is not given to many to preach the word, nor is that necessarily the most telling way of spreading the truth of the Gospel. There is another way, much more powerful too, by which we teach, willy-nilly, and give testimony either for or against Christ. It is by example, a most potent testimony to what we actually believe. We are told that 'example is better than precept,' and are invited 'to practise what we preach.' It is of little use for a preacher to urge: 'Do as I say, but not as I do!'

It is common knowledge that the spoken word carries but little weight unless it is backed up by corresponding deeds, by example. It is not what we say but what we do that is most noted by others, and the good done by a sermon may be totally undone again by the bad example not only of the preacher but also of those who profess to believe in what has been said. It is not 'what we call ourselves' but 'what our deeds prove us to be' that convinces others. As St John writes: 'My little children, let us not love in word or in tongue, but in deed and in truth.'

St John the Baptist sent his followers to ask our Lord: 'Art thou he that is to come or look we for another?' Jesus could have answered simply: 'Yes I am he.' But that was not his answer. He replied: 'Go and relate to John what you have seen and heard. The blind see, the lame walk, the deaf hear, the dead rise again, the poor have the gospel preached to them.'

187

He knew that a mere declaration is not convincing, hence he bids them judge by his example which is the real proof of what he is and claims to be.

Our Lord never taught what he did not himself fulfil to the utmost. Suppose someone asks: 'Are you a Catholic?' Dare we answer: 'Look at my life. I go to Mass and keep the commandments of God and the Church; I deny myself; I love my neighbour as myself; I take up my cross daily; I practise what I profess to believe.' Could we truthfully give such an answer? It might seem to be pride if we did, but that is the answer that we ought be able to give in truth. In fact we are giving that answer unconsciously day by day through the force of example either for or against the tenets of the Catholic Church. If our conduct does not correspond to Catholic ideals and teachings, we are giving false testimony to Christ. If we are not 'all a catholic should be' we are unfaithful to our trust, not giving witness to Christ and his Church.

We have been warned that the world will hate us, even as it hated our Lord; but though it hates, it yet looks for the high standard of conduct demanded by the Catholic religion, and it rightly demands that catholics shall live up to the standard they profess to accept. Have we realised that? Possibly we have never given it a thought, but it is true that the world, those living round us, those working with us, those acquainted with us, do expect a higher standard of conduct, a more perfect goodness, from the professed catholic than from others. Much harm is done to religion by careless catholics who do not practise what they profess; the Church is judged by its known members. Wherever your daily life takes you, into the office or the factory or the fields, to those round you you are the CHURCH. By your conduct its reputation is upheld or falls into disgrace; the good name of the Church is in your keeping. This may seem unfair, perhaps it is unfair, but nevertheless the Church is judged by the conduct of those known to be its members. Often we find mentioned in the public press the fact that 'the accused' is a Roman Catholic. It makes no mention of the religion other accused may profess, unless perchance it be a 'minister of religion' who has fallen from his high profession. This goes to show that the world demands a higher standard from catholics than from others. A catholic criminal is matter for special notice. Woe to those catholics who fail to live up to the high standard demanded even by the world, who in failing stain the spotless robe of the Bride of Christ.

A young woman who was being instructed in the faith with the purpose of becoming a catholic, had explained to her the doctrine of the real presence of Jesus in the Blessed Sacrament. After that she did not return for any further instructions. Later the priest met her by chance and inquired why she had not come any more for instructions. She told him that after learning about the real presence she had gone to Benediction and during it had noticed certain girls talking and giggling in what they were said to believe was the actual presence of God on the altar. She thought that if catholics could so behave there could hardly be faith in the reality of God's presence, so that the catholic religion was not worth much after all and she was as well off where she usually attended. Poor reasoning indeed, but the force of bad example was enough to turn the scale and prevent the beginnings of faith from fructifying in that soul. Instruction in word carried little weight in the face of concrete example. It shows how little we are aware of the effect on others of our conduct. Yet a grave responsibility lies on us in the example we are unconsciously giving to those around us.

Consider this further instance. A working lad on a holiday of obligation asked permission to take time off to go to Mass. His employer could hardly credit such a request being genuine in a lad and giving the permission, he sent another to watch this lad and report on what he did. Afterwards it was reported that the lad did actually go to church and returned to work as soon as the service was over. This so edified the man that he made enquiries into the catholic faith, which resulted in his becoming a catholic and building a church in thanksgiving for the grace of faith. Little did that youth know how his example was to bring a soul a God.

Truly example is better than precept. We read in the Gospel

that 'they watched to see what he would do.' We also are watched! Our workmates watch us and woe to us if our conduct is not more moral than theirs. They may tell lies but they expect us to tell the truth; they may take small items from the factory, we may not do the same; they may swear, talk filth, but no catholic may do these things and yet expect his Church to be respected. At times they may tempt us to see what we will do. Knowing that catholics are forbidden to eat meat on Fridays, they will offer a share of their meat pies. Woe to us if we fail our Lord even in these apparently unimportant things.

Our example is continually before our fellows for good or evil. We must live a truly catholic life, must be catholic in deed as well as in name. Scandal, so severely condemned by our Lord, is simply bad example which leads another to sin or to fail to learn truth. 'Woe to the world because of scandals, for it must needs be that scandals come, but nevertheless woe to that man by whom the scandal cometh.' Woe to the catholic who brings the Church into disrepute and causes others to lose the faith they might otherwise gain because of the bad example shown.

This responsibility may seem a great burden, but actually it demands no more from us than our ordinary duty. If we call ourselves catholic and do not live in accordance with our professions, we are but frauds. It is the frauds that give bad example and bring the Church into disrepute. Since we cannot help giving example either good or bad, it behoves us to be on our guard that we live a truly catholic life and avoid being unfaithful even in small matters.

The giving of example does not mean that we are to be always thinking about it. We do not set out of intent to give example; it is largely unconscious on our part. It is of no use to say that others ought to mind their own business, that it is their fault if they misjudge the Church through what we do. The fact is that unless we live up to what we profess we cannot avoid giving bad example, just as a man who is doing his best to be a true catholic gives good example and bears witness to the truth of the catholic faith by the goodness of his life. We influence others; they influence us in turn. It is a talent for which we must give an account to God. Liberty of action may be very dear, but we are held responsible for the consequences of such action. But if we do nothing unbecoming to a catholic we need not bother about example; it will look after itself. We must remember that to our acquaintances we stand for the Church and by our conduct the Church stands or falls. They have no other means of judging; they know so little about the truths of faith except insofar as they see them in action. This they see in our conduct and thus there is a grave responsibility for us to bear, one which we cannot escape. There is so much ignorance of faith and religion about us, so little attraction in the many false religions presented that few have any idea of serving God or know how to serve. From our conduct they can be led to see the beauty of a holy life, and when they watch us, they may be unconsciously seeking for truth. If we fail them, where shall they go to be taught the way to save their souls?

Remember always that YOU ARE THE CHURCH! She will be judged by what you are in your daily life.

'My little children let us not love in word nor in tongue, but in deed and in truth.' (St John I. Ep. ch. III, v. 18).

XL OUR LADY—OUR EXAMPLE

Holy Church puts the lives of her saints before us not only to do them honour but also to give us ideals on which to model our own lives. But whilst we admire them some of the saints frighten us by the extraordinary austerity of their lives, the severe penances they inflicted on themselves, such as we of weaker natures could not possibly imitate. Yet the most perfect of all the saints, Mary the Mother of God, as far as we know adopted none of these awful austerities; she lived a quite normal human life and nevertheless is beyond all others of God's holy ones. She is thus the perfect saint for us to imitate. Does it seem presumptuous to choose the sinless Mother of God as our exemplar? Are we not aiming too high? She was sinless; for the rest of our lives we could be sinless if we corresponded perfectly with God's grace as Mary did. As she gave herself over without reserve to the workings of grace, so could we. It is in this above all that she is our model.

That she was conceived without sin, that she was chosen to be the Mother of God, this was the ineffable work of the eternal God. 'He that is mighty hath done great things to me.' But, as with all the saints, her sanctity was in some sense her own and the secret of her sanctity was her full and perfect submission to, and acceptance of, the will of God. 'Be it done unto me according to thy word.' Whatever happened she accepted it as the will of God and conformed her will to his. If we did the same, we should indeed be saints. The appeal of her life is its natural simplicity; we know of no extraordinary penances practised, of no outstanding works of charity, of nothing very big accomplished to any outward seeming. Our Lady was a married woman, a working-man's wife, who looked after the needs of her husband and the Child, was occupied with the ordinary cares of a house, cooking, washing, cleaning and mending. The holy family was, to the outward view, quite a normal human family with nothing to distinguish it from the other families of the village.

Leaving aside for the moment the purely supernatural elements in our Lady's life, let us consider what we know of her life as it would have appeared to the relatives and friends who knew her. At an early age she was espoused to Joseph, the carpenter. Her womanly charity is shown in her eager visit to her cousin Elizabeth. In due course she gave birth to her own child. To save his life she was taken by Joseph into Egypt and lived there for some time, but of their actual life there we know nothing. Other mothers have had to leave country and friends for the sake of the family. Returning to her native land, she no doubt settled down to the village life again; we hear no more until, at the age of twelve, the Child is lost in Jerusalem for three days. It is not an uncommon thing for children to get lost and cause anxiety to their parents. After they had found him he went back home with them 'and was subject to them.' This brief phrase in the Gospel covers the next eighteen years, but during that time it seems that Joseph died and the Child, growing to manhood becomes, no doubt, the breadwinner for his mother. His public life is inaugurated by the very homely happening of his being invited with his mother to a local wedding. But little is heard of her during the three years of his ministry; such references as there are suggest that she followed her Son in his preaching journeys, as we should expect. After his ascension she lived on for some years, still in a very hidden way, taking no public part (as far as we know) in the spread of the Gospel, but assuredly helping all by her sympathy and her prayers, mothering the infant Church, until God calls her to himself.

Looked at from that angle this simple human life is just the life of millions of other mothers, and yet how different when regarded from the spiritual point of view! Mary is indeed the perfect model for every human being, for she shows us how, by perfect submission to God, an apparently ordinary human life can provide the means of supernatural perfection which is demanded of us too: 'Be you perfect, as also your heavenly Father is perfect.'

The practical question arises, therefore, as to how we can make this example fit into our own lives. What must we do to imitate the perfection of her who has so well been called 'our fallen nature's solitary boast'? Let us take some care in looking for a sane and helpful answer, one which embodies her out-look on life in relation to God. A certain preacher, speaking to children of Mary, was guilty of the following absurd argument: 'Our Lady never·smoked, therefore you should not smoke.' That is a ridiculous criterion of conduct; followed to its logical conclusion it shows its own absurdity. If we exclude from our lives all the things that our Lady did *not* do—sin of course excepted—we should find ourselves in some strange predicaments under present conditions of life. Innumerable items of our daily lives and our whole civilization were, of course, entirely unknown to her. But the vital and practical question about such items is: How would our Lady have behaved if she had lived in our own times? In 2,000 years and in different lands customs and modes of life change. Nevertheless, change as they may, the law of God and our duty to him is unchanging; heaven and earth shall pass away, but not his word. It is in her attitude to these laws and to God, and her application of this to her daily life, that we must imitate our Lady. We are not required to go back to her days, but we must bring her into our own days. Let us make a practice of asking ourselves: Would the Mother of God do what I propose to do? If we appreciate in any degree this handmaid of the Lord, the answer will be found easily enough in our own conscience.

Our Lady was certainly no kill-joy. At the marriage feast of Cana, noticing the absence of wine and realising the embarrassment it would cause to their hosts, the cloud it would bring over the rejoicings, she appeals to her Son, who miraculously supplies the deficiency. Let self-styled 'temperance' advocates and narrow-minded kill-joys disapprove if they will! Mary would never prevent, would rather encourage, innocent enjoyment. She could appreciate the good things given by God for man's use, though she would never abuse them as we so often do. We can therefore imitate her by trying to save others embarrassment, furthering their happiness by kindly thought, refraining from criticism. Had she lived in our own day, would our Lady have taken her cup of tea? Certainly she would: she would do as others in the ordinary things of life. But she would not have made a cup of tea the occasion of uncharitable gossip. It is said: 'Given two chairs, two cups of tea and two ladies—and God help the parish!' At least we can be sure that this would not be the case if our Lady were one of the ladies, or if the ladies tried to model their lives on hers. She would use God's gifts or refrain from their use for her own good reasons; she would never deny their reasonable use to others. Only in things sinful or leading to sin would she have no part.

If our Lady had lived in one of our modern streets in a working-class quarter she would have been unnoticed, except for her sweetness and goodness. She would have gone about her household duties, have gone out to do the shopping, have cooked the meals, have kept her house neat and clean; and it would have been a real home. She would never have been found gossiping on the doorstep, nor criticising her neighbours. She would not have pretended to be other than she was, a working-man's wife without airs or pretensions, content with what God had provided for her. Charitable to all, helping in need, tending the sick, being neighbourly, doing good in an unobtrusive way, the perfect wife and mother—that would be our Lady's life now, as it was in Nazareth.

Fashions in dress change and must to some extent be followed to avoid singularity; but there is a happy medium between the ultra-fashionable and the dowdy. We may be sure that Mary would always choose that medium, remaining modest and inconspicuous, being neither a leader of fashion nor its slave nor yet ill-dressed.

This is the way then, that our Lady is to be imitated; by avoiding always whatever is sinful or the occasion of sin, being diligent in the work we have to do, charitable and helpful towards others, never a killjoy nor interfering with the lawful recreations of others, by cultivating true humility and not being obtrusive or self-assertive in manner or opinions, by showing modesty and care in dress, in short by being an ordinary person to all outward appearance, yet always conscious of one's obligations to God and of the true purpose of life. In his eternal wisdom God has put us where we are, given us a particular kind of life to lead, a certain kind of work to do, duties that we have to perform and obligations towards others. As with our Lady, this is the humdrum stuff out of which he desires us to fashion our whole life into one of serving and loving him. Like her, we must be ready in all circumstances to say to him: 'Behold the handmaid of the Lord; be it done unto me according to thy word.'

XLI ST JOSEPH—OUR MODEL

Just as the simple life of our Lady gives us an ideal on which
to form our own lives, so too St Joseph is a model patron
whose life as an ordinary working-man gives inspiration and
encouragement to ordinary folk in the home and at work.

In holy Scripture he is described as 'a just man' (Matt. I),
which is indeed high praise. But little else is known in detail
of this great saint. Even more than our Lady, he was so
wholly in the back-ground, yet was so necessary in the scheme
of redemption as the protector of the Virgin Mother and the
Holy Child. Since he was chosen by God to be the head of the
Holy Family he must have been endowed with very special
graces and great holiness to fit him for the dignity of his great
office, next to that of Mary herself, being the 'reputed father
of Jesus.' To all his associates, St Joseph was the husband
of Mary and father of the child, who was thought to be 'the
son of Joseph the carpenter' by all who knew him.

Though so little is known of St Joseph, he is yet a perfect
model of what each of us ought to be in our own lives. He did
nothing which by God's grace we cannot do; he led a simple
human life supernaturalized by grace. Born in Bethlehem of
the royal house of David, by descent a prince of the House
of Juda, he was but a poor labouring man supporting his
family by the work of his hands, being by trade a carpenter.

Two fathers are ascribed to him in holy Scripture; St Matthew calls him the son of Jacob, whereas St Luke describes
him as the son of Heli. How comes this strange difference?
The explanation is that 'by nature' he is the son of Jacob, but
'by law' the son of Heli. Heli and Jacob were brothers of the
same mother; Heli the eldest, died without children, hence
by the Jewish law Jacob was bound to take Heli's widow to
wife and raise up offspring through her to Heli. Her children
though having Jacob as their natural father, were by the
Jewish law the children of Heli. Hence St Joseph is the possessor
of two fathers. He was born of Heli's widow as the natural
son of Jacob, but the law counted him as the child of Heli.

By the symbol of the rod blossoming he was indicated as

the one to be chosen by God and destined to be the spouse of Mary.

We know of little but sorrow and labour in the life of this great saint. Soon after his espousals, he realises to his amazement that the young virgin Mary, his wife, was to become a mother by no act of his; the child could not be his own. Can we imagine the anguish of soul caused by this knowledge? What could he do? According to the Jewish law, he could no longer continue to live with her under these circumstances, he was bound 'to put her away,' no longer acknowledge her as his wife. Scripture tells us 'that being a just man he was minded to put her away privately' so that she should not suffer the indignity of public exposure for what seemed to him strange and unexplainable in such a one as Mary.

Herein we learn our first lesson, not to be eager and ready to expose what we discover about the faults of others, but rather to keep secret anything that may be known against a neighbour's character, not to judge him, not to gossip about him, not to make a public exposure of his apparent misdeeds. Like St Joseph we should strive to make every possible allowance, especially if we do not know all the facts; if anything must be done, let it be done as privately as possible so that few may know. To preserve Mary's good name St Joseph in his perplexity was silent about what he could neither understand nor explain.

In his agony of mind an angel of the Lord appeared to him in sleep saying : 'Fear not Joseph to take unto thee Mary thy wife, for that which is conceived in her is of the Holy Ghost and she shall bring forth a Son; and thou shalt call his name Jesus, for he shall save his people from their sins.' (Matt. I, 20). Joseph rising from sleep did as he was commanded. Ready obedience to the will of God was his chief characteristic; he never questions, never debates in his mind the fitness of things or the consequences; he gives instant obedience, to him the will of God is paramount; no matter what difficulties may be entailed, it is obeyed without question.

This sorrow passed he is found next seeking a lodging in the city of Bethlehem for his young wife who is about to give birth to her child. In vain he seeks a suitable habitation; nothing is to be had, every house is full, and there is no one to give shelter to the poor couple in their need. All he can provide is a humble stable in which perforce he must shelter his spouse with the beasts of the field. There the child is born and laid in a manger. It must have caused intense sorrow to him that a more suitable lodging could not be found for his young spouse at such a time. But he had done his best, had done all that was possible to him; the rest he leaves to God.

May we not learn from this to be considerate for the comfort of others and their well-being, to make every exertion to give the best, and having done our utmost leave all else to God without repining, in resignation to his will? Too often we have little or no sympathy with others, do not try to help them when it entails self-exertion or inconvenience, try to put off with some paltry excuse those who need our help, and complain about the difficulties to excuse our want of real exertion. Always we should do our best for others in their need, and then leave the rest to God who will accept our efforts no matter how unsuccessful they may appear to be.

The next event related is that an angel again appears to him in sleep bidding him rise and take the Child and his mother into Egypt to save him from those who seek his life. Again there is instant obedience, no delay, no tarrying to make suitable preparations for so long a journey and for an indefinite period of exile. 'He rose from sleep and took the child and his mother by night and retired into Egypt.'

Once more the lesson of instant obedience is presented. How dilatory we are in carrying out God's commands, delaying for our own convenience, weighing up the prospects, debating whether it is really necessary, taking time to make preparation, even at times excusing disobedience through worldly wisdom in providing for the future. Does not this show a great want of trust in God, a fear that he might forget our needs? St Joseph acts so differently; he rises instantly in the night and does what he is bidden without question, without any preparation, trusting God to the full.

When the child is twelve years of age, he goes with his parents in obedience to the law to keep the Pasch in Jerusalem. After the feast, unknown to his parents,' the Child remains behind when the company leaves. As soon as his absence is discovered they return filled with anxiety to seek him. When he is found in the temple amid the doctors, it is the Mother who gently chides him: 'Son, why hast thou done so to us? Behold thy father and I have sought thee sorrowing.' St Joseph keeps silent; not one single word of his has been recorded, nor is there any other mention of him in the Scriptures. All we can surmise is that he lived at Nazareth the life of a working-man supporting his family by daily toil, teaching the growing youth his trade as a carpenter, accepting a just price for his labour, working without complaint in the state of life to which he was called by God. Of his work we can be sure that it was done to the best of his ability, that he could allow nothing faulty or badly made to pass, that he would not cheat his neighbour by unjust profits or poor material; he was a 'just man.'

Surely there is a clear lesson for us here. St Joseph was a great saint but he was by no means in the lime-light. He works in the background, hidden and unnoticed. We do not know the time of his death; when his task was done, God took him to his reward. We might say that St Joseph was just a convenient instrument used by God to look after the minor details in the scheme of redemption, and when no longer needed was removed. We conclude that he died, with Jesus and Mary by his side, a most holy death and has therefore been chosen by the Church as the patron of a happy death. A simple ordinary human life, full of humility and instant obedience to the will of God, that is the foundation of all sanctity.

St Joseph can so readily provide a model for the ordinary catholic. A working-man supporting a wife and child by the labour of his hands, as so many millions must do in our own day, living a life of obedience to God, accepting his state of life as God's will and striving by doing all things well to sanctify himself day by day, and growing daily more holy thereby.

That is what we also must do. It matters not what our work may be, whether we sit at a desk or sweep the gutters or toil at a bench with our hands, all can be done well for God in acceptance of his will. By doing all for the glory of God and not simply for 'the meat that perisheth,' in reasonable obedience to those in authority who are the means whereby God's will is made known to us, our lives will be sanctified day by day.

St Joseph had great dignity in being the head of the Holy Family, but he worked out his salvation not by his dignity as the 'reputed father of Jesus' but by his humility and obedience to whatever was God's will. That must be the foundation of our own sanctity. So may we be obedient to all who have the right to command, fervent in the service of God by our daily toil, obedient to the obligations of religion, all forming a natural human life supernaturalized by the help of his freely given grace.

'He sanctified him in his faith and meekness, and chose him out of all flesh.' (Ecclus. XLV, 4.) 'Joseph was a just man.' (Matt. I).

XLII HABITS

We are all creatures of habit! We hardly realise how many things we do out of habit. What is a habit? It is an acquired facility, or ease, in doing things so that such things become almost mechanical and are done without thought. Life is greatly a matter of habits; were it not so, many things would be difficult and burdensome to us. As tiny children, being unable to walk, we went about by crawling on hands and knees; then came a day when we stood on our feet for a few seconds, feeling very proud; perhaps we toddled a few steps, and then sat down suddenly or fell on our face. Gradually more steps were managed with fewer falls, until the day came when we had learnt to walk. In other words we had acquired the habit of walking. It was not that walking had become easier in itself, but we had gained a facility in it which made it no longer difficult to us; we had acquired a habit by a frequent repetition of the same action. Even then we had still to be dressed and undressed by someone; our small fingers could not manage tapes and buttons. Now we manage those things without thinking. Again it is an acquired habit.

Life would indeed be tiresome if it were not for this power of habit. There are so many things that are done by habit, like reading, writing, cycling, sewing, or knitting, each of which was gained by the frequent repeating of the same act. Let us carefully note that important fact: habits are acquired by the frequent repetition of the same act. Practice makes perfect. That is a truth which affects life seriously. Another truth that must be grasped is this: a habit makes an act easy to do but does not force us to do that act! Thus I do not walk because the habit of walking forces me to do so, but if I wish to walk, then the habit makes it easy for me to walk without any difficulty. I can still sit quietly, even though I have the habit of walking; I walk only when I will to walk. So with all habits; though they give facility, they cannot compel action unless it is willed. That truth has a vital bearing in the consideration of habits in the spiritual life. Just as in the corporal life, so in the spiritual life, habits play a great part. There are good and bad spiritual habits, which are termed 'virtues' or 'vices.' We speak of virtues and vices as though they are rare, and we hardly credit ourselves with possessing either. Virtues seem such difficult things to acquire; vices are only too easy, and seem much too harsh a name for our own failings; so we prefer not to think much about the possession of them in our own spiritual life. But in actual fact these words are simply the way in which a distinction is made between good and bad spiritual habits.

Many virtues are given to us directly by God. They are supernatural and we could not acquire them naturally. Thus in baptism we are given, faith, hope, and charity, and these are then called 'infused virtues' because God gives us freely a facility in believing in him, hoping in him, and loving him. The Holy Ghost also infuses the cardinal virtues of prudence, justice, fortitude and temperance, and all the other moral virtues which flow from them. Though there are no 'infused vices,' yet owing to the inborn proneness to evil in our nature, as the heritage of original sin, vices are only too easy to acquire. Both virtue and vice, then, imply a facility and tendency to certain acts that have a moral value. That facility and tendency is kept alive in us by the repetition of the acts concerned. To do the same good act frequently will give us an 'acquired' habit; thus we may develop the habit of obedience because we have tried consistently to obey orders until it has become a second nature and we have no difficulty in obedience. In the same way we contract a bad habit or vice by frequently repeating the same bad action until we hardly notice that we are doing wrong. Such habits imperceptibly gain hold on us through our failing to be on our guard and not resisting the inclination to some bad act. We may in time not revert to the fact that we are doing something evil. Nevertheless we are responsible for each bad action done under the influence of habit because we should never have allowed the vice to grow.

It was particularly noted above that a habit does not compel action, it provides facility and inclination, but the act of the will is still necessary before we actually perform some action. Whether under the influence of habit or not we are responsible for what we do. Because through non-resistance and frequent repetition it has become fatally easy to perform the act without adverting to its evil, that does not excuse us from sin; and we are bound to destroy that habit as soon as we are aware of it. We may fall into some sin once or twice, but that does not produce a vice; neither does the doing of a good act a few times produce a habit of virtue. It is the continual repetition of the bad or good act that produces the one or the other. Again the possession of a virtue does not merit of itself, but the acts which proceed from it are all meritorious since the consent of the will to an act is chiefly what gives it moral value. Thus I may have the virtue of obedience, but if I have no one to obey I do not gain merit from its mere possession.

Many bad habits are rooted in us in childhood and in some cases we may hardly be to blame for acquiring them, whether because of ignorance of the evil therein or for want of correction by parents for wrong acts. In such cases there may be some excuse for us; but as soon as such acts are known to be evil, there is an obligation to fight against the sin and destroy the bad habit. Take selfishness for instance; some do not consider this a vice, but it is one of the commonest. It is a vice because it is self-indulgence, and therefore contrary to temperance, and probably contrary also to justice as far as others are concerned. Parents are much to blame for not correcting the natural tendency to be selfish which is in every child. When every whim is gratified by its too fond parents, if it is never taught to give way to others or consider their needs, a child grows self-centred and insistent, gives way to temper if thwarted. It thus acquires the vice of selfishness. Had such a child been taught to be generous to others, to give way at times so that it did not always have its own way, made to do without things it cried for, it would have learnt to be unselfish and generous and so acquired a virtue instead of a vice. When that child grows older it will have to learn that selfishness is a vice, and then will arise the duty of uprooting that vice, no easy task. Only by continual acts of generosity and self-denial can the evil be corrected and uprooted; the only way to destroy any vice is to practise the opposing virtue.

Hence just as vice is acquired by frequent acts of evil, so

it can be uprooted only by frequent acts of the opposite nature, and by acquiring the opposite virtue in the process. Pride must be destroyed by acts of humility; anger and bad-temper by acts of meekness; sloth by diligence; selfishness by self-denial; each vice has an opposing virtue and the effort to develop such a virtue will end in the destruction of the corresponding vice.

How shall we set about the process?

(1) By avoiding as far as possible the occasions which give rise to the indulgence in the habit. Some vices need solitude, others certain company.

(2) By seeking opportunities of doing the virtuous act which opposes the vice, by seeking humiliations to destroy pride.

(3) By never making any exceptions to the rule, until the vice is destroyed completely. We may say 'just this once,' but it grows to twice or thrice, and we slip back into the old habit and lose all that has been gained. This will not be easy and many lapses must be expected before the vice is finally overcome; but perseverance will win in the end and we shall free ourselves by diligence and the help of the grace of God.

Life, both natural and supernatural, is a question of habits that enable us to do things easily and ease the burden of living which otherwise would be even more difficult than it is. Habits cause differences of character in individual persons; thus one will rise quickly from sleep as soon as called, another will be slothful and stay in bed till the last minute. Some are obedient or patient; others rebellious or petulant and irritable. Some have stronger tendencies than others to certain vices; this is a matter of temperament frequently and for them it is more difficult to acquire the opposite virtues. Each has his own special difficulties. Early training or want of it, environment, circumstance and temperament all affect habits; but in spite of all adverse inclinations, all vices can be uprooted by practising opposing acts of virtue. We need constant watchfulness and persevering effort, helped by fervent prayer and the grace of God without which all our efforts will be in vain.

Habits of virtue can be acquired in the same way as good

natural habits. Just as we learnt to walk, dress, read, write, cycle and so on, so we can learn to be obedient, kindly, self-sacrificing, gentle or patient, and the rest, by frequent repetition of the acts exercising the virtue. In regard to vices we must not be discouraged by frequent lapses. Obviously the habits of years will not disappear in a moment; but we must go on trying, trying, and trying, never relaxing effort, until gradually the lapses grow less frequent as the facility in doing good increases and the habit of virtue is at last acquired. 'Watch and pray'— that is the advice given by our Lord. It is the only way to succeed in the spiritual life. We must make full use of the infused virtues since these are the foundations on which all our habits of virtue are formed. God gives the foundations: the building up is our task.

XLIII PRUDENCE

One of the chief tasks of our spiritual life is the practice of the virtues and the formation of virtuous habits, many of which hinge on the four cardinal virtues (*cardo*, hinge). These cardinal virtues are prudence, justice, fortitude and temperance. Here the first of these is to be considered.

Prudence is the capacity of the intellect to apprehend what ought to be done or not done, and to direct as to the best means to be adopted. It is a good habit which directs a man's reason so that in every action he tends to choose what will best serve him in the end. In practice it simply means making a correct decision about what is to be done for the best. Prudence enters into the natural as well as the supernatural life in all decisions that are made. True prudence is able to relate both aspects of life, so that the prudent man always has his final end in view whatever the proposed line of action may be. It is most important since reason guides the will in its choice; if the mind fails in judging correctly between right and wrong, what is good and what is less good morally, the will chooses wrongly and sin results.

St Thomas Aquinas calls prudence the 'eye of the soul.' Without eyes we cannot see the way to go. It has also been called 'the rudder which guides the ship.' Without prudence we make shipwreck of all virtue. Worldly wisdom is the opposite of true prudence since it discerns only what will bring temporal advantage or sensual enjoyment and leads to sin. The wisdom of the world is foolishness to God.

Prudence depends on several things: (a) memory of past events, such as occasions which have proved dangerous and led into difficulties or sin; (b) knowledge of the true principles of action; a man without principles cannot judge wisely; (c) respect for what has been determined by the wise, or what is called 'experience,' for experience is the father of wisdom, memory the mother of it; (d) application of the principles to the matter in hand and foresight as to the consequences of what is about to be done; (e) precautions against failure to obtain what it is desired to accomplish.

That sounds a great deal and may seem to involve a lengthy process, but it is in fact swift in action. For instance, I wish to cross over a busy road. (a) Memory reminds me that accidents happen in doing this, there are certain dangers involved which must be avoided if I am to cross in safety. (b) My principles urge me to take every care of my life. (c) Wise people through experience of past events advise 'safety first,' therefore I must act according to their advice and not run foolish risks. (d) Foresight bids me look both ways to see if the passage is possible and the way clear of fast-moving traffic. (e) Precaution against failure advises me not to dawdle across but to get over as quickly as possibile and keep my attention on what I am doing, not gazing aimlessly about me. As a wise man I understand the principle of acting under these circumstances and do what is necessary, so that when reason is satisfied that it is safe to cross the road, it prompts the will to act and I pass safely to the other side. All this is done in a flash, but true prudence observes the whole routine. Once we have this virtue developed it acts as a second nature. We should have fewer worries in life, if we were always prudent in all things.

Every sin is the result of want of prudence, since sin is always the outcome of a wrong decision concerning the best way in which to act. Some are very foolish in the way they disregard their own experience. A man knows that every time he eats pork, he suffers pain through indigestion, but tempted by the tastiness he eats it in spite of past experience—that is imprudent! He causes himself unnecessary suffering, unfits himself for his work, is unable to enjoy other good things, is probably irritable and disagreeable to others; he may irritate them by his manner, and so fail in charity, by vexing and making others angry; thus he falls into sin because he ate pork! To gratify his sensual appetite in a food not good for him and by experience known to be so he takes risks which are not prudent. Foresight of the consequences should have made him realise the probable danger of irritation and vexation of others, for which he must hold himself morally responsible. Pork and the spiritual life may seem to have little in common, but common sense bids us judge otherwise.

PRUDENCE

We can gain considerable insight into the working of prudence by observing the sins directly opposed to this virtue. Virtue stands between the two extremes of excess or deficiency, which might well be classed under the general name of imprudence and which can be a mortal sin in grave matters. A deficiency or want of prudence may be shown in hastiness, lack of thought, inconstancy, or negligence.

Hastiness is acting too quickly in making a decision and not taking sufficient care in acting. Rash judgments are the result of hastiness which itself may arise from anger. Lack of thought is the neglect of the consideration necessary to form a balanced judgment. Thus to leave a bucket or broom on a dark staircase may result in a bad accident to someone coming down the stairs. We are responsible for such accidents by imprudence since we ought to have foreseen the possibility of such an accident. Inconstancy is a want of adherence to a decision, changing one's mind without good reason or through hastiness in making the previous decision. Some are undecided through weakness of will and cannot carry a project through. Others again make promises and then fail to keep them, either through being forgetful of the promise itself or failing to remember obstacles that will prevent the promise being kept.

Negligence is the failure to act in accordance with the decision of the practical reason; it is the destruction of all real virtue. In external acts it shows itself as sloth or laziness and leads often to other sins. Thus, when I awake on Sunday morning I am aware that I am under obligation to assist at Mass and prudence dictates that, in view of this obligation, I should rise without delay. But laziness or sloth persuades me that I am too tired to get up, or at least yet awhile. If I reject prudence and give way to sloth I miss Mass, and add to my sin of sloth that of grave disobedience to the law of the Church and of God.

There is a counterfeit prudence which shows itself in other failings. It is concerned with the attaining of some apparently good, but actually evil, end or with the use of unlawful means to secure what in itself is not evil. It is manifest in slyness, deceit and fraud, which often pass for prudence notwithstanding that they involve injustice towards others. If I break or damage an article belonging to another, it may seem like prudence to escape the consequence by hiding it or by pretending ignorance of the matter. But that is a wholly false prudence that condones or covers an injustice. In the so-called 'business world' there is many an instance of 'prudence' that ought to be called by its proper title of fraud.

There is also a kind of false prudence that shows itself in excessive solicitude or exaggerated caution. Many suffer from this vice, being continually worried about the future, concerned with temporal affairs to the detriment of the soul, with little or no trust in God's providence and his promised care of them. We ought, of course, to take reasonable care about the future, save for things we may need or for old age, but not to the extent that it becomes an obsession. The extreme example of this vice is seen in the miser who hoards for the sake of hoarding and loves money for its own sake. But a flagrant and all too common instance of false solicitude is provided in the usual plea for the justification of artificial birth-prevention. Reasons often given in defence of this abomination are want of means to rear a large family, fear lest the children should not get a good education, or anxiety about the wife's health. Even if they are sincere they show not only a lamentable ignorance of God's law but also a complete want of trust in his providence. 'Be not solicitous,' says our Lord. 'Your heavenly Father knoweth that you have need of these things.' If God provides so generously for the birds of the air and the lilies of the field, will he not have at least as much care for our needs? Learn the true prudence: 'Seek first the kingdom of God and his justice and all these things shall be added unto you.'

Why do we not trust God? Is it that we do not believe that he will be faithful to his promises? Do we think that our Lord did not mean what he said? It would seem so from our reluctance to give God the opportunity of proving his care of us, from the false solicitude and overwhelming anxiety we display about the future.

It behoves us to be truly prudent in all things, not failing either by defect or by excess, taking a balanced and sane view of life based upon a practical trust in the providence and care of God. Prudence is the keystone of all the other moral virtues, since it alone enables us to fit the details and events of daily life into God's ultimate design in creating us; it shows us how to make spiritual profit out of all earthly things, how to turn our whole life into one of prayer and service of God.

'Be prudent, and watch in prayer.'

XLIV JUSTICE

The second of the cardinal virtues, justice, covers so much ground that it is impossible to deal adequately with it outside a long treatise; therefore but a summary treatment can here be given, which may, however, be sufficient to enable us to understand our personal obligations in this important matter. Justice controls our actions in relation to the possessions of others. It is often represented as a blindfolded figure holding scales equally balanced, and this is a true and helpful symbol. The blindness denotes that in matters of justice there must be no respect of persons, no favouritism, likes and dislikes must be disregarded. The evenly balanced scales denote that to each must be given what is exactly his due, so that the balance remains undisturbed.

Justice is concerned with the right of each man to his own existence and to those other possessions which he holds by right of natural law; and further it is concerned with the rights of society as a whole. The object of justice is to give every man his due, and this includes the grave obligation of restitution where any injustice has been done, in order to restore the just balance between the parties concerned. To give a simple example: if I take £5 from another man, my side of the scale becomes heavier by £5, his side lighter by the same amount, and the balance of justice is disturbed. Only by taking the extra weight from my side and replacing it in his scale, will the balance become even again and justice be satisfied. Therefore before the sin of stealing can be forgiven this restitution of the balance to equality must be fulfilled under grave obligation if the matter is serious, or at least there must be the sincere intention of so doing as soon as it is possible.

Justice affects both existence and possessions. A man has a right to his life as his most valued possession, hence murder is the gravest crime against justice, and it is an injustice not only against the one whose life is taken away, but also against society as a whole. Further, a man has the right to keep his person intact; hence any assault against a man's person not only against his body, but also against his good name, is injustice. A man has also the right to his possessions and the use of them without interference, though he himself is also under obligation to make proper use of them, to take care of them. Even in respect of what is our own property we can sin against justice by abuse. Common sins against the right of possession are robbery and stealing, fraud in buying, selling or making things to be sold, usury or charging too great an interest on loans, defrauding workers of their just wages, not paying a living wage, and failing to pay just debts.

Even if we do not fail in these obvious ways, we may fail in other less obvious ways, as for instance in the want of care given to the property of another. People are often very careless about borrowed books. It is against justice to leave such a book lying about where it may be damaged, to lose it through carelessness, or to lend it to another without the consent of the owner, unless we have good reason to think that he will be agreeable. Because I lend an article of any kind, I do not thereby lose ownership of it, and I have the right to expect that reasonable care will be taken in its use and that it will be returned in due course. Some people are very dilatory in repaying loans of goods borrowed. We are bound in justice to pay debts and payment must come before personal enjoyment; it is not just to buy luxuries or pay for pleasures when it entails keeping another waiting for repayment of what belongs to him by right. When we are in debt the money we may have is not strictly ours, since it is owed to another, and we are bound to repay him as soon as we have more than sufficient to obtain the necessities of life.

Other sins against justice are known by specific names.
(a) *Invective*. This sin injures another in his honour and in the respect due to him by words used against him. Such words are uttered in anger, and intended to cast opprobrium, censure, or reproach. In a lesser degree railing and abuse are to be included here. Our Lord says: 'Whosoever shall say to his brother, Raca (a word of contempt), shall be in danger of hell-fire.'

(b) *Calumny, detraction, backbiting, tale-bearing*. These are

213

also sins against justice because every man has a right to his good name and character as most precious possessions. We offend too by imputing false charges, by exaggerating defects, by revealing unknown faults and by accusations of evil intentions, all of which injure a man in his relationship to others.

(c) *Whispering.* This kind of injustice attacks a neighbour by dishonest or cunning words in order to cause discord and misunderstandings between friends. St Thomas Aquinas calls this 'a most odious sin against a neighbour which merits the just reproval of God and man, being directed against the virtue of friendship.' Jealousy is a common cause of this degrading, underhand and mean sin.

(d) *Mockery.* This is a sin against justice because it reviles a man by exhibiting his defects and short-comings in such a way as to cause him to lose confidence in himself, causes 'an inferiority complex' which can do grave injury to his character, and lowers him in the esteem of others.

(e) *Cursing.* In its true sense this is a grave sin of injustice for it wishes spiritual evil to another.

(f) *Scandal.* Again in its true sense this is a very grave injustice for it is 'soul-murder,' since by bad example it leads another to sin and perhaps to eternal damnation. It is an odious sin severely condemned by our Lord. 'If any one scandalise one of these little ones, it were better for him that a millstone should be hanged about his neck and that he should be drowned in the depths of the sea. Woe to that man by whom scandal cometh.'

On the other hand there are specific virtues which spring from justice as their root having particular relation to God or to man in various matters. They are:

(a) *Religion,* which unites man to God and includes all acts of religion, prayer, adoration, sacrifice and all the ways in which man strives to get into contact with God. Sins against this virtue are superstition, want of respect for sacred persons, and sacrilege.

(b) *Filial respect,* which gives to parents and country the honour and respect due. After our duty to God, nothing is more sacred than the duty to parents and to country. Reverence for all lawful authority is part of this virtue. St Peter bids us: 'Be subject to every human creature for God's sake, whether it be to the king as excelling, or to governors as sent by him . . . honour all men, love the brotherhood, fear God, honour the king.' All lawful authority is held in trust from God.

(c) *Gratitude*, which is the recognition of favours received, chiefly those from God, and also from all other persons. From it springs the desire of returning favours to the best of our ability. Ingratitude which is opposed to this virtue is a most odious sin, hateful to God and man.

(d) *Truthfulness*, consisting in showing ourselves as we really are in word and in deed. Lies are a common offence against this virtue. A lie is never permissible even to bring about good. Officious lies are those told to aid oneself or another, usually as excuses, and which do no harm to another. Malicious lies are told with the intention of injuring another, their worst form being 'perjury' or a lie told when under oath to tell the truth. In its worst form this is a sacrilege since it is calling on God to witness to a deliberate lie. It may be noted, however, that it is permissible to conceal truth by silence if there is just reason for so doing, as, for instance, where the questioner has no just right to the information. Thus it is generally recognised that no man is bound to incriminate himself. Pretence is a form of untruthfulness which often arises out of vanity or envy. In its worst form it is hypocrisy, which is pretence in spiritual matters and seeks to give a false idea of one's piety; it was the vice of the Pharisees which our Lord condemned in no uncertain terms.

(e) *Friendliness* is that virtue which makes a man try in word and deed to treat others in such a way as to bring mutual joy and charm or happiness into life. St Thomas Aquinas calls it 'the flower of justice and charity.' We offend against friendliness when we do not trouble ourselves to try and bring pleasure to others, nor care if we cause annoyance to them. We also offend by flattery which approves in another what is blameworthy in him.

(f) *Liberality* is the readiness to give material goods, especially money, to promote the well-being of others. Opposed to it is avarice, or miserliness, which leads one to retain one's possessions in a selfish manner rather than to use them for good works. We may also be liberal to excess, as when we are wasteful or extravagant in using or giving immoderately what we possess, of which we are in fact stewards of God.

Justice covers a wide field, including civil justice as administered by the state and retributive justice which gives due punishment for crime.

Justice must be shown to all without exception and without respect of persons. No matter what our personal feelings may be towards any other, we are bound to give him his just due, to avoid any injury to his person, good name, character, or possessions.

'Give to every man his due.'

XLV FORTITUDE

Fortitude could be best described as 'courage;' it is that perfection which keeps a man firm in the presence of great fear, especially that arising from danger of death. Hence it gives courage to endure or to attack evil in the pursuit of good, or readiness to meet the greatest evil rather than turn aside from the path of good. It demands patience and constancy and often heroism. Fortitude was perhaps the most conspicuous characteristic of St John the Baptist. He fearlessly upbraids the pharisees, calling them ' a brood of vipers;' again he stands up boldly to King Herod rebuking him for his incestuous marriage. He was the champion of the divinity of Christ and by fortitude lived his hard life in the desert, endured the sufferings of imprisonment and finally martyrdom for truth.

This virtue is the support of all other virtues. Without some degree of fortitude none can be saved, since the life of man is continual warfare against evil. It combines in itself such qualities as strength, vigour, endurance, self-sacrifice, and perseverance, thereby supporting the spiritual life through all difficulties. Life is one unending struggle between good and evil; prone to evil, we find it so much easier to do evil than good, the circumstances of life often incline us to evil, and courage is needed to overcome the many obstacles in the way of doing good. By nature weak, inconstant, easily discouraged we need fortitude to sustain us in the long struggle throughout life.

Fortitude has many aspects. Thus mortification of the passions, e.g. anger, lust, and such like, is accomplished through fortitude. We know to our cost the difficulty of controlling self once any kind of passion is roused and we need courage to attack the evil within our nature. Always within us, enemies of our peace, the passions incline us to evil on the least provocation. How can we hope through the years of life to overcome the onslaughts of passion unless we have fortitude and its handmaids to help us in crushing the uprisings within our nature.

The endurance of grave difficulties, labour, hunger, thirst, danger to soul and body, for the sake of a neighbour needs much fortitude. St Paul describes himself as enduring such difficulties for the sake of others; he needed all his fortitude to carry on his work of teaching the gospel and saving souls. Again fortitude is necessary to endure unforeseen trials such as the death of those dear to us, the loss of friends by separation or misunderstandings, the loss of possessions, sickness, poverty and hardship, all of which are likely to be met with at various times in life. The supreme act of fortitude is to be found in martyrdom, steeling a man to acceptance of death in testimony of true religion and fidelity to God. Little less than this are the persecutions suffered because of religion through taunts, ridicule, contempt and calumnies; life can be a veritable martyrdom and it may be more difficult to live for Christ than to die for him. We need all the courage possible to face the many difficulties and hardships that life brings to one and all, and this we find in our virtue of fortitude.

Fortitude is opposed by two vices: rashness, which is excessive fortitude, and cowardice, which is the defect of fortitude. Rashness is acting under the impulse of excessive boldness unrestrained by reason; it is not true courage at all. It is presumption as to our powers, too much self-reliance, which takes unnecessary or dangerous risks. One who goes into dangerous occasions of sin without need is guilty of such boldness, since he risks the grave danger of falling into sin. There are probably many occasions when we thus rely on our own strength and sin in consequence of our own rashness. We ought to remember from experience what constitutes danger for us and avoid it, not by trusting to our own strength but rather to the grace of God. We do not realise the force of temptation, the great strength of our enemies; and when we fail to see the real danger and pit our puny strength against the powers of evil, is it any wonder that we fail miserably? Only by the grace of God exercised in true fortitude can we hope to overcome the temptations lying in wait for us.

Cowardice on the contrary is want of confidence, the lack of due courage in the face of danger. It shows itself in us when we are afraid of standing up for our religious or moral convictions; hence we are weak in faith, afraid of criticism or ridicule, we stay away from the sacraments through false shame, and though ready to defend our political opinions or fight for social rights we are ashamed to confess our religion or defend our catholic principles. Human respect springs from want of fortitude and through it we are led to do what we know to be vrong, weakly give way to sin, or condone what we know to be evil. How different the conduct of St John the Baptist who was no reed shaken by the wind; he stuck to his principles and feared not to speak the truth.

Similarly when through love of comfort we shrink from penance and mortification or try to escape the obligations of fasting and abstinence, we must recognise the cowardice in our nature and the need of fortitude to overcome this miserable shrinking from necessary hardships.

Fortitude has various subsidiary virtues attached to it such as magnanimity, magnificence, patience, and constancy. These also are opposed by corresponding vices.

Magnanimity is a readiness of soul to do great things for God and is characteristic of the saints. It means 'greatness of soul' and implies a fine spirit of generosity and bigness of vision. Contrary to this virtue are:

(a) Over-confidence, ambition and vainglory. Over-confidence inclines one to attempt what is beyond one's power and ability, and ends in failure to accomplish anything worthwhile; ambition seeks honour and glory greater than are deserved; vainglory rejoices in worthless possessions and attainments, or those which are not directed to the true end i.e. the glory of God and the welfare of man. These display themselves in boasting, hypocrisy, discord, strife and disobedience which all arise through having too great an idea of one's abilities.

(b) Pusillanimity or meanness of soul is sinful because it is contrary to the natural law which inclines a man to act according to his full capability. It is blameworthy in not making due use of the power and means given by God, because of a false mistrust of self. It is not to be mistaken for humility which is the recognition by the soul of the truth regarding itself in relation to God.

Magnificence presupposes wealth and is especially the rich man's virtue. It is the disposition of soul to expend one's wealth in great and worthy undertakings, such as the building of churches, the endowing of hospitals or other similar works for the glory of God and the benefit of humanity. Opposed to this virtue are the vices of stinginess and extravagance which need no further elaboration; they are all too common.

Patience is especially helpful in the daily trials of life, giving the power to accept with resignation to the will of God the disappointments, vexations, and sorrows that are the common lot. It differs from fortitude in that it applies to brief periods, whereas fortitude covers the whole of life. Patience must not be confounded with apathy or stoicism which arise from sheer indifference.

Constancy strengthens the mind against imminent evils and prolonged difficulties, enabling us to remain true to our principles and obligations. It is opposed by fickleness and stubbornness.

Akin to constancy is *perseverance*, which enables us to continue our efforts, undaunted by fatigue, difficulty or boredom, and spurs us on towards the goal we have set ourselves. Mere length of time brings serious difficulty in working out salvation; everything becomes monotonous through continual repetition, interest flags or ceases altogether; and the prospect of struggling against evil for an indefinite period is apt to discourage. It would be easier if there were some time limit to exertion, if after keeping free from vice for a month or so, we could relax from effort and rest. But life demands unceasing effort for an unknown period; hence the need of perseverance to arm us against the tendency to relax or give up the struggle.

Waywardness is the opposite of perseverance and through it we soon tire of fighting and struggling, and take to any path that will lead us away from them. Thus we may join some guild or society attached to the church; but when initial fervour has worn off, we tire of attending the meetings, slacken off and allow ourselves to become absorbed in some other less exacting interest. We do not persevere. It is a common story in our spiritual life—the fervent beginning, the gradual slackening off, and the final cessation of the good work entirely.

Obstinacy is another vice contrary to the true virtue of perseverance. This means persisting in some work when it is no longer reasonable to do so. Thus a form of penance may be begun which later threatens health. If, being advised to cease this penance, we still persist, then it becomes mere obstinacy, and contrary to true perseverance.

Thus throughout life fortitude with its handmaids sustains, helps and encourages us to face all difficulties and to persevere to the end.

XLVI TEMPERANCE

Temperance is the virtue of moderation, avoiding both excess and defect in physical and spiritual undertakings. When temperance is mentioned many at once think of teetotal societies or the abolition of strong drink; but temperance has, in any case, a far wider scope than the question of alcoholic drink.

Like the 'temperate zone' lying between the 'torrid' and 'frigid' zones, temperance is the choice of the happy medium between too much and too little of anything. To be 'teetotal' is not true temperance, even though in some cases it may well be strongly advisable in order to overcome an inherent weakness, especially that which leads a man to indulge more than is reasonable in strong drink.

Temperance is the virtue which keeps a man's sensitive appetite in check, under the control of reason, so that he is not carried away by passions, particularly those which concern the senses of touch and taste in those acts which are necessary to preserve or to reproduce bodily life, that is to say those of eating and drinking or the use of marriage. A temperate man eats and drinks no more and no less than is reasonably necessary to support life, preserve health, and gain strength to fulfil his duties. This does not exclude the enjoyment of eating and drinking; but it does exclude indulgence in that enjoyment for its own sake. St Paul bids us 'use this world as if we used it not.' St Francis de Sales says: 'I desire very little, and that little I desire but little.' Temperance does not consist in refusing necessary things in such a way as to make one unfit to do one's proper work. That would merely be imprudence.

Temperance in the matter of food is opposed to gluttony. Not only does it prevent over-indulgence in food, but makes for contentment with food in ordinary form. Some consider themselves free from gluttony because they do not over-eat, but they may be guilty of it by being too particular in the choice of food, of the way it is cooked, being too finicky, thus pandering to the sense of taste.

To find pleasure in eating and drinking is not gluttony, since God gave to the palate the power of enjoying food as an incentive to eat—hunger is given to incite the desire for needed food, the pleasure of taste to give enjoyment in the satisfying of the natural desire; but to eat and drink merely for the sake of indulging the pleasure of taste may be gluttony. It can be a mortal sin in the case of those 'whose God is their belly,' who live for the pleasures of the table; or if one gorges to the extent of injuring health; as well as if one disobeys the law of fasting or abstinence. It is a venial sin if the indulgence is not grave. The consequences of gluttony are stupidity of mind arising from a brain made dull and torpid, incompetence and indolence in the management of affairs and duties. It leads to to the rousing of passions in other forms thereby causing real danger of sin; it may also bring on disease and consequent shortening of life.

For the furthering of temperance in this matter the Church has laid down the laws relating to fasting and abstinence, binding under a grave obligation; to ignore these is to be guilty of grave sin.

In the matter of drink temperance is called sobriety; a temperate man is always sober, using intoxicants in a manner which is decent and reasonable. Wine is a gift of God 'which gladdens the heart of man.' At the marriage feast of Cana our Lord worked his first miracle of changing water into wine for the enjoyment of the guests. There is no harm in wine or other drinks provided one is temperate; it is not the use, but the abuse which is sinful. Want of sobriety induces drunkenness and this state supervenes when a man loses the capacity to reason normally or make proper use of his senses. It is a mortal sin when deliberate or when the nature and effects of the drink are knowingly disregarded. The consequences of excess must be foreseen and to choose such consequences rather than be deprived of the sensual enjoyment of drinking is to be guilty of mortal sin.

It is debasing and unnatural, since a man knowingly deprives himself of the use of reason and puts himself below the level of the brute beasts, a traitor to his own manhood.

There are various stages of drunkenness. A man may be 'tipsy' and thus be unsteady on his feet, or he may lose control of himself so far as not to be able to walk without staggering and falling. He may become uncontrolled in speech and blurt out things which he ought to keep secret. He may become quarrelsome and rowdy, unable to control his temper. Drink affects different people in different ways; some become angry, others over-affectionate and maudlin; others become tearful, some grow very quarrelsome. A man ought to know what effect strong drink will have on him and he is responsible for whatever he does under the influence of drink deliberately taken to excess.

Men also differ in the capacity of remaining sober; one man may take double the amount that another can take and yet remain sober. One cause of evil is the custom of 'treating' or standing a round of drinks in turn, which for the sake of good fellowship tempts a man to take more than he can stand, while many are too weak to stand out when they have taken the safe amount. If a man is unable to refuse drink when he has reached his limit of sobriety, then he should give it up altogether. Human respect and the weakness of will to resist invitations to have more are often the downfall of many in this respect.

Temperance also controls the natural impulses to the pleasures of the flesh in matters of sex. Under this aspect this virtue is called chastity. It not only guards against all impulses towards unlawful pleasures of this nature, but even against excess in those acts which are lawful. Continence is a less perfect form of chastity. It is concerned with the resistance to existing impulses towards unlawful pleasure, but is not concerned with eliminating these impulses altogether, as chastity is. The vice of incontinence arises from giving way to those impulses, as a man becomes a slave to his passions.

Clemency and meekness are part of temperance. The first moderates the degree of external punishment to be meted out to an offender so that all danger of vindictiveness is overcome. Meekness controls the passion of anger. There are times when one is justified in being angry; thus our Lord was angry at the desecration of his Father's house; also we are bidden 'to be angry and sin not.' Anger is sinful when the irascible passion seeks unjust avengement or punishment with too much temper in it. There is the anger of those who are fretful and become irritated at the least provocation; the anger of those who are bitter, forgetting with difficulty an injury done to them; the anger of the revengeful and unforgiving which leads to the taking of revenge in an immoderate way. The offspring of anger are indignation, excitement of mind, contumely, blasphemy and quarrels.

Modesty springs from temperance and restrains the desire of one's own excellency, curiosity, exterior actions, and manner of dress.

Modesty encourages the growth of humility which makes a man repress all over-estimation of his own worth so that he sees himself in his true relation of dependence on God, and pride is thus avoided. Modesty further develops in a man the desire to know only those things that he ought to know and guards him against the vice of curiosity or undue desire for knowledge of matters that are not his concern. This latter vice is shown in the inordinate desire to get all the news of the day, to listen to gossip about neighbours, to know the latest scandals and to be informed of all that is going on whether it is one's business or not; it is also manifest in the feeling of being hurt when deprived of such knowledge.

Lastly comes modesty in its strict sense which regulates external conduct. Modesty in this sense ensures a proper fitness in movement, in gesture, in the tone of the voice, in laughter, in posture and dress so that nothing in these be offensive or suggestive to others. It includes also moderation in the use of amusements and recreations. Immodesty, on the other hand, induces a disregard for all or any of the things above mentioned in external comportment. Herein there is to be considered the responsibility towards others arising out of such disregard. Base passions may be easily roused in others by wearing dress that is beyond the recognised bounds of modesty or in the postures we assume in the presence of others. It is futile to say that it is no fault of ours if passion is roused in others; we should know the weakness of human nature, and it is a strict duty to avoid whatever may be the cause of temptation or sin in another. Raucous laughter and noisy conversation, as well as immoderate desire for such amusement as dancing, theatre-going and the cinema, are to be traced to this same evil disposition. St Paul bade the Philippians: 'Let your modesty be known to all men.' Both for their own sakes and for that of others it is the duty of christians to be modest and moderate in the use of all things that pertain to the body and the pleasures of life.

Thus the cardinal virtues control our lives in all things, and are the hinges on which the other virtues work. Prudence enables us to choose the right course of action, justice gives to each what is his right or due, fortitude sustains in all the difficulties of life, and temperance controls the use of all things pertaining to bodily needs. Each has its special virtues springing from it as from a root. These four infused virtues are the foundation of the spiritual life.

XLVII PEACE

One of the titles given to our Lord is 'prince of peace. There can be no doubt as to the value which Jesus Christ attached to peace, a most precious gift from God. His birth took place at a time when the temple of Janus in Rome was closed, signifying a world at peace, an event so rare that it had happened twice only during the 750 years after the foundation of Rome. Angels heralded his birth by singing 'Glory to God in the highest and on earth peace to men of goodwill.' Jesus in his teaching said: 'Blessed are the peacemakers.' He bids his disciples on entering a house to salute it with the words 'Peace be to this house.' Weeping over Jerusalem, he laments: 'If thou hadst known and that in this thy day, the things that are to thy peace.' After the resurrection his greeting was 'Peace be to you,' not security from enemies, not reputation or honour, but simply peace since this is the foundation of happiness. Before his death he had said: 'My peace I leave with you, my peace I give unto you.' But he added: 'Not as the world giveth, do I give unto you.'

The peace offered by the world is false and without security; it has no foundation, since it rests on false ideas and principles opposed to the teachings of Christ. Moreover it is not 'peace at any price' that is promised by our Lord, but only such as results from friendship with God. Our Lord seems almost to contradict himself; though he insists on peace, he yet says: 'Do not think that I came to send peace upon earth. I came not to send peace but the sword. For I came to set a man at variance against his father, and the daughter against her mother . . . a man's enemies shall be those of his own household.' The explanation given is 'he that loveth father or mother more than me, is not worthy of me, and he that taketh not up his cross and followeth me is not worthy of me.' The peace offered by Christ is not to make life easy and pleasant; on the contrary it entails suffering and separation from the world and its tenets, from parents and friends when they are in opposition to truth, and demands perfect loyalty to Christ and his doctrines. How often has the love of Christ set enmities between the members of a family for the sake of the true faith, caused loss of home and friends for the sake of conscience, brought persecution and death to his followers. Peace worth possessing can only spring from a good conscience. How true are the words spoken by our Lord: 'Think ye that I am come to give peace on earth? I tell you, no, but separation,' separation from all the world offers, from ambition, honours, riches, perhaps even from home and friends because everything that may turn one away from the teachings of Christ must be cast out. Hence the peace offered must be a true peace founded on friendship with God and enmity with the world.

This peace that the world knows nothing of is from the first an essential idea in the Church. St Paul usually begins his Epistles: 'Grace be to you and peace from God.' St Peter writes: 'He that will love life and see good days let him seek peace and pursue it.' The Church uses similar expressions; the newly baptised are told to go in peace; in confirmation the bishop says: 'Peace be to you;' when a priest enters a house in his official capacity he greets it with the words 'Peace to this house and all that dwell therein.' We pray that the dead may 'rest in peace.'

Does not all this reference to peace prove its value as a precious gift from God? There can be no other reason for so much insistence on it. To enter a house where there is discord and dissension is to realise what the absence of peace means and the evil presence of strife and unhappiness

What is peace? It is the absence of discord; it is a state of serenity, free from disturbances; it is unity and concord. Though we may feel no peace in the body because of pain or grief, this need not disturb the inner serenity of the soul. It is this peace which God wishes us to keep within ourselves and with all men. We hear of persons being 'bound over to keep the peace,' meaning that they must not disturb others. That is what God demands of us; we are all 'bound over to keep the peace' with all men as part of the great duty of charity. How shall we obey?

We keep the peace:

(1) by having patience with the failings of others. All are

subject to faults and failings varying with their particular traits of character; we must bear with them. To bear the burdens of another as well as our own is an essential exercise of charity, the bond of unity and basis of peace. Dissension arises because we will not yield; we complain of the faults of others, forgetful of our own, and refuse to bear with them or make allowances for differences in temperament. If we see faults in others, they likewise see faults in us and so also we must show patience and a forbearance to others. In that way we keep the peace.

(2) We keep the peace by taking interest in the prosperity or adversity of others. It does good to find sympathy in trouble and kindly interest in prosperity; it makes joy sweeter and adversity more bearable when these are shared. St Paul bids us 'rejoice with them that rejoice, weep with them that weep.' By the sharing of joy and sorrow we become as one family in God. Sympathy unites, but want of sympathy disturbs the harmony necessary for peace. Just as we are hurt when others have no care for our well-being, so we hurt others.

(3) We keep the peace by condescension in conversation with others. Stubbornness, adherence to one's own opinions, self-assertion, these are often destructive of peace, whereas by condescension and consideration peace is kept intact. Most people are gratified when notice is taken of their opinion; likewise they are hurt by frequent contradiction. To keep the peace we must be ready to yield to others where there is no question of sin. In an argument which is of little importance we can keep peace by gracefully giving in when danger of heated temper or anger approaches; an argument should never be allowed to develop into a quarrel. There are always two sides to a question and we must not force our own ideas on others, always excepting occasions when this entails sin or condonation of evil. Peace can only be maintained when consideration is shown and there is no stubbornness in holding to personal opinions.

(4) We keep the peace by kindliness. Harsh words rouse evil temper. We do not like to be spoken to in a harsh manner; no one enjoys being ridiculed or called foolish names. The

Book of Proverbs says: 'A mild answer breaketh wrath but a harsh word stirreth up fury.' If angry words are spoken to us we must guard against retaliation in kind. 'A spoonful of honey attracts more flies than a barrel full of vinegar;' so a mild answer to an angry retort may keep the peace: at least we shall have done all that is possible.

(5) We keep the peace by minding our own business. It is not prudent to interfere unduly in another's concerns. Busybodies cause dissension. One speaks of a neighbour's faults to another who in turn repeats it with perhaps some addition of his own. What has been said may get back to the person concerned, peace is destroyed. Had the first offender kept silent, there would have been no occasion for discord. Tale-bearing is most odious and inimical to peace; it breeds mischief, foments discord, and so destroys peace. 'The whisperer and the double-tongued is accursed, for he troubles many that were at peace.' Unhappy are the married who have not peace and tittle-tattle is often the cause of discord between husband and wife. Trust no longer exists, quarrels and strife creep in, and unhappiness besets the home. 'Every kingdom divided against itself shall be brought to desolation.' This is true of the home where peace does not abide. It is an accursed thing to cause trouble in a home by tale-bearing, thus ruining peace therein. 'Blessed are the peace-makers'—they are the children of God.

Some, through personal prejudices, interfere with the lawful occasions of others to the breeding of resentment and anger. Some people see evil where none exists, express disapproval simply because what is done does not agree with their own particular ideas. People who are doing their best in a good cause are criticised and accused of trying to gain unmerited praise. If people would only mind their own business, much discord would be avoided and peace would be more easily preserved. Peace is one of the greatest blessings of life and the foundation of all contentment and happiness. What salt is to food, so is peace to life. Without salt the best food becomes insipid, loses its savour; so, though we possess health, honour, reputation or wealth, there is no happiness in them without peace. We should understand the value of peace by the insistence with which our Lord desires peace to be kept among his followers, who are in turn commanded to pass peace on to all others, as a precious gift. 'Grace be to you, and peace from God, our Father.'

By all the means in our power, therefore, we must endeavour to promote peace among men. Human nature is difficult to control, anger is so easily aroused and is followed inevitably by discord. We can do our share towards preserving peace by being indulgent to the frailties and foibles of others, keeping in mind that we also have our disagreeable traits that jar on other folk; we are none of us free from faults nor do we see ourselves as others see us. Each has a right to his own opinions, so we must avoid trying to dominate others and forcing them to accept our views. Ready sympathy in joy or sorrow keeps unity and friendliness between men, whereas coldness causes antipathy. By minding our own business and leaving others alone we can avoid discord, and tale-bearing must be abhorred as destructive of all peace. It is only by avoiding the obvious causes of strife that we can hope to keep the peace as our Lord commands.

'As much as is in you, have peace with all men.'

XLVIII PEACE OF MIND

Everyone has an innate desire for happiness, and one necessary factor for this is peace of mind, the absence of any disturbing influence in the mind. When we are troubled and uneasy about some matter or discontented with circumstances, we are not happy. Usually there is some definite cause for this state; by removing the cause the effects are banished and happiness is restored. The want of peace in the mind usually arises because we would have things different from what they are at the time. If such things are under our control, well and good, we can alter them; but if they are outside our control, then the inevitable must be accepted as the only way to keep peace of mind. This may be difficult, but we can train ourselves to see in all happenings the will of God in our regard. There is a little verse which runs: 'It ain't no use to grumble and complain; it's just as cheap and easy to rejoice. When God sorts out the weather and sends rain, why! rain's my choice!' There is sound wisdom in those few lines, a great philosophy; if we would see every incident as 'God's choice' and make it our choice also, we should keep peace in mind and heart, and be happy.

The first requisite for this peace is a good conscience. There can be no sort of peace when there is enmity with God—sin and peace cannot exist together. At times conscience may become deadened to the sense of sin and so allow a spurious peace for a time, but it cannot last; conscience will wake and destroy peace in the end. Anyone with the least desire of goodness must be troubled in mind by the presence of sin and will not enjoy peace until the sin is washed away by repentance. Such loss of peace is definitely under our control—avoid sin and conscience will be at rest.

But many things beyond our control may disturb us, such as pain, sickness, the loss of one dear to us, and other ills of life. Yet in spite of these the mind can be at peace if we accept them in the right attitude of true resignation to God's will. Sad at heart, we may still have peace in the mind by turning to God for consolation.

'What cannot be cured must be endured;' but we lose peace of mind by letting many things which are not under our control dominate us and disturb our inner serenity. Peace of mind depends largely on our attitude towards persons and things. One common disturbing factor is worry or anxiety about the future, fear of the unknown which may or may not happen. Some natures are given to worrying much more than others; it is often a matter of temperament. It is no use telling such persons not to worry; they must cure themselves by seeing the foolishness of it. Worries may spring from some imprudent act from which we fear ill effects may result. This entails loss of peace through our own fault. Had we been prudent there would be no cause for anxiety and no loss of peace. Hence for our own peace of mind we must learn to be prudent.

Want of confidence in God, or want of resignation, bring fear and worry. To worry over what cannot be changed is surely foolishness, since we can do nothing to prevent future events that depend on God's will. We must be ready to accept them calmly as part of God's design, knowing that no harm could come from God, keep ourselves resigned to whatever he deems best, and go on unafraid trusting in God's care for us. No amount of worry or anxiety can alter these things, and a moment's consideration should teach us the foolishness of losing peace of mind about future happenings beyond our control. 'Don't worry; it may never happen!'

Many are troubled by the anxiety 'What will people think?' Human respect! What does it matter what people think? Obviously we cannot make others think of us as we would have them think. If they misjudge us, dislike us, impute wrong motives to our actions, what of it? We cannot change their ideas; it is impossible to please all. Does it really matter so much what people think? What does matter is what God thinks of us. But many are far more concerned about the opinions of their neighbours. A work-mate may offer a share of meat to us on an abstinence day. If we refuse, what will he think? If we accept, then we offend God and conscience is troubled. It is 'out of the frying-pan into the fire'! Had we no worry about what others think of us, we should do our duty to God and keep our peace of mind. What others think of us should not be a guiding principle. Let us do the right thing and let others think what they will. In any case we are none the happier for worrying over it; but we do please God and that should always be our one guiding principle.

Similar to this is the desire for popularity; we want to be friends with everybody. In a discussion some will try to side with both opinions, hoping it will not be noticed, afraid to say what is their real opinion lest they become unpopular. If such insincerity is found out, all popularity is lost, because insincerity is cowardly and despised by all. Let us have the courage of our convictions; if we do not wish to be involved in a dispute, let us say so and be done with it. Let us be true to those who are worthy of trust and let the rest go. Cheap popularity is not worth having, much less worth worrying over.

Keep truth as a motto. 'Tell the truth and shame the devil!' Never be afraid to admit the truth, let the consequences be what they may, and in the end you will be the gainer. One lie has to be bolstered up with another, one has to remember what lies have been told or contradictions will arise and the lie be found out. Lies cause worry and anxieties, and involve the loss of peace of mind. If the truth be told in the first place, there is nothing more to worry over, the worst is past, no more lies follow, and though it may be a case of a penalty being inflicted, yet if we are to blame we should be ready to take our punishment.

Though we be surrounded by those who constantly show defects of character and conduct, if we yield to a complaining and impatient spirit, we shall mar our peace of mind, yet benefit none. People do 'get on our nerves,' but simply because we are on the lookout for defects and allow ourselves to be upset by them. All people have their own peculiarities; one makes a lot of noise, another bustles about full of self-importance, one sniggers in an irritating manner, another is always in the dumps; we cannot change such traits of character, so we had best grin and bear them; as was quaintly said by a wise man, 'I go on taking a lot of no notice!' If we took 'no notice' of defects such trivial things would not disturb our peace. But we are apt to take too much notice and allow ourselves to be upset; better to forget them all and refuse to allow ourselves to be moved by petty trifles of this sort. We have probably the same effect on others by similar tricks of temperament of our own of which we are blissfully unaware. Let us accept such irritations in a spirit of mortification, grin and bear them and keep our peace of mind.

To rely too much on others for happiness is dangerous. We should take care not to let the desire for one person's company weigh too much with us. It breeds jealousies, and in these there is no peace, causes brooding over fancied slights where none are intended, and often produces an unforgiving spirit. If we try to own another person in this way the result is heart-ache, resentment and loss of peace of mind. We must not brood over fancied slights or injuries, not allow any person or thing to become so much to us that we cannot do without the object of our desire. The more we place reliance on others, the more we put our peace of mind under their power. It is always a risk and the cause of much unhappiness when we feel that we have been 'let down.' We reap hours of misery because we set our heart on changeable and fickle mortals.

Disappointments are sure to happen; that particular treat we arranged to enjoy and anticipated has to be foregone because of unforeseen circumstances. Why let such disappointment disturb our peace of mind and sadden us? It may be expected that children will feel disappointments keenly, but grown-ups ought to have sense enough to be prepared for the eventualities of life and be prepared for plans to go amiss. Then is the time for self-reliance to fill the gap. To go about feeling sad and at a loose end will not bring peace; the sensible course is to get something else to do and leave the rest to God's will. It is foolish to set such store on something that, should it go wrong, we lose all peace and contentment. Nothing in the world is worth it; nothing is so essential to happiness as keeping the mind serene and undisturbed by the vagaries of life. We must learn to put all things in their proper relationship to mind and soul, to get everything in a proper perspective. The more we rely on external objects, the more we become their slave; so the more we can cut off external delights, the more free we become, the less power they have to influence our peace of mind.

The prime necessity is to keep a clear conscience; without the friendship of God peace is impossible. Sin and peace are incompatible.

We must not be anxious about mere human respect which is of no value and often leads to wrongdoing. Cheap popularity is worthless; it makes us insincere and despicable. It is far better to be honest and accept friendship from those only who are trustworthy. Never fear to tell the truth and there will be no fear of being discovered in a lie, and other lies are avoided. The true secret of peace of mind is to trust in God and leave the future confidently to his loving care. Though others may fail us, God never will.

'Don't worry, it may never happen.'

XLIX DAILY FAULTS

Our divine Master has given us a precept : 'Be you perfect, as also your heavenly Father is perfect.' Humanly speaking this precept seems to be impossible of fulfilment; but since God never demands the impossible, it follows that we can attain to such perfection, not by our own efforts it is true, but by the help of grace. We all fall short of this standard of perfection; we commit faults daily but consider them of little or no account; we do not class them as sins, but call them imperfections—which after all is an admission of failure in carrying out the precept imposed on us. These imperfections, of which we reck so little, are a great hindrance to holiness, having a pernicious influence on the spiritual life. Doubtless they are less serious than deliberate venial sin. We hardly think of them as sins at all. Yet what do we know of sin? How can we judge what is to us an evil mystery? We put our own values on what we little understand, so that faults are glossed over without any attempt at correction, forgotten in the examination of conscience, perhaps not considered wrong at all. Then we wonder why we do not make any spiritual progress or grow closer to God. Though we go frequently, perhaps daily, to Holy Communion we seem none the better in spite of being so closely united to the giver of all grace. The probable reason is carelessness about these so-called imperfections. 'Catch me these little foxes that destroy the vineyard.'

The grace of God, all-powerful, is able to work wonders in the soul so long as no obstacle is put in the way of its work. If it seems to have little effect in us the fault lies in our imperfections.

Just as the sun pours its light and heat upon the earth, so the grace of God is poured forth on the soul. The sun is always shining, though at times it is hidden from sight by a barrier of cloud which it cannot penetrate. Mortal sin has a similar effect; it places a barrier between the soul and God so that his love and grace, though still poured forth, can have no effect because of that barrier of sin. Let us now suppose that the sun is shining brightly without any cloud to prevent its light and heat, but we are in a room in which the windows are covered with dust and dirt; it then follows that though the sun does light the room, its power is dimmed by the coating of dirt on the windows so that it cannot have its full effect. The thicker the dirt, the less illumination there will be. Daily faults have a like effect on the soul; they form a coating of dirt that prevents the full effect of grace on the soul. True, these imperfections do not deprive us of sanctifying grace, but they do prevent grace from exercising its full power to enrich the soul and so they prove a hindrance to spiritual progress.

Carelessness about little faults prepares the way for greater ones, for deliberate venial sin, by dulling the conscience; and venial sin disposes to mortal sin for the same reason. Did we take care about imperfections we should be more likely to avoid any deliberate sin; 'take care of the pence and the pounds will take care of themselves.' How truly this old adage can be applied to the soul and sin. Take care not to allow imperfections and there will be little danger of giving way to mortal sin. A soul that is starved of God's grace by the dust of imperfections may well find the struggle against temptation hard and wearisome, and because of weakness falls may be only too frequent.

Why do we take so little heed of these imperfections? It is again a case of judging by 'feelings. Such imperfections do not make us 'feel' guilty! A man who has over-indulged in strong drink feels the after-effects in a sense of shame, causing him to feel that he has done a great wrong. But to make some small uncharitable remark about a neighbour gives no such feeling of shame and is soon forgotten, and conscience fails to suggest any sin to us. Too often in examining our conscience we judge by feelings rather than by knowledge of the law and thus disregard small sins as being of no account. The standard by which we shall be judged is: 'Be thou perfect.' We must account for every idle word, for each thought harboured in the mind, for every deed however small in our own estimation.

Let us consider some common daily faults, the kind we

deem of no account. How often we are impatient over trifles that do not suit us! Do we even advert to the fact that impatience is a defect? Probably we do not take count of the number of times in the day we give way to irritation, perhaps vent our displeasure in explosive words and hurt another's feelings, and then forget that we have been impatient at all. We think little of such falls; but if a greater trouble befall us we are the less prepared to meet it patiently by our failure in smaller matters. The first thing in a morning many are impatient and irritable, the day is begun badly by want of self-control; but as the day passes and our lapse is forgotten, there is no sorrow for it; nevertheless it has been noted in heaven and the penalty must be paid. It has had some effect on our spiritual life, and if another has suffered through it, the effect has been so much greater by want of charity.

How often we fail in self-denial, give way to self-indulgence and are without any spirit of mortification. Yet the effect of this is a weakening of the will and consequently of the power to avoid small lapses. Often this want of mortification is shown in grumbling about petty things, causing bothers over trifles that have upset us and making ourselves disagreeable to others. Do we realise that this is a want of perfection?

Then such faults as small jealousies shown in various ways; quarrels over trifles; angry expressions of temper; tiny lies of excuse; mean deceits; rash judgments; evil thoughts, unchaste, envious, proud thoughts; vanities; human respect; self-complacency; negligence in the care of things borrowed; laziness or indolence; hastiness; stubbornness; unkindness; thoughtless words about others. By these and a host of such like failings we fall short of what is demanded by perfection.

What of the 'sins of omission' also? The kind word left unsaid that might have helped another in distress; the sunny smile that could have cheered another; the helping hand to one in need; graces offered only to be ignored; the many opportunities of doing something for God that are allowed to pass; all these are failures on our part to live up to the precept of perfection.

Do we ever give serious thought to these small faults or

THE EVERYDAY CATHOLIC

make any definite effort to lessen the number of times we fail? Perhaps these all appear too small, too insignificant, to bother about when there is so much to do in other ways; yet these faults are the root-cause of want of spirituality, the dust lying on the soul that prevents the full action of God's grace. All must be accounted for, atoned for, sooner or later. Do we even express any sorrow for such faults? If not, it proves how little we heed them, how wanting we are in determination to amend our lives. Maybe perfection is considered to be the concern only of those who 'enter religion,' of those who profess to be striving after perfection; but the precept is laid on all without exception or qualification.

Holy Communion is the daily antidote to venial sins, but we must make use of the graces gained. Holy Communion gives all the necessary help, but we must do the positive work ourselves; we have to work out our salvation by our own efforts aided by grace; it will not be done for us without our co-operation. Neither will it be brought about by wishful thinking, but only by steady persevering effort day by day to lessen the number of our falls.

Carelessness about these daily faults may be of serious consequence and there is a grave duty of making some real effort to lessen their number until our evil tendencies are gradually overcome. It can be done by watchfulness and prayer. 'I can do all things in him who strengtheneth me.' It needs much watchfulness, since we fall almost before we notice the occasion of a fall; a sudden circumstance intervening, our natural propensity to evil, the least provocation will cause failure unless we are on the watch continually and ready to resist the sudden onslaught. We need much more self-control to withhold the angry word, to suppress the venting of impatience, to check impetuous resentment.

Such tendencies demand careful watching and effort, so easy is it to give way without thought or consideration of evil when feeling is roused. Probably we offend mostly in word, since St James says: 'If any man offend not in word, the same is a perfect man.' We so often speak without any thought, the words are out before we realise the evil therein; the angry

240

expression, the spiteful remark, the uncharitable bit of news, all slip out because we are not watching, keeping a ceaseless guard over the tongue. Much of this is due to spiritual sloth, to a disinclination to make serious effort against natural propensities and a failure to persevere in good resolutions when made. It is no easy task to struggle continuously against natural inclination, so easy to be overcome if we relax; the bias in nature is all towards self-satisfaction and gratification of all inclinations. Only the grace of God aiding the efforts made by us to correspond can bring about any improvement.

We shall have to give an account of each thought, of every idle word, of each imperfect act, of the many omissions of good, when we come to be judged by God. We may forget or disregard these small daily faults, but God cannot forget and will demand payment to the uttermost farthing. God never asks the impossible, so with his help we can overcome evil and fulfil the precept:

'Be you perfect, as also your heavenly Father is perfect.'

L HAPPINESS

The desire of happiness is man's most natural instinct and it might be true to say that everything he does is intended in some way to promote happiness for himself. Each one seeks happiness where he imagines it can be found, usually only to discover illusions and emptiness, since satisfaction such as man desires is not to be found on earth. God wills it so, since he would have us understand that an immortal soul hungering after perfect unceasing happiness can only be satisfied by the vision of himself. Unwittingly we seek heaven where it is not to be found, putting our hope in transient joys that may suffice for a time but soon fade and leave heartache instead. Does this mean that life must always be unhappy? By no means; life can know its own happiness so long as we accept its limitations and do not expect too much. In this life perfect happiness is impossible; we must be content with something much inferior, a happiness that will soothe the passing hours but never satisfy. The things of time cannot satisfy an immortal soul; made for God, he alone can fulfil all its longing and desire. The first principle of happiness is to realise the limitations of life on earth, then find some mean of happiness in things as they are, until God gives perfect eternal bliss hereafter.

A grave mistake is made in seeking things as an 'end' instead of simply as a 'means' of making life endurable until the true 'end' is obtained. A certain measure of contentment can be found in looking at things from the right standpoint and not expecting more than finite objects can give. Happiness consists in an attitude of mind towards things as they are. An old adage says 'Happiness generally depends more on the opinion we have of things than on the things themselves.' If we can accept the truth of this it will help much; it is our attitude to things that spells happiness or discontent.

Peace of mind and conscience are vital. Where there is no friendship with God, there can be no true happiness—that is certain; that is why peace was the gift of our Lord because it is the foundation of all happiness.

Another need is contentment with things as they are, and not as we would have them to be, especially when we have no control over them. If we examine our unhappy times, we shall find that discontent is chiefly at the root of our joyless state, which in turn can be reduced to 'self.' The more we depend on external objects, persons, or things, the less likely we are to find happiness, because we cannot mould persons or things to suit our ideas or desires. To place our hope of happiness in things outside our control is to put ourselves in their power with consequent risk of disappointment and discontent.

Let us consider some of the causes of unhappiness, by removing which we shall have a better chance of happiness.

Discontent with our state of life is one cause. We envy those who possess more; we want fine clothes, amusements, a motor-car, or riches. Because we cannot have these we are discontented with our lot, grow jealous of those that have wealth and enjoyment beyond our means. By thus putting our happiness in things beyond control, instead of being master of our soul we lose peace of mind, grow discontented. This does not deny us all ambition to get on in life; we can legitimately expect happiness in striving to better our lot, but it will be rather in the striving than in the attainment. No one desirous of possessions is ever satisfied with what he already has; no 'collector' is ever satisfied with his 'collection,' he always wants the more to add to it. Riches bring worries and anxieties in their train, breeding fears of loss which are the ruin of happiness. Hence the wisdom of our Lord: 'Blessed (i.e. happy) are the poor in spirit' those who have the right attitude to wealth.

Too much dependence on another person is also a fruitful source of unhappiness. It may be a lover or a friend to whom we have given our affection, but we demand more than any human being can give. We become afflicted with jealousy because we fear to trust, are resentful when they fail us. We demand in them the perfection of God, compliance with all our wishes, expect unspoken whims to be known and are displeased when they fall short. How can we expect such perfections in an imperfect human being? Why expect man to supply what only God can give? Unconsciously we look for the perfect love that can be found only in heaven .Often enough we are loving 'self' in another. We become too possessive of the object of our love, deny freedom of action, try to enslave, and reap unhappiness thereby. Because we are not able to control another, bend him to our will, we lose peace of mind, we do not love truly, but selfishly; happiness is found in giving, not in receiving, but so many have the 'receiving' type of love and give nothing in return. It is not that 'I love you' but that 'I want to be loved by you,' to get, not to give; it is not a friend we require, but a benefactor to minister to our wants. We call it mutual love, but it is all 'take' on our part, no 'giving.' The less we seek self, the more we shall be happy. To seek happiness for self is to lose it; to give happiness to another is to find it.

Lack of self-reliance makes for discontent. People of the past generation were happier since they were not thus afflicted Necessities were fewer, there were no cinemas, there was no craze for speed, external amusements were rare, life was simpler with less nerve strain. The fewness of outside attractions meant more self-reliance on creative work to fill in time and the simple joys of home and the fireside rather than external attractions provided recreation. Civilization in its progress has but increased men's needs, made them lazy in exercise so that they want transport instead of using their legs, made them dependent on the external amusements for recreation; but it has not added to real happiness in the end. The joy of self-reliance is unknown to many who suffer from boredom and discontent through inability to occupy their spare time; they have lost the creative instinct and must have everything done for them to keep them amused and occupied. Idleness is a great source of boredom and discontent; self-reliance is an asset to contentment and happiness.

The death of a loved one is a very natural cause of grief and sorrow, but much of this sadness is selfish, a hard saying but true! Why should it make us unhappy because God has called a loved one to eternal bliss? Would it be a real kindness to bring back to this vale of tears one whom we love? Think you the sainted dead could possibly wish to return? The real cause of our sorrow is not sympathy for the dead, but self-pity for the gap in our lives, for our personal loss of accustomed companionship, not real love for the departed. This grief is natural, but still selfish, and happiness can be regained only by recognising and accepting the loss as God's will, and by the knowledge that the loved one has gone to a truer, richer life in eternal happiness in which we may hope to meet him again.

Spiritual writers tell us that 'detachment from all things' is the way to true happiness. That is true, but most of us dare not risk it! We are afraid to credit the truth of it. Yet the more we are detached from externals, the more chance there is of real happiness because we grow more independent. We fear detachment because we fear it means self-sacrifice. Those who have attained some measure of detachment know the possibilities of it. What does it really mean? Detachment is to free ourselves from so setting our heart on anything that it has no power to disturb our peace of mind or serenity, to desire nothing so much that it can bring discontent and disappointment if not forthcoming, to see in all the will of God and find joy in its acceptance.

Here are a few truths which will help us to be happy if we try to practise them, difficult though they may appear.

(a) The less we covet things, the more happiness we shall find. Contentment with our lot is the first step to peace of mind, the essential of happiness. Hankering after what we cannot get, or what when obtained breeds anxiety and worry, is not conducive to happiness.

(b) Independence of external objects out of our control frees us from discontent. If we allow external objects to control us, we reap unhappiness. We must be masters of our soul and refuse to let disappointments rob us of happiness and make us sad.

(c) Kipling says 'Love all but none too much.' No human being can give perfect love and satisfy us; man is too imperfect never to fail nor disappoint us at times; we must not expect too much from friendship. Possessiveness leads to jealousy; there can be no joy in a jealous love. No human being can be ours absolutely, nor can we mould another to our desire.

(d) Avoid idleness; it gives too much opportunity for brooding over fancied wrongs, bringing bitterness to the soul. The happiest man is the one who is too busy to know whether he is happy or not. A hobby is a source of happiness in giving an object in life, especially if it brings out the creative instinct and makes for self-reliance in recreation.

(e) Develop detachment from all external things. Let not peace of mind be dependent on things out of our control so that they can sadden us by disappointment and discontent. See in all the will of God.

No doubt it is difficult to carry out these ideas, yet in such methods lies the best chance of happiness. Forgetfulness of self is the true road to happiness. The glory of life is in loving, not in being loved; in giving, not in getting; in serving, not in being served. To bring happiness to others in self-forgetfulness always increases our own and self-reliance makes us independent of others.

Happiness is an attitude of the mind to persons and things; by creating the right attitude we gain happiness.

LI HUMAN RESPECT

St Paul writes (I Cor. IV, 3.): 'It is a very small thing to be judged by you or by man's day.' The Corinthians were quarrelling about the merits of their various teachers, praising this one, blaming another, and accusing St Paul himself of evils. The saint shows how little value he puts on the opinion they may have of him. Unfortunately we do not imitate St Paul, but lay far too much stress on what others may say or think of us. In the *Imitation of Christ* (Bk. III, Ch. 36.) Thomas a Kempis warns us of this: 'My child, fix your heart firmly on God and have no fear of the opinions of men, as long as your conscience declares you devout and innocent . . . to please all is impossible; though St Paul tried to please all men in the Lord and became "all things to all men," yet he held it a very small thing to be judged by men.' This submission, this slavery, to the opinion of others is what is called human respect—fear of what men will think or say of us and allowing this fear to influence our actions.

An eminent philosopher on his death-bed said: 'Listen, my children, to this last lesson which I am about to give you. I confess and deliberately attest in the presence of God, whom I am about to receive and before whom I am about to appear, that if I have shown myself but little of a christian in my words, actions, and writings, it has not been through conviction, but through vanity and because of the opinions of men.'

Do we sometimes show ourselves 'but little of a christian' because of the opinions of men?

Human respect is not a sin in itself, but it is an attitude of mind that inclines us to sin through fear of what may be said of us. There are times, it is true, when it will prevent us from committing the grosser classes of sin lest they become known, but through fear rather than from the love of God. It is definitely a weakness of character, a fertile source of temptation to sin, and the cause of infidelity to the faith and religion.

It paralyses character in as much as we wait to see or hear what others will do or say before we dare act or state our own opinions. We agree with the majority or stronger party, right or wrong, being afraid to differ. If however a more power-ful party comes in, we change over so as to be with the stron-gest. When it is not a matter of faith or known truth each one has a right to his own opinion. But when we give preference to the esteem of men rather than to the will of God and to his commandments it is an insult to God; we serve God when it is convenient for us to do so without being criticised by others whose opinion we value too highly. It is mean and cowardly and mental slavery to allow ourselves to be ruled by what others may think. It is moral cowardice, a want of fortitude, when we act against conscience out of deference to the wishes or opinions of others.

How does human respect lead us into sin? By causing us to act against the rulings of conscience in order to please others or through fear of being singled out for taunts or ridicule if we do what we know to be right, or through unwillingness to lose their good opinion or esteem by being true to conscience. (In actual fact that is the quickest and surest way of losing all esteem and all respect, since others notice our want of courage and despise us).

Let us take a few examples of sins often committed through human respect.

(a) We may be drawn into a conversation, then realise that it is an unfavourable criticism of some person, perhaps a personal friend, and statements are made that we know to be quite untrue. Instead of defending the absent and sticking up for a friend, we stand by without any protest through fear of offend-ing the gossipers; by silence we become a partner and give consent to the lies and defamation of a friend's character, we join in the sin of uncharitable gossip and are disloyal to our friend simply because we are too cowardly to stand up in defence of truth and loyalty, afraid of what others will think! 'Silence gives consent.' Is it not cowardly to be thus afraid of the opinions of men? (b) At times we act in the opposite way; we speak when we ought to keep silent. At work conversations are not always of the cleanest; talk becomes immodest and unchaste; we know it is sinful to join in—'Let such things not be so much as named among you as becometh saints'—

yet we do take part, not daring to keep silent, afraid lest they should taunt us and jeer at us for being pious and goody-goody if we protested against such talk even by silent disapproval. We are not ready to suffer for conscience sake. Conscience may protest, but it is ignored. We prefer to join in the lewd talk to please men rather than be loyal to God and conscience. Bad language in other forms is used. It may be foul words or God's name taken in vain, and we dare not be different from our companions. We want to appear bold and manly, to talk big as they do, to be popular with them, one of them, entirely failing to see how far this cowardice is from real manliness. It shows the weakness of our character in that we have not the moral pluck to stand out against evil; we are so afraid of what others may think that we sink ourselves to their level. (c) Again the familiar example of accepting meat on an abstinence day to please another. We may visit some acquaintances, be asked to share a meal in which meat is served. Dare we refuse and say 'I am not allowed to eat meat to-day'? Or should we weakly accept through fear of what would be thought? Plausible excuses are forthcoming of course: it would seem to be uncharitable to refuse; it might hurt the person's feelings; it might make things awkward; hence we give in. We disregard the fact that we are unfaithful to the law of the Church and to God; we take meat through cowardice to avoid comment on our religion; the opinion of our acquaintances is worth more to us than God's. (d) Clothes are responsible for sins of weakness. Why was Mass missed last Sunday? Because I had no clothes to go in! Often that old excuse is brought out, but what it really means is that we were afraid of what the neighbours would think if we had nothing better than our working clothes to wear to church. They would think we were too poor to afford good clothes. We do not want them to think we cannot afford to be in the latest fashion, unable to get a smart frock or dainty hat. Hence Mass is missed, the soul is deprived of grace and clothed in the vile vesture of sin, because of what neighbours might think of us.

Girls are afraid to be out of the fashion. Money is wasted

when it is needed for more urgent things and even theft is committed to be in the fashion. Parents are disowned in public because others may think them dowdy or old-fashioned. Public opinion is of so much more value than the respect and honour due to parents and the love they have given to their children. (e) 'Come and have a drink.' Many times this invitation ought to be refused, but how often a man has not the moral courage to say 'NO.' It means that he must stand his turn in treating, he may easily take too much, may spend money needed by his family. But what will the others think if he refuses? What a terrible thing if they think he is not 'a sport.' Bad company often leads us astray simply because we are afraid to be different, to have a mind and will of our own.

Enough of these examples; there are so many ways in which human respect plays its evil part in our lives, deluding us into committing sin through want of moral courage to refuse the proposed evil. Have you heard the story of the man and the donkey? The man was riding in a cart drawn by a small donkey when he heard some one say: 'Look at that lazy lout making that poor little animal drag him along in the cart.' He got out and walked alongside the cart. Another said: 'Why does not the silly man get in the cart and save his legs?' He got in the cart again. Forthwith someone said 'That hulking man ought to put the little donkey in the cart and give it a rest.' Again he complied, and caused roars of laughter along the road. After that he no longer cared what others said; he got into the cart and the donkey pulled him along. He realised he had been trying the impossible—to please everybody. A silly story perhaps, but no more foolish than the things done because of human respect, no more foolish than to take so much notice of what people may think or say of us. Why not have the courage of our own convictions, have a mind and a will of our own and act on it, instead of being like a weathercock twisted all ways by every wind that blows?

We read of our Lord that 'he was watched to see what he would do.' Did he ever fear to do what he knew was right because of the opinions of men? He knew that the so-called holy ones of Israel were watching to accuse him of evil deeds, to criticise him and make him of evil repute, and in the end bring about his death in a shameful manner. But never by a hair's breadth did he ever deviate from his chosen path of doing good, no matter what others might think of him or do to him. In this he set us an example that we should follow in his footsteps and do what is right always. God has given us a conscience to guide us and this we are bound to follow no matter what may be said or what opinions held about us by men. If we remember the presence of God we shall not worry about the judgments of men. God is our judge, not men.

Though human respect is not a sin, yet it is the prolific cause of sin. Always we must be on our guard, watching this insidious thing less fear of others leads us astray from God.

'Fix your heart on God, and fear not the opinions of men.'

LII LOVE OF OUR NEIGHBOUR

To the Galatians (V. 14) St Paul writes: 'All the law is ful-filled in one word—thou shalt love thy neighbour as thyself.'

After the love of God, our chief duty is to love our neighbour. Indeed our love of God cannot be sincere unless love of our neighbour is included, for, as St John says, 'If any man say, I love God, and hateth his brother, he is a liar. For he that loveth not his brother, whom he seeth, how can he love God, whom he seeth not?' (I Ep. IV, 20) It is not always fully real-ised how much we are bound by this commandment, that we cannot truly love God unless we love all men without excep-tion. No command is so frequently impressed upon us in holy Scripture, none so often ignored.

Our divine Saviour taught this precept by his own example. He was always ready to do good to others, was full of sympathy for human ills, nothing was too much trouble; love drove him to serve and ask no reward save gratitude to God for his favours. At the Last Supper, having given his own flesh and blood to be the life of the human souls and a mark of his infinite love, he said to the apostles: 'A new command-ment I give unto you, that you love one another,' and the extent of this love 'even as I have loved you' i.e. with a perfect unselfish love. It is moreover to be a sign by which his followers are to be known: 'By this shall all men know that you are my disciples if you have love one for another.' Could a stranger from another world easily find the disciples of Christ to-day by their mutual love? So many profess to be 'christians' yet have little love for others. Even amongst catholics is mutual charity so marked as to be an unmistakable sign of the followers of Christ? It is much to be doubted; and res-ponsibility lies at the door of each one who fails in this grave duty of neighbourly love. In the Epistles the apostles insist strongly on the duty of christian love among all who profess to follow Christ.

Many will say it is impossible to love all men. Some we love; others we dislike intensely; between the two are many shades of feeling. How can we love one for whom we feel a natural antipathy, have an instinctive dislike and aversion? To ask that question shows a misunderstanding of the quality of the love which must be given to one's neighbour. That dislike or aversion is merely a physical feeling, akin to moods and emotions, over which we have little or no control, but which can be counteracted by the will so that it does not influence our actions. It has no concern in spiritual love. We confuse emotional love, which rests in the feelings, with 'appreciative' love which is the deliberate choice and adhesion of the will to what is known to be 'good,' being based on judgment and esteem, or on some reasonable ground. Love of a neighbour need not be emotional, i.e. there need be no warmth of feeling or attraction such as is found in physical love. We are nevertheless bound to have that calm judgment and esteem which leads us to treat all others as we treat self: 'Thou shalt love thy neighbour as thyself.' That is the standard to which our love must conform in our relations with others.

We do love self; it is our most natural instinct dominating all action; yet we do not 'feel' this love for self, there is no emotion in it nor do we advert to it, being wholly unconscious of it. How does it show itself? By the care taken to promote only what seems for our benefit, or to avoid all that seems harmful or is distasteful to us. Hence we try to escape pain, do ourselves no injury, seek happiness, strive to keep our good name and reputation, hide the evil we do, fear to lose esteem, keep silent about misdeeds, do not criticise ourselves or tell tales against ourselves; we wish to be respected by all, to be helped in time of trouble, to have kindness shown, to be appreciated and praised, to receive consideration for our feelings. All this is simply the result of love for oneself. We feel no glow of attraction, have no desire to hug ourselves or show ourselves tokens of love. That would seem to be folly. Love of self is a movement of the will, based on calculated judgment, to avoid harmful things and promote whatever appears to be a source of contentment and happiness. That is the love we must show to all men. 'Do unto others as you would have them do to you.' There is no other way of truly loving our neighbour. Hence, though we feel physical aversion from or dislike of some person, that does not, or should not, affect the will to do good towards him or to avoid whatever may be a cause of distress or unhappiness.

We can test ourselves by what we expect from others. I am gossiping about another uncharitably, criticising his faults. Suppose I knew that some other was gossiping about me in a similar manner, what would be my reaction? Should I resent it? If so then it is ample proof that I am doing a wrong in such gossip, I am allowing my will to be dominated by emotions and feelings, the will is consenting to evil against a neighbour, I am not showing him that love which I give to myself, and I thereby offend God by want of charity. That example can be applied to all thought, word, or deed affecting a neighbour. All feelings and emotions can, and must, be dominated by the will so that in our conduct nothing causes harm to another but always leads to doing good and treating a neighbour as we wish him to treat us. Moreover we must remember that Christ takes to himself whatever is done to another; 'Whatsoever you do to one of these my least brethren, you do it to me.'

There is this difference between the love of God and the love of a neighbour—the love of God is 'friendship' because it is known to be a mutual love (that is essential to friendship), but, the love of a neighbour is 'benevolence,' the disposition to be kindly and well disposed to him. In its perfect form this love ought to be mutual, as it is in the case of those who are real friends.

Obviously it is not possible to love all equally and there is a definite order to be observed. 'Charity begins at home.' That is quite proper. St Paul says 'Let us work good to all men, but especially to those who are of the household of the faith.' (Gal. VI, 10).

Parents, members of the same family and relatives have the first claim; then fellow-workers, then all catholics; lastly all other human beings. The closer the tie that binds, the greater the claim on charity. St Paul gives us a true idea of the workings of neighbourly love in daily life and how it is to be shown in a practical way.

Charity is patient, he says (I. Cor. 13): this means bearing ills without complaint when caused by others, enduring without irritation the foibles and mannerisms of others which at times get on our nerves and incline us to irritability.

Charity is kind; it spends itself in doing good, in promoting happiness helping others in need, sympathising in trouble or sorrow and avoiding what might sadden or distress another.

Charity envieth not; envy implies sadness at another's good with the desire of depriving him of the enjoyment of it, though one may gain nothing by such deprivation. Also all jealousy must be avoided.

Charity dealeth not perversely; we can be very awkward at times and difficult to get on with, being obstinate in wanting our own way, or annoying and vexing others, especially those we dislike.

Charity is not puffed up; where love liveth, pride dieth; pride makes us unforgiving and resentful, nursing grievances; moreover it despises or belittles others, criticising and finding fault in what they do.

Charity is not ambitious: ambition desires superiority and to gain its object has no consideration or thought for the well-being of others.

Charity seeketh not her own; how we do like to have our own way; selfishness is rooted deeply in us so we find it hard to give way and not demand what we think to be our rights or privileges or proper dues.

Charity thinketh no evil; if we think no evil, we shall not speak nor do evil. Probably we offend more by speech in gossip, tale-bearing, or backbiting, than in any other way. We need to keep guard over our speech.

Charity beareth all things; it shows forbearance to all; does not get into a temper when thwarted, but bears slights and want of consideration in a spirit of meekness without desire of retaliation for fancied injuries.

Charity believeth all things; not idle rumours or tales, but the good intentions of others, and trusts the goodness to be found in all.

Charity hopeth all things; it has confidence and does not despair at the apparent want of charity shown by others, but always hopes for the best.

Charity never falleth away; it knows no end, never weakens, but remains steadfast and loyal through all the trials of daily life, always seeking to do good, to be helpful and kind, persevering to the end of life.

Is that what charity suggests to us? Do we practise it in that way? If we have unfailing charity towards all, we have begun on earth the life of heaven where all is perfect and eternal mutual love and esteem.

We must have a true idea of charity, realising that it has nothing in common with feelings or emotions, but is an act of the will determined to give to all the treatment we would wish to receive ourselves in the same circumstances. It has nothing to do with dislikes or aversions which must be ignored, but for love of God strives to avoid all that might harm, and to promote all that is good and helpful. Charity to neighbours is a personal obligation on each one of us, no matter what others may do. We cannot be excused from the obligation because others fail in charity to us.

'A new commandment I give unto you, that you love one another as I have loved you. By this shall all men know that you are my disciples.' (John XIII, 34, 35).

LIII UNCHARITABLE GOSSIP

Unkindly talk about others is a common sin of ordinarily good people, who, without any intention of doing harm, forget how evil may result from such gossip and that it is contrary to the law of charity. This is no new sin. St James has a lot to say about it: 'If any man offend not in word, the same is a perfect man, he is able also with a bridle to lead the whole body . . . the tongue is a little member and boasteth great things . . . the tongue is a fire, a world of iniquity . . . the tongue no man can tame, an unquiet evil full of deadly poison. By it we bless God and the Father; by it we curse men who are made after the likeness of God. Out of the same mouth proceedeth blessing and cursing. My brethren these things ought not to be.'

Ages before St James, Ecclesiasticus warns of the same evil. 'A man full of tongue is terrible in his city, and he that is rash in word shall be hateful . . . the whisperer and the double-tongued is accursed for he hath troubled many that were at peace. The tongue of a third person hath disquieted many . . . hath cast out valiant women and deprived them of their labours. He that harkeneth to it shall never rest, neither shall he have a friend in whom he may repose. The stroke of a whip maketh a blue mark, but the stroke of the tongue will break bones. Many have perished by the edge of the sword but not so many as have perished by their tongue. Hedge in thy ears with thorns, hear not a wicked tongue . . . take heed lest thou slip with the tongue.'

Such inspired words should make us think of the many times we have offended in speech, or listened to unkind talk, which is just as sinful and gives encouragement to the gossiper. Excuse is made that no harm is meant, but the evil happens just the same, and the responsibility remains. Once words are uttered they cannot be recalled; injury that is incurable may result and the responsibility lies at our door. We are careful about some sins, but fail in matters of speech. We do not steal a neighbour's goods, but we steal his good name; we do not kill him, but we destroy his happiness. Nor do we call these sins by their correct name. Calumny and detraction are known to be grave sins, but we never use those names to describe our sin. We call it 'speaking uncharitably' or telling tales, backbiting, but never calumny or detraction which is what it is. Calumny is to speak untruly, detraction to say what is true, of a neighbour's defects. The gravity of the sin is measured by the harm done, and restitution is of obligation for pardon. Whatever evil thing we say about a neighbour is either false or true, and is therefore either calumny or detraction, no matter what less evil-sounding name we give the talk.

Seldom do we know the harm done by evil gossip. Peace is destroyed, sadness caused, and bitterness of soul results. Uncharitable words are poisoned arrows which not only wound, but cause these wounds to fester with them. Homes are filled with disagreement, marriages wrecked, congregations split in twain by evil gossip. Many are discouraged in their good works by the imputation of false motives, lives are burdened by tales repeated. What use is it to say that no harm was intended? The harm is done and we are responsible because we have not loved our neighbour as ourselves.

Harm is done by hints. One says 'I could tell you something about him,' or 'I would not like to say what I know about him.' Possibly less harm would result if the truth were told instead of this hinting at evil. The evil may be slight, but those who listen may think the worst. Damage can be done very thoroughly by such hints. Others wonder what the truth is, try to find out, or invent what they cannot discover; but the 'hinter' may not reflect what harm has been done.

The clergy and consecrated persons are not respected by gossipers. As we treat a priest in his priestly capacity, so we treat God. 'He that despiseth you despiseth me.' Much harm is done to religion by such gossip and it is akin to sacrilege as being directed against consecrated persons. Few would strike a priest, but many flay him with their tongue. Bishop Vaughan wrote in a pastoral letter: 'Priests have their faults, no doubt, or they would not be human. When these things are seized upon by the uncharitable, magnified, and distorted, a dislike is engendered in the hearts of the unwary which may tell against religion itself. Because of stupid misunderstandings and the havoc wrought by bitter tongues, people are estranged from their priests, stay away from Mass and the sacraments, and sometimes drift into irreligion. Time after time we have had to see and lament the way in which these uncharitable people hinder the work of the priests of God and prevent the spread of the gospel.' Unfortunately his words are only too true and religion suffers by such gossip. Who are we that we should dare to uncover a neighbour's faults, be he priest or layman? Are we so free from faults that we can discuss others and thank God that we are not as other men? 'He that is without sin, let him cast the first stone.' There is a certain smug satisfaction in speaking of another's faults, since it implies that we ourselves are free from such faults, yet often we see most easily in others the very faults of which we ourselves are guilty.

Paschal Germaine wrote: 'I have learned to doubt the truth of any story of evil of the absent. People mix convictions and evidence, and it happens that the most horrible mischief in the world is made by conscientious people who speak from belief, instead of facts; and their listeners forget that though 'good' they are not discriminating. Of course we all err; but when it comes to saying of one man that his error is deliberate, or even that he is guilty of the thing as it looks, I for one would never judge.' We are too apt to judge things by their face value, knowing nothing of the facts, or to think what we believe on doubtful appearances to be evidence.

Why do we so readily give way to odious and hurtful gossip? (a) Eagerness to display knowledge, to be the first to relate a bit of 'spicy news,' love of causing a sensation, of surprising or shocking some one, all these are causes of gossip. No harm is intended, or adverted to, but harm is wrought, a neighbour's reputation is blasted, he is saddened and grieved by loss of esteem; for whatever he suffers, we are responsible and are bound in conscience to put right the wrong done. (b) Curiosity is another cause. We like to know what is going on and so encourage the gossiper; later we retail what we have heard, perhaps with additions of our own. To encourage and listen to evil gossip is just as sinful as the actual talking; we are a partner in the sin. Did we not listen, there could be no gossip; it requires at least two for gossip and they share the guilt. (c) Self-love leads to disclosing the faults of a neighbour in order to show our superiority and goodness. We hope by a display of zeal for good to create a good impression of ourselves, imitating the pharisee who thanked God that he was not as other men, a sinner. We see the mote in a brother's eye, but fail utterly to see the beam in our own. (d) Jealousy is a prolific cause of gossip. Frequently we are made sad by hearing another praised, when we wish to have the praise ourselves. How we dislike to hear the praises of another sung in our unwilling ears; how easy to stop this by showing up the one praised in a poor light, belittling his achievements, stealing away the honour given by displaying his faults, exaggerating his failures. Jealousy is always ready to find fault and talk disparagingly of others. (e) Pride makes us judge rashly. In revealing another's faults we are passing a judgment on his actions, blaming him for a failure to live up to a certain standard (which may be of our own setting), allowing our own prejudices to bias our judgment, and blaming others because they do not comply with our own ideas of what is proper. Paschal Germaine again says: 'I have learned to distrust all evidence of personal evil. The most searching tone of our Lord's utterances, and one that grows every day in its significance upon me, is "Judge not, that ye be not judged;" and not on the grounds of charity but truth. It is unmanly, impossible to judge of another: we do not even understand ourselves.' If we cannot understand self, how can we judge any other person, merely by what we see or imagine? (f) Resentment for injuries, fancied or real, is often at the root of want of charity in speech. Brooding over an injury magnifies it out of all proportion, and to relieve our injured feelings we break out into venomous talk against the one who did the injury, perhaps unconsciously. The injury is exaggerated and made to appear as grave as possible and with the intention of showing up a neighbour in a bad light. The repaying of evil with evil is not adverted to at all, nor the failure to forgive injuries as we hope for forgiveness of our own sins from God.

This tendency to gossip and find fault spoils otherwise spiritual lives of many good pious people who take no heed of the words of St James 'If any man think himself to be religious, not bridling his tongue, that man's religion is vain.' Pious people do harm to religion by critical fault-finding, thereby making their own religion vain. Misery and harm are caused by tittle-tattle, making others suffer cruelly; sensitive people feel intensely what is said against them, so that they become unhappy and saddened thereby.

There is an old saying 'De mortuis nil nisi bonum' (of the dead, nothing but good). The dead are respected and seldom is evil spoken of them. Yet words cannot harm the dead, they are beyond all human interference. Would that as much respect were shown to the living who can be and are grievously harmed by ill-spoken words. 'Charity thinketh no evil.' If we think no evil, we shall not speak it; talk is the expression of our thought, hence ere evil is spoken it must be thought and that is the first breach of charity. Train the mind to think only good of others, and no evil will be spoken.

'If any man offend not in word, the same is a perfect man.'

LIV FORGIVENESS OF INJURIES

Everyone sins, all need forgiveness and pardon from God; but the first condition essential for pardon is to forgive one another. Our Lord was most insistent on this condition, teaching it in season and out of season. 'If you will forgive men their offences, your heavenly Father will forgive you also your offences, but if you will not forgive men, neither will your heavenly Father forgive you.' (Matt. VI). That is a definite statement of fact—pardon from God depends on first forgiving men the injuries they do to us. To show the enormous difference between personal injury and sin, Jesus told the story of the unforgiving servant. This man owing a huge and unpayable debt pleaded for mercy and time in which to pay. This debt was wholly forgiven him by his master. Going forth he found a fellow-servant in his debt for a paltry sum, of which he demanded immediate payment. The man was unable to pay, so was cast into prison, to the great indignation of other servants of the same master. They made complaints of the vile, unmerciful treatment accorded to a fellow debtor by one who had himself been forgiven a huge debt. The master, justly incensed by such conduct, withdrew the former pardon and cast the unmerciful debtor into prison until he settled his own debt. No one could quarrel with this decision; the man deserved it.

This is an exact picture of our own conduct when we refuse to forgive injuries. Let us go deeper into this example. It is not said that this man frequently asked pardon; he did not profess a religion of love and mercy, but one which demanded an eye for an eye and a tooth for a tooth. He made no bargain that if forgiven, he would also forgive; but the master was justly incensed at his unforgiving conduct in spite of this. We owe an infinite, unlimited debt to God in penalty for sin for which we ask pardon and expect it to be mercifully granted. When man injures man, he injures an equal, the guilt is finite, limited to man's capacity and often paltry. There can be no comparison between the infinite guilt of sin and the finite injury done by another. Man can atone for injuries to man;

262

but he cannot of himself atone for the least sin.

God has made a contract—'Forgive and you will be forgiven,' i.e. forgive the finite injury done by man, and you will be forgiven the infinite guilt of sin against God. We cannot complain of any injustice in that; it is so wholly in our favour. In saying the 'Our Father' we accept this contract, but often do not advert to the meaning of what we say. A certain man told a priest that he could not forgive some injury done to him. The priest asked: 'Do you say the "Our Father"?' The man replied that he said it daily. The priest then advised: 'Never say it again until you have forgiven your enemy. Do you not understand that you are asking God not to forgive you?' The man went away in a different frame of mind! Let it be a warning to us. If we bear resentment towards another because of some injury and say 'Forgive us our trespasses as we forgive them that trespass against us,' we are asking that we also should not be forgiven. We are apt to forget that when we repeat the 'Our Father.'

What a perfect example of forgiveness is given by our Lord when being nailed to the cross! 'Father forgive them, they know not what they do.' He cannot deny that a grievous crime is being committed by his enemies, but he excuses them on the grounds of ignorance of what they do. Do we make excuses or allowances for others who injure us? If Christ on the cross can forgive, surely we also can forgive the petty injuries done against us. We refuse because of pride, resentment, little-mindedness, meanness of soul, hurt feelings and for such-like paltry reasons. There is something magnificent in forgiving, since thus we rise above our petty feelings and the littleness of human nature and become God-like. 'To err is human, to forgive divine.'

There is no limit to the number of times we must grant forgiveness. Just as we expect and hope for infinite mercy from God, so we in return must set no limits to our pardon of others, no matter how often they offend. St Peter asks, Lord, how often shall my brother offend against me and I forgive him, till seven times?' Our Lord answers 'I say not to you till seven times, but till seventy times seven times,' i.e. an unlimited number of times. This is brought out also by St Luke: 'If thy brother offend against thee reprove him, and if he repent forgive him, and if he sin against thee seven times in a day, and seven times be converted to thee saying I repent, forgive him.' To weak human nature this may seem hard, but the teaching of our Lord admits of no choice but to accept.

No matter how many times we are injured, we must forgive without limit. No man will ever injure us so frequently as we sin against God; a lifetime of such injuries will never equal the guilt of a single sin against God.

So long as we are in an unforgiving frame of mind, God will accept nothing from us. 'If when thou offerest thy gift before the altar thou remember that thy brother hath anything against thee, leave there thy gift and be reconciled to thy brother, and then coming thou shalt offer thy gift.' It would be well to remember this when we come to offer ourselves to God in the Mass, to offer our submission and surrender of self to God. If we are unforgiving it will avail us nothing; our gift is not acceptable to God; we receive no graces or benefits from the Mass.

Sometimes we hear people say 'I forgive, but I cannot forget.' That is not true forgiveness; it is not God's way. In the 24th Psalm David pleads: 'The sins of my youth and my ignorance do not remember.' In Psalm 78, 'Remember not our former iniquities.' Not to forget, is to remember! It has been well written: 'Merely to forget an injury is not to pardon it, I prefer pardon to forgetfulness. Pardon is voluntary forgetfulness, while forgetfulness is involuntary pardon.' If we say that we forgive but cannot forget, it means that the injury is still rankling in the heart like a festering wound; it means that we still bear resentment against the one who injured us and it is impossible for our nature to refrain from allowing this to influence our attitude towards the offender. True forgiveness must include forgetfulness of the injury, the putting away of all resentment and bitterness, otherwise it is only partial pardon.

The spirit of resentment has embittered many lives. Secret resentment against another is a festering wound that grows worse with time, though the injured one may try to deceive himself into thinking he has forgiven. The impulse to resent injury is quick and obstinate; there is an instinct to punish injury; pride will not forget but by brooding magnifies the hurt so that we grow bitter, desire to vindicate self and to retaliate in some way. Thus we meet people who are 'not on speaking terms' or who admit to being 'out of friends' with someone which simply means that resentment is being retained which is incompatible with forgiveness. Yet such people say the 'Our Father' without a thought of what they are asking from God, and will go to Mass thinking they are doing their duty in every way.

Suppose a person humbling himself asks pardon which is refused, it will tend to make him bitter and further injury is the result. Two are then unforgiving about some paltry trifle out of all proportion to the offence. Families are much disturbed when two members are unforgiving. Two sisters refused to speak to each other for years, sending messages through the mother or pointing to what was needed at table instead of asking. To such lengths will an unforgiving spirit lead. In family life this causes embarrassment to all, the innocent suffer, but what matters it so long as pride upholds its dignity and achieves vindication!

These so-called injuries are mostly trivial and petty; one has not received the consideration expected or been passed over for another; one has been asked to do some work beneath his dignity and he feels insulted. A friend has failed to do a service through inability or other good reason and the friendship is broken off. We take offence where none is intended. Then we feel hurt, brood over it, foster resentment, become bitter, speak uncharitably, possibly resort to detraction, air our grievances and then kneel down and say 'Forgive us our trespasses as we forgive.' God forgive us indeed, we know not what we ask! Great injuries may be done at times, but probably few are really intentional. It is mostly a question of thoughtlessness and want of consideration. Nevertheless, even the greatest injury fully intended must be forgiven, if we hope to be forgiven in turn for the many sins against God laid to our account. The greatest human injury done to another cannot equal the guilt of any sin against God. The fact that the injury done entails sin is not our concern; that belongs to God who will repay and demand the full penalty. We can leave all our injuries in his loving care and forget whatever may have been done against us.

There is no need to go into motives for forgiveness of injuries. We have no choice, if we hope for pardon ourselves. God has laid it down as an essential condition of our own forgiveness for sin. That is sufficient motive in itself. Forgive and you will be forgiven. Refuse to forgive, and pardon will be denied to you in turn. To know all is to forgive all; but in this world it is utterly impossible for us to know all. How little we understand one another; we cannot judge what is intended, we do not know from what motives another acts, we cannot assess any injury at its true value, any more than we can assess the guilt of our own sins against God. Could we do this, then we should forgive, because we should know all. Hence it is that God demands that we forgive because we cannot judge the guilt of any act done by another.

An unforgiving spirit is usually the result of pride and forgetfulness of our own sins against God. If we learn to be truly humble, we shall learn to forgive.

'To err is human—to forgive divine.'

LV   REVENGE

St Paul writes to the Romans (XII, 18): 'If it be possible as much as is in you, have peace with all men ; revenge not yourselves, my dearly beloved; but give place unto wrath for it is written: Revenge is mine, I will repay, saith the Lord . . . be not overcome by evil, but overcome evil by good.'

Few would admit acting from motives of revenge or thinking of taking revenge; at times we may 'try to get our own back,' but revenge? Oh no, we should not think of it! We do like to call evil by nice-sounding names that veil the guilt in our estimation, and so delude ourselves that we are not guilty of the forbidden act.

A teacher once asked a small boy what revenge meant. The boy answered: 'Revenge is a low mean wish to pay back; revenge is mine saith the Lord.' The coupling of these two ideas may cause a smile—a low mean wish, and God's prerogative! Yet both ideas are perfectly true. Revenge belongs to God as an act of strict justice; but on our part it is a low mean act.

Revenge belongs to God alone because he alone is able to judge justly of the guilt of an offence according to its exact merit. 'Man seeth the thing that appears, but God seeth the heart.' When we punish, we can neither assess the guilt nor exact strict justice in the penalty, being always biased in our own favour or by other motives, nor do we know the facts fully. We do not see into the heart but judge from external appearances.

These are many things that influence acts. The 'crime' may be deliberate; it may be an accident; it may be caused by circumstances beyond our control; it may be the result of fear, persuasion or force; or there may be other causes that excuse or lessen guilt. We cannot know all the relevant facts in a case nor mete out justice in the exact balance required. How can we for instance gauge exactly how much fear entered into the act to excuse it? Only God can do that. God knows everything entailed and exacts penalty to the uttermost farthing, no more, no less. We, because of the bias in our own favour, magnify an evil beyond its deserts, demand more than the just due in payment. Hence God reserves to himself the right to take revenge. 'The anger of man worketh not the justice of God.' It is not fitting that man, so biased in his own favour, should punish any act against himself.

God having reserved this right of revenge to himself, if we presume to take revenge we steal what belongs to God alone; it is therefore a 'low mean act' on our part. Again, it it is 'low and mean' because it is not doing unto others as we would have them do to us. Should we err, we are ready with excuses to palliate the evil; we do not wish to be judged by what appears on the surface but by what we intended in our own hearts, known only to God and ourselves. God we cannot deceive, but others can only judge by what we say; therefore we try to make the evil appear less, try to explain it away, plead non-intention and so forth. We expect to be believed, to be excused; but are we willing to grant the same to others? It is low and mean to excuse oneself and refuse to accept excuses from others. It is that bias towards oneself that causes us to act in such manner, but it also proves how totally unfit we are to exact punishment from one who offends against us.

Revenge makes us hypocrites. We plead 'forgive us our trespasses as we forgive them that trespass against us' but still hope 'to get our own back on them' somehow—not in revenge; just 'paying them out.' We are hypocrites since we try to get revenge by calling it another name, by pretending it is something different. This desire 'to get our own back' is simply revenge and nothing else. It is also against charity which 'seeketh not her own.' Revenge paves the way for dissensions, quarrels, and such like. It divides families, societies, and parishes; creates divisions by enticing people to take sides in a dispute for the sake of petty revenge.

Usually methods of taking revenge are mean and paltry, and so are not grave breaches of the law. We do not resort to personal injuries of a grave nature, but what we do is certainly sinful, call it what we will; it is revenge and filching from God what belongs to him alone. It only escapes grave sin by its own pettiness, though if grave consequences do follow we are then guilty of grave sin. We try to make offenders feel uncomfortable in our presence, aware of our displeasure, we ignore them, refuse to speak to them, and do not answer when they question us—petty and trivial things but pointing to the desire for revenge.

Perhaps someone denies us the loan of an article we wish to borrow or refuses to do some favour we request. We consider it a slight and we wait till the 'offender' needs a similar favour and refuse it. Thus we 'get our own back' on him. It is mean and petty to act in such a way. Probably little harm is done, but the spirit of revenge is there. We cannot justify such acts as punishments; we have no right to punish equals. It is not unknown for persons to take revenge against God himself. The death of a child is made a cause of neglecting religion; the parents are angry with God for taking away a loved child, so they 'get their own back' by neglect of prayer and religion. It may be that someone has been offended by a priest, who is then 'paid out' by a refusal to attend the church at all. Instances of this can be found in many parishes; revenge is taken against God and his Church for fancied injuries. What a grave act it must be, to revenge oneself on God himself!

Our Lord gave us striking examples of refraining from revenge against those who injured him. In the garden when Peter struck off the ear of a servant, our Lord heals the wound and bids Peter lay up his sword. On Calvary he excuses his torturers on the plea of ignorance of what they did. Shall we who profess to follow him, do less than follow his example in our trivial affairs? Strangely enough the old law counselled revenge. Thus in Exodus XXI we read, 'an eye for an eye, tooth for tooth, hand for hand, burning for burning, wound for wound, stripe for stripe.' Such was the rough justice which meant doing to others as they do to you, and no doubt it prevented much evil. Our Lord completely reversed this old law. He says :'You have heard it said an eye for an eye, and a tooth for tooth, but I say unto you not to resist evil; but if one strike you on the cheek turn to him the other, and if a man contend with thee in judgment and take away thy coat, let go thy cloak also unto him . . . You have heard it said thou shalt love thy neighbour and hate thy enemy, but I say to you, love your enemies, do good to them that hate you, and pray for them that persecute you.' We are given a precept of love; we are not to seek revenge but to do good to any that injure us, to repay evil with good.

St Luke tells us that when our Lord came to a certain Samaritan town the people refused to receive him since he was a Jew. James and John were full of indignation and wanted to punish these people forthwith in no uncertain manner. 'Lord wilt thou that we command fire to come down from heaven and consume them?' Jesus rebuked them, saying: 'You know not of what spirit you are.' At times neither do we remember of what spirit we are, that we are ruled by a law of love and not by retaliation for injuries. Nothing could be plainer than the law that we must love our enemies, do good to those who hate us, and pray for any that do us an injury. That is the only way in which it is permitted to 'pay back.'

There is no other way for those who claim to be followers of Jesus Christ to repay injury except by kindness and prayer, leaving to God all the claim of justice to be satisfied. We avenge ourselves by returning benefits for injuries, and such vengeance is divine. St Stephen prayed for his murderers. He was much more grieved at the injury they were doing to their own souls than at anything they were doing to him. The Acts of the Apostles describes it thus: 'They stoned Stephen invoking and saying Lord Jesus receive my spirit. And falling on his knees he cried with a loud voice saying: Lord, lay not this sin to their charge. And he fell asleep in the Lord' (Acts VII). Thus did the first martyr to die for Christ follow faithfully in the footsteps of his master, by pleading forgiveness for his enemies, by returning good for evil.

He who refrains from returning evil for evil, or confers benefits on the one doing him an injury, puts such a one to shame and pacifies him. He who returns good for evil wins for himself an increase of grace, a fuller reward in heaven, and benefits his own soul. But he who seeks revenge is guilty of sin and injures his own soul.

It would be well to consider our actions in this matter. It

is quite possible that whilst we do not think nor admit that we seek revenge, at the same time we try to 'pay out' the offender, 'get our own back' on him, or return evil in some kind for the petty and trivial injury that we may have suffered. No matter how we may describe what we do, it amounts to taking revenge even though we call it by some other name and seek thus to lessen the appearance of guilt. When we try in some petty way to 'get our own back' on another, we are stealing from God a right that belongs to him alone, that he has reserved solely to himself. However small and paltry may be the way in which we thus repay evil, it shows an underlying spirit of revenge that is unchristian and definitely contrary to charity; we are returning evil for evil, seeking an eye for an eye and tooth for tooth. We must be on our guard against this tendency to exact penalties for injuries fancied or real. Resentment is quick to spring up in our nature, to retaliate in kind and seek to punish and only by watchfulness can we overcome and destroy this revengeful spirit, so often the outcome of pride and an unforgiving heart.

To seek revenge in any form is utterly opposed to the spirit of fraternal charity which is the mark of our Lord's followers. Be not deluded and self-deceiving by calling revenge by other names.

'Revenge is mine, saith the Lord. I will repay.'

LVI   CHEERFULNESS

The Book of Proverbs says: 'A glad heart maketh a cheerful countenance; but by grief of mind the spirit is cast down.' Some people think it a sign of piety and goodness to go about with a doleful mien as though they bore a world of woe on their shoulders, and pretend to be shocked at others who enjoy life with a smile; they look solemn and grave as though religion were a sad sort of affair with nothing cheerful in it. Nothing could be further from real piety. Holy Scripture bids us to be glad and rejoice, since nothing is so helpful as cheerfulness, nothing worse than gloominess of spirit. Being gloomy certainly does not aid spirituality, and our Lord bids us be of 'good cheer.' All spiritual writers insist on cheerfulness in religion and in the service of God. Religion was never meant to be a thing of gloom and sadness. To serve God should be a joy to us, otherwise it can scarcely be pleasing to God, who is supremely happy himself. The saints served God in joy and gladness of heart. This gladness of heart is very important in the spiritual life. The psalmist sings 'Be glad and rejoice ye just . . . sing joyfully to the Lord, serve ye the Lord with gladness.' Ecclesiasticus says: 'I have known that there was no better thing than to rejoice and do well in this life.' St Paul counsels the Philippians: 'Rejoice always in the Lord, again I say rejoice.'

The saints were noted for cheerfulness. St Francis of Assisi was known as 'the happy saint'; St Ignatius urges his disciples to gladness; St Dominic was always joyous. St Francis tells us that, with the exception of sin, nothing does so much harm as sadness and melancholy.

To a young poet who found it necessary for his art to go about looking sad and melancholy in order to create 'atmosphere,' St Catharine of Siena writes: 'Is not sadness the greatest of sins?' That seems rather a strong remark to make but the meaning is clear. Sorrow or sadness is not actually a sin in the real sense but its effect can be more harmful, because sadness, melancholy or despondency has a discouraging effect that inclines one to give up in despair.   Maybe we

CHEERFULNESS

are much tempted to a certain sin; after a long struggle we give in to the temptation. Then comes a feeling of hoplessness; we ask what good it is to try when we fail in the end; so sadness of spirit causes discouragement and slackening of effort, thus making another fall more easy. Even though we have failed, we can be cheerful about it and hope for better success next time; the effort to be cheerful in spite of failure will spur us on to greater efforts in the struggle; we shall continue to fight in spite of the fall. That is the only way to succeed; if we fall, we must rise again with a smile and a cheery spirit, refuse to be downcast by failure. It is no use worrying about what cannot be undone, better to repent and carry on cheerfully though maimed, with a smile refusing to be 'down and out,' to admit final defeat. Sorrow for sin does not mean melancholy and discouragement. We can be truly sorry and yet 'rejoice in the Lord,' since he is understandingly merciful: he will forgive and offer grace to carry on the struggle against evil. Cheerful striving in spite of falling will carry us further than despondency.

Joy gives glory to God, sadness in serving God deprives him of the glory—'the Lord loveth a cheerful giver!' Joy makes our service more perfect, more acceptable to God. We ourselves value service done cheerfully more than a grudging, grumbling service which robs it of any merit.

Joy helps us to persevere, we are glad to go on when we are happy in doing our allotted task. Never think that gloom and religion go hand in hand, nothing could be further from the truth. Our greatest joy in life should spring from religion, our relationship to God. There is no need to be sad and gloomy about serving God. 'Be glad and rejoice in the Lord.'

Cheerfulness pays also in our ordinary life; even though things go wrong it does not help to be sad about it; either we can change what is amiss, or it is beyond control; being 'blue' won't help matters in either case. As well as the effect sadness has on us personally, it also affects others with whom we come into contact; a long face gains no friends, no one cares for doleful company, for a 'wet blanket.' If we are given to grumbling and grousing, unloading our troubles on to others, we shall be shunned and avoided. So true is the saying 'Laugh and the world laughs with you; weep and you weep alone; for this brave old earth must borrow its mirth; it has troubles enough of its own. Rejoice and men will seek you; grieve and they turn and go; they want full measure of all your pleasure, but they do not want your woe.' Cheerfulness is infectious; so too is gloom which is not wanted. We cannot feel gloomy among cheery people; they will make us smile in spite of our troubles and help us to laugh trouble away. We must line up with the cheery folk, and get rid of dolefulness.

Cheerfulness can keep a lot of sin out of our lives. Grievances and long faces are inseparable. We cannot harbour a grievance with a smile; they don't fit together at all. The smile makes the grievance look silly.

If we see people talking and laughing together, we can be sure that they are not harbouring grievances, for people do not talk uncharitably when they are smiling. They may laugh at a person's whims and foibles, but there is no venom behind it, they are amused and think none the worse of the person. Hatred, jealousy, back-biting, scandal-mongering and such-like evils need gloom to make them seem real; a smile would take all the sting out of such sins and make them appear foolish which indeed they are. Next time a grievance is felt, try a smile; and the grievance will probably evaporate at once.

Look at nature. The day is dull and gloomy, rain falling, trees dripping, birds silent, the flowers appear listless, all looks miserable and there is no cheeriness anywhere. Then the sun shines. What a transformation! Clouds take on new forms, trees glisten with diamonds, birds break into song, the flowers riot in colour, and nature is glad—because the sun has smiled. A smile is the sunshine of life chasing away morbid thoughts and exorcising the gloomy spirit, turning all to cheeriness and joy.

Out of charity we ought to keep our sorrows to ourselves. If we have a bad headache, there is no need to pass it round in the form of gloom; others are not interested in our small aches and pains, they have their own to bear. Some one asked 'Does your father still suffer from neuralgia?' and the reply was

'Yes, but not so much as the rest of the family!' The meaning is obvious. If a person is really ill and in need of help, it is a different matter and help will be readily given; but the ordinary little discomforts of life should be borne in silence. We gain no sympathy by grumbling and complaining about trifles, yet how often we indulge in it.

If cheerfulness is infectious, gloom is infinitely more so. When we have been cheerful, we may have met a grumbler and a gloom descends on us; he has passed his gloom on, the joy has gone out of life. It is so much easier to affect a person with gloom than to cheer him up. Charity therefore demands that any such tendency in ourselves should be corrected. It is strange that, after a night's rest which should have refreshed and recreated the whole system, many rise in an irritable frame of mind, ready to find fault, and spread gloom over the household. This shows a great want of consideration. If it is difficult to be cheerful we can at least refrain from infecting others with our gloom, keep a still tongue so that we do not speak irritably. If we are shunned by others, it is probably often because of a gloomy disposition that we display.

We can cultivate cheerfulness as a habit by looking at the bright side of things and making the best of everything. An old lady was so cheerful always that people wondered. A friend asked her: 'You must have many clouds in your life, do you not?' 'Clouds,' she replied. 'Why yes, if we had no clouds where would all the blessed showers come from?' There is good in everything if we look for it, and therefore a reason to be cheerful.

There are times when everything seems to go wrong and life becomes burdensome. That is the time to smile! Brooding over things in a spirit of discontent and sadness will never improve the outlook; on the contrary it will tend to make things worse than they are. If all seems wrong and the future gloomy, and we are then tempted to give up whether in the spiritual or the natural order, let us try the effect of a smile. It will be like a ray of sunshine piercing the clouds; it cannot make things worse, but it may make them appear considerably brighter and help us to go on. Others, too, must be considered;

we have no right to infect them and rob them of their joy. It is far more helpful to ourselves and to others to make an effort to smile and be cheerful over troubles and difficulties. We all have at least a little bit of sunshine in our lives, something to be thankful for. By turning our faces to the sunshine instead of keeping in the shadows we can manage to be cheerful. It contributes to mental and bodily health to look always at the bright side of life, to live in the sun rather than in the shadow. To people who indulge in fits of the 'blues' everything seems wrong. Much would disappear if we could get into the habit of taking all cheerfully and seeing the bright side of things.

The inspired writer in the book of Ecclesiasticus says: 'There is no pleasure above the joy of the heart . . . better is death than a bitter life . . . give not up thy soul to sadness and afflict not thyself in thy own countenance. The joyfulness of the heart is the life of a man and a never-failing treasure of holiness, and the joy of man is length of life. Have pity on thy soul, pleasing God, and contain thyself. Gather up thy heart in his holiness and drive sadness far from thee, for sadness has killed many and there is no profit in it. Envy and anger shorten a man's days and pensiveness will bring old age before time . . . a cheerful heart is always feasting.'

LVII FORBEARANCE

'Bear ye one another's burdens and so you shall fulfil the law of Christ. Everyone shall bear his own burden' (Gal.:VI,2).

This is the practical application of charity in daily life. But at times we are at a loss to know how this law of charity in daily life is to be carried out.   Forbearance with others is practical charity, the carrying of another's burdens, the bearing of our own. What are these burdens?

All differ in character and temperament, no two persons are alike in these; this obvious fact is responsible for much want of charity, and the cause of burdens. Some are impulsive, others cautious; some affectionate, others cold and undemonstrative; some are active and lively, others sluggish and slothful. These diversities of character or temperament are found even among members of the same family, more so between fellow-workers and others with whom we come into contact during the day. When people of varied character are thrown together, especially in family life, there is bound to be some reaction, perhaps friction, between temperaments. One may 'get on our nerves' and often unpleasantness is caused, perhaps a quarrel breaks out over some trifle, unless we are forbearing and make allowances for differences of character.

What does forbearance mean? It means the exercise of patience, self-control, or keeping oneself in check. It is the patient endurance or toleration of what offends us in others, the refraining from retaliation or retribution, indulgence towards the fads and foibles in others, excusing the effects of temperament. Forbearance makes a great demand on charity. Take an example: One member of a family may have a very tidy disposition and hates to see the house disarranged. He or she takes trouble to put everything in a proper place (tidy persons can be a great nuisance!) and gets a sense of satisfaction when all looks neat and tidy in the home. In comes a careless member; a hat is thrown on a chair, a coat or parcel tossed on the table; papers are dropped on the floor and the tidy appearance of the room is disturbed. Naturally the first one has something to say about it, and it probably will not be too pleasant hearing. What happens? That will depend on forbearance being shown or not. 'A soft answer turneth away wrath.' Should the untidy member show forbearance, that is express regret quietly and remove the cause of offence, all will be well. But if the one chided blurts out 'Oh bother you and your tidiness!' then there are the elements of a family quarrel. Others may join in siding with one or the other; arguments get acrid and bitter; there is a rift in the family; harmony is destroyed, and charity is gone, simply through want of forbearance in the first place. It needs thought for other people, a realisation of difference in temperaments and mutual forbearance, with readiness to admit being in the wrong. Many unpleasant incidents in family life could be avoided by forbearance; it acquires a guard over the tongue, over the words used, over the tone of voice, over the whole demeanour, each of which may mean the difference between peace and discord. Much watchfulness is needed, and should one fail the other must be prepared to overlook the fault and by meekness keep peace.

Impulsive people want everything done at once, they cannot wait, do not know what patience means. Others are expected to set aside whatever they may be doing and give immediate attention to the demand made, or a harsh remark is uttered to hasten on the dilatory. Another feels that there is no need for hurry, to-morrow will do just as well. Think what a clash of temperament can result between two such opposite characters. There is much need of forbearance between them. The impulsive must learn to curb impatience; the dilatory learn to get a move on so that no cause for grievance arises, and peace is preserved between them.

There are numberless similar incidents in home life. How easily one who is affectionate is repelled and hurt by coldness shown to him. Another may be inclined to worry over trifles, but it does not help him if he is laughed at and told not to be silly; that only adds to his torment, whereas kindly sympathy and interest, pointing out the fruitlessness of such worry may be of real value to him.

Why is that we so often show less forbearance to the members of our family than to the casual stranger? Charity begins at home! We have the right to receive consideration from those nearest to us by ties of blood, we expect to be helped in bearing our burdens, especially such as are the result of the natural propensities in our nature. The bearing of another's burdens often means making due allowance for the difference of character in each individual and thoughtfully avoiding conflict by watchfulness over our own conduct.

Forbearance must be mutual, since we react on one another, and the duty of charity is binding on all. If a person 'gets on our nerves' the probability is that we in turn get on that person's nerves; but we forget how we may afflict him in the same way as we are afflicted by him. Some attract us; we get on with them easily; others repel us, and nothing they do is right in our eyes, but with such people there is a greater need of forbearance on our part. It needs constant watchfulness and care to avoid giving offence, and taking offence also. The untidy must learn to appreciate tidiness in others and take care not to offend in the matter. The impulsive must learn self-control and patience. Those who are sluggish and indolent must spur themselves to action so as not to irritate those who are more active. It is by thoughtfulness of such differences in others that forbearance is established and peace is preserved.

'But let everyone bear his own burden.' This is perhaps the real way in which to show forbearance, especially by not inflicting our whims and fads on other people. Each has his own peculiarities of character and temperament which may well be regarded as his own burden. We must know ourselves; our own temperament and inclinations and the way we give offence to others. Maybe we are too apt to blurt out angry words; a silent tongue would help there. Life would be happier if we were more thoughtful and learnt from past experience. Could we but see ourselves as others see us, we might get a rude shock; we might realise our own jarring peculiarities, manners or fads that disturb others, just as others disturb us. We may put a great strain on their forbearance with our mannerisms.

It is of no avail to say 'I can't help it' or 'I am made that

way, it is my nature' or to offer similar excuses. We must
overcome nature by grace. Life is a continual struggle against
deficiencies of nature and character. We are prone to evil
from childhood, it is our business to overcome that tendency
and we have no excuse for giving way to evil. We must fight
against and control the evil within whether it springs from
habit or temperament, and that applies to whatever may be
a source of annoyance to others. In modern days there is too
much talk of suppressed instincts, inhibitions and such like,
which is too often the excuse for what is merely bad temper,
self-indulgence, sloth and so on. Often we hear of people,
especially actresses, musicians, or painters, though they are
not the only ones, who give exhibitions of uncontrolled temper which is excused on the grounds of 'artistic temperament'
whereas it is simply want of ordinary self-control when things
do not suit. They have no right at all to trade on 'temperament' and cause others to suffer by their tantrums; they need
to learn self-control.

We may think how nice it would be if everyone did show
forbearance and made allowances for differences of character.
We agree, and then do nothing; we wait for someone else to
begin. But in this case we may wait for ever. St Paul wrote
on forbearance almost 2,000 years ago. How much heed has
been taken? It is a personal obligation laid on each one of us
to carry out this duty of charity. We must start with ourselves,
no matter if we are alone in the attempt. The world will be
just that much better at least for the effort we make. No matter
what others may do, each is bound to show forbearance as a
personal matter, to try always to return good for evil, to be
considerate for others, to remember their difficulties and peculiarities and make allowances for them. Each must also bear
his own burden, remembering how he may afflict others, bearing with patience the small trials thrust upon him by others.
'Blessed are the peace-makers for they shall be called the
children of God.' Each must make concessions for the sake
of peace by the avoidance of what offends and causes strife.
Some are peaceable enough so long as they get their own way
but the least contrary thing irritates them—like stagnant

water, which is well enough when left alone, but emits a horrid stench when stirred up. If we knew more of one another, how much more love, pity, compassion and generous feeling there would be in the world! It is from ignorance of one another's trials and afflictions that we judge so hardly and sometimes most unjustly. Want of understanding is the cause of much unpleasantness between people. Did we try to understand, we might be more easily able to bear the burdens of others as well as our own. Forbearance is the outcome of true charity, and we are each personally bound to do all we can to keep peace and concord with all.

'Bear ye one another's burdens—let every man bear his own burden.'

LVIII SELFISHNESS

Probably the most prevalent vice of the present day is selfishness or excessive self-love. Many think that selfishness is
simply want of generosity in sharing things with others; but
that is only one aspect of this vice. Selfishness means the putting of self in the first place regardless of others; seeking one's
own interest, pleasure, or personal advantage without any
consideration of the needs of others. This is contrary to
charity which 'seeketh not her own.' The selfish person always
seeks his own. St Paul writes to the Corinthians: 'Christ died
for all that they also who live may not now live unto themselves,
but unto him.' To live unto oneself is selfishness.

The idea of 'self' is coupled with many mo.e words and
nearly always means something vicious—thus self-love, self-
indulgence, self-willed, self-seeking, self-importance, self-
gratification, self-complacency and a host of others. Love is
the strongest of all motive powers, but it needs directing
into a proper channel lest it centre in self alone. Why do we
lose our temper, get sulky, remain obstinate, become covetous?
Because of self. Vanity is self-love; idleness is self-indulgence;
opposition to authority springs from self-importance. Thus
self enters into many faults and is their underlying cause:
we 'live unto ourselves and not unto God.' This vice, especially
if strongly marked, is odious; yet many hardly consider it a
sin or vice, though obviously it is contrary to 'self-denial'
which is obligatory on the follower of Christ. It is the root-
cause of most of the great evils of the day through self-seeking.

By a fundamental and ineradicable law of nature we all desire
happiness. God, who fashioned our nature, wishes us to be
happy as he is happy, even more than we wish it ourselves,
but more wisely. He has given us the true means of happiness,
which is usually the very opposite of what we seek. In great
measure selfishness springs from the desire of happiness,
hence in seeking self-gratification we hope to find happiness;
self is the centre of all things. Strange as it may seem, but
unquestionably true, the very opposite is the best means to
happiness. The real secret of happiness is to forget self and be

unselfish to others. We all admire unselfishness—in others; we all dislike selfishness—in others; but we cannot see that it would pay us to be unselfish in ourselves. It is a mistake to imagine that some are endowed with unselfishness as a natural virtue. Those who are less selfish have become so by overcoming natural tendencies. The more selfish a person is the quicker he is to suspect selfishness in others lest they thwart his own desires. He sees selfishness in others as inimical to himself, and is ready to accuse others of it. The world, of course, always contrary to the teachings of Christ, advocates seizing all for self to advertise self. Self-advancement is one of the world's tenets, to get on in life regardless how others may suffer in consequence. It may perhaps appear that the selfish get on best in this life; but they certainly do not find happiness. 'Let a man deny himself' is a key to happiness, amongst other things.

Let us see how selfishness grows from childhood. The untrained child is naturally selfish, his only notion of happiness is to have all he wants as soon as he wants it. It is a matter of some trouble to teach him and make him understand that it is not good for him to have his own way all the time. Too many parents fail to teach their child to be unselfish, rather teach him to be selfish by giving in to his whims and tempers. Selfish and comfort-loving themselves, these parents find it too much trouble to teach a child to be unselfish, not to expect every desire to be gratified; it is easier to take the line of least resistance and let him have what he wants to save trouble. In consequence there is a spoilt child' who is a nuisance to all, irritating others by his continual wants, crying with temper when denied and in general discontented. To save bother the parents give in to him and selfishness increases. One sees utter disregard on the part of some parents to the annoyance caused to others by such a child. Thus when in a train travelling with others, such a child makes a nuisance of himself to all. First at one window, then at the other side, treading on people's feet, putting sticky hands on their clothing, making noises or crying, and being a nuisance generally. The parents take no notice, being themselves too selfish to be considerate of others.

THE EVERYDAY CATHOLIC

So long as they are not bothered, such parents care little whether the child is annoying other people. In years to come they have to pay the price of this neglect; but the blame lies entirely on themselves and they deserve no sympathy at all.

Cardinal Newman defined a gentleman as 'one who has consideration for others.' No selfish person has the right to be styled a gentleman (or a lady) since thought for others is only gained by unselfishness. At home many are very selfish; that is the place where we are 'ourselves' in truth. We are not selfish with the casual stranger, because experience teaches that selfishness does not always pay; but to the home-folk such consideration is not shown. If harmony is to be preserved there must be mutual consideration, but at home the need for this is not recognised and we become 'natural,' selfish and inconsiderate. The selfish one leaves the burdens to others, he does not like disagreeable tasks, others can do those. After a meal, instead of helping to clear away, to wash up and tidy the place, he will get a book to read, or go out, leaving the work to others; but if asked to give a hand becomes unpleasant about it; therefore he is left alone. The selfish person makes as much noise as he likes, but complains if others make a noise. At table he takes the best, or as much as he wants, without considering whether there will be sufficient for the rest. If asked to make up a number for a game, he refuses because he wants to do something to please himself. In most circles the will of the majority counts, but not to the selfish person who cares nothing for majorities but only for himself. He alone is to be considered in his own estimation. Little wonder that selfish people are not popular with others!

Why should we be unselfish? Because it is virtuous and meritorious and pleasing to God. Also it is part of the law of charity to give way to the needs of others, to be thoughtful and considerate; most of all because it is a precept laid on all. 'Let a man deny himself.' Our Lord has told us: 'He that loseth his life, for my sake, shall find it.' In its widest sense this means that we shall find our true life, and also true happiness, in the emancipation of the soul from the narrow bonds of self-seeking. Only by setting aside the narrow self can one find his true self, that nobler, greater self, which is born of the realisation of the true relationship between God, ourselves, and our fellow-man.

The man who is selfish lives a narrow existence bounded by his own outlook, centred wholly on himself and his desires. He is always afraid that he will lose his happiness if he cannot satisfy his desires, or that someone else will take what he wants for himself. He is shunned because of his want of consideration, and becomes bored and miserable because he is confined by the narrow bounds of self. He is to be pitied in a sense. He that can please nobody is not so much to be pitied as he whom nobody can please, which is often the state of the selfish man. No one can please him because he is suspicious that he may be the loser by their good intentions.

In olden days the world was thought to be the centre of the universe about which all else revolved. Later it was discovered that the world is but a small planet in the great solar system. The selfish man thinks that he is the centre of his own world with others to minister to his needs. We have to grasp the truth that we are very diminutive units in the whole and that the general good is of far more importance than individual good. This is true of the family, society, the Church. In a word, the more we sink self in the interest of the whole, so much the more do we become true to our better self, and raise the whole tone of our character. This does not mean that we must give way to others on every occasion. Thus parents make a grave mistake in giving way to their children always. But we must be prepared to give way where principle is not involved.

We have only to look round the world to-day and see the great evils produced by self-seeking on the parts of individuals and of nations. Marriage is wrecked by selfishness on the part of husband or wife who takes all and gives nothing. Home life is made uncomfortable by the selfishness of the children. Workers are paid niggardly wages so that the profits of the wealthy may be increased for their own selfish ends. Nations oppress the weaker and filch their lands by force to gain more wealth and power. The world verges more and more towards chaos and oppression.

By unselfishness man best serves God and his neighbour. Never need we fear that our own interests will suffer if for God's sake we put self in a subordinate place. It may appear that the self-centred get on best in this world, but they are not truly happy and gain no merit in the life to come. True happiness comes from forgetfulness of self; thus the selfish miss all true happiness. Unselfishness pays because it begets happiness that will not grow stale, nor leave regrets in passing, but gives a sweet memory of joy given to others. It saves us from disappointments if we cannot have our own way, and removes anxiety about our own desire. The Master gives us an example—'He emptied himself.'

LIX ENVY AND JEALOUSY

Envy and jealousy are two prevalent vices which do much harm between individuals and in society. Usually these vices are kept secret since no one cares to admit to being guilty of such mean and despicable faults of which all are ashamed. Much good work can be spoilt through the effects of these sins by the interference and annoyance of others.

What is meant by envy and jealousy? Envy is sadness at another's good, as though it were in some way an evil to oneself. Jealousy is sadness at not being able to keep exclusively for oneself what is claimed as one's own. Thus to dislike hearing another praised instead of receiving the praise oneself is envy. Disgruntledness resulting from some friend's being with another instead of oneself is jealousy. In practice little difference is made in the use of the terms, but it is best to have a clear understanding of what they actually indicate.

Envy is sadness, displeasure, or resentment felt against another because he possesses some good, e.g. esteem, honour, rank, success, or ability, the lack of which in oneself is considered to be our injury. This reference to 'self' is the characteristic sign of envy. Displeasure at another's good without any reference to self is 'hatred.' If such displeasure refers to an undeserved honour being given to someone thought to be unworthy of it, but without any reference to self, it is indignation. Envy considers the possession of 'good' by another to be an injury to self. It is always unlawful to consent to envy.

Jealousy concerns itself with an apparent violation of one's right to exclusive possession, arising from a love which desires to have the sole ownership of what is loved. Jealousy may be quite lawful! If one has in fact the right to exclusive ownership of any good, then jealousy is lawful. In the book of Josue (Ch. 24), God is said to be 'a holy God, mighty and jealous,' because he claims the exclusive right to be served by men. St Paul wrote to the Corinthians (II, XI): 'I am jealous of you with the jealousy of God,' because they had been unfaithful to his teachings. A wife who is saddened because her husband

287

pays attentions to other women, having vowed fidelity to her alone, is lawfully jealous. If, however, one is jealous because a friend takes notice of others, such jealousy is unlawful, since friendship does not confer exclusive right of possession. Of their nature these vices are mortal sins, being included in the seven deadly sins, and prolific causes of other sins. Both are seen more in their effects than in themselves since they are secret vices. Both are contrary to charity and mercy.

Holy Scripture warns us against these vices. 'Let us not be made vain-glorious, envying one another.' 'Charity envieth not.'

Envy rejoices over another's misfortune, grieves over another's prosperity, grows into hatred seeking revenge, tries to belittle by whispering and detraction, gives way to mean and petty acts of annoyance. If the sins are not always mortal sins it is because they may be concerned with trivial and petty matters, or there may be want of advertance or only partial consent of the will. These vices are much too common, and often we are quite blind to their presence and to the sins that spring from them. We can see the result and can understand the gravity of the sin from its effect. The downfall of the human race was the result of Satan's envy of human happiness; Cain, envious of the preference shown to the sacrifices of Abel, slew him. Joseph was sold by his brethren into captivity, though they first intended to murder him. Christ was put to death on the cross through the envy of the pharisees. Is there any length to which these vices will not go?

Envy and jealousy spring from the idea that in our opinion our self-esteem is diminished by what some other enjoys. They are such mean vices that we try to keep them hidden, but they display themselves in a variety of ways. As the Canticle of Canticles has it: 'Love is as strong as death, jealousy as hard as hell.' The jealous person is capable of going to any lengths, no matter how sinful, to vindicate himself. Attempts are made to destroy or deprive another of the good he enjoys by detracting from his reputation or honour, by pointing out his faults, by minimising any good he may do, by trying to make him sad or unhappy, rejoicing if ill befall him, and in many similar ways. Hence though either envy or jealousy are hidden, they become apparent in the effects resulting therefrom.

Envy tries to appear as zeal for good, pretends to be shocked at the behaviour of another, exclaiming 'It is not right!' or imputing evil motives so that honour or esteem is withheld. So often things are 'not right' because we cannot have the enjoyment of them ourselves. It is merely envy posing as zeal for right.

Though we try to keep these mean vices secret and hidden, we are given to brooding over wrongs; as a worm gnawing at the heart, poison is working in our lives, and though outwardly we may appear happy yet within we are seething with discontent and desire for revenge and vindication. In some moment of provocation these vices burst forth, unable longer to be contained, and the inmost feelings are displayed in some petty revenge. If we would only air our grievances at the outset instead of brooding over them and magnifying them in secret, we should probably see the foolishness of it all. Envy or jealousy, both are foolish because no good can come out of them; and secret brooding simply increases and aggravates the mischief within. It is said that there can be no true love without jealousy. That is false. Of its very nature jealousy is utterly selfish, whereas true love ought to be unselfish and consider first the happiness of the one loved. Jealousy always takes away the happiness of both parties.

We are jealous because we fear that we are missing something, the happiness of the beloved counts for nothing unless such happiness comes through us alone. Is not that selfishness? When the one we love is happy, we ought to rejoice in such happiness no matter whence it springs; but we grieve over it, try to hurt and quarrel because some other has been the giver of happiness. Jealousy springs from want of trust; true love is always trustful. Jealousy is self-love, not love for another, and deprives of happiness instead of giving it.

What is the effect on us? Jealousy makes us sad, destroys happiness and peace of mind, causes us to hurt others, to be irritable and brood over a fancied slight, drives us to self-pity, to speak uncharitably—it makes fools of us! What is the effect of our jealousy on others? It turns them against us, makes them unhappy and angry with us for being so unreasonable. It utterly defeats its own object by alienating all affection for us, instead of attracting that esteem which we desire. Nothing can be so foolish and inimical to our own good. No one likes a jealous person, since such a one is always 'touchy' in his feelings, ready to see slights where none are intended and unreasonable in his demands on others.

We cannot claim anyone exclusively as our own outside the bonds of wedlock. Even in marriage there must be reasonable cause ere it can be lawful. But often there is petty and unreasonable jealousy between husband and wife. For envy no justification can be possible at all.

We have to admit that we cannot help feeling jealous at times since our feelings are entirely not under control. But we need not consent in will to the vice. We can prevent jealous feelings from overcoming reason and forcing us to act in so foolish a manner. We must withhold all consent to feelings of jealousy or envy lest they rob ourselves and others of happiness and cause us to sin. Like all other temptations, such emotions can and must be fully resisted and crushed down, ignored and fought against lest they influence our actions and lead us into sin. To overcome them we must seek that aid from God without which we are helpless. To do anything good we need God's help; all success comes through him. Others owe their esteem or rank to the will of God, and we, by recognising God's will, can avoid envy of another's good. Moreover it may be a great trial to human nature to find that others are preferred to us by the friend we love, but even friendship is a gift of God. Christ himself suffered in this way. Barabbas was preferred to him by those for whom he had done so much. Can we not find consolation in being like Christ in this and overcome our hurt emotions?

Much harm is done to religion by envy and jealousy in societies, choirs or sodalities connected with the church. Good work is hindered, cliques formed and factions war against each other. One is jealous because another sang a solo; another

290

is envious of one elected to a position of authority in a guild; there is envy of praise given to hard work, and so on. Where there should be naught but charity and zeal for the good of the whole, we find discord, petty bickerings, strife and bitter feeling, spoiling the work for God among souls. Each should search his own heart for any sign of envy or jealousy concerning his rights as a member of a society or guild. He may find that good work is being hindered by his envious or jealous attitude. Capable people are held back and dare not use their many talents since they know from bitter experience that they may be misjudged and criticised through the envy or jealousy of others, when only charitable co-operation should be found. Thus much harm is done; workers become cynical and unwilling because of the deep-rooted spirit of envy or jealousy among Christ's followers.

Well, indeed, are these mean vices classed among the deadly sins.

'Charity envieth not.'—'Jealousy is as hard as hell.'

LX PREJUDICE

Jane Austen wrote a novel which she entitled *Pride and Prejudice*. These are two faults that often go hand in hand. Prejudice is quite a common thing and affects persons, actions, customs and various other items. Pride steps in to prevent prejudice being admitted or corrected, and causes stubbornness in clinging to false opinions. Prejudice may be defined as an attitude of mind towards persons or things producing a bias in favour of, or adverse to, such persons or things and a judgment on them before adequate knowledge of the facts has been obtained. The word is derived from the latin *prae* meaning 'before' and *judex* meaning a 'judge.' Thus opinions formed on mere hearsay, or when but little is known of the facts, or refusing to be influenced by those better informed, are prejudices.

Take a simple example: A person is to start work among strangers. Almost immediately he forms the opinion that 'A' is a cantankerous person, irritable and quarrelsome, but 'B' is charming, sociable, and affable. Influenced by this information, the newcomer will have a formed opinion adverse to 'A' but biased in favour of 'B.' He is prejudiced. 'A' is placed at considerable disadvantage to 'B' since he will have to contend against an adverse bias, whereas 'B' enjoys a predisposition in his favour. 'A' has to break down prejudice which is always a difficult matter. Now the original opinion may have been quite incorrect, resulting from a meeting with 'A' and 'B' in circumstances which gave an entirely erroneous impression of their true characters. Hence it is obvious how much harm can be done by prejudice in favour of or against any person by forming an opinion of their characters without sufficient knowledge, perhaps on the mere word of another person. When we receive any information about a person, we must always reserve judgment until we have sufficient knowledge to form a balanced opinion. It is unjust to form a prejudice judgment, which may later be very difficult to break down.

The same notion is applicable to actions. Our objection to

others doing certain things may be simply the result of pre-judice. Much in the social code depends on prejudice. At times someone is courageous enough to flout social customs but at the risk of ostracism. Not so many years ago it was unheard of that ladies should smoke. Many, chiefly old folk, are preju-diced against it and say that it is 'wrong.' That word 'wrong' is much overworked and misused; it means so many things, from real sin to what is no more than personal dislike. Many so-called 'wrongs' are simply prejudice because we feel a per-sonal disapproval, often unreasonable, of certain modes of action. New customs are generally held to be 'wrong' by the old regime through prejudice.

Prejudices are found even in regard to sin; not that good can ever be evil, or evil become good, but that erroneous judg-ments are made as to the guilt of certain types of sin, or because some ecclesiastical law is changed. The Church has the power and the right to change any law which she has made. When the Holy Father changed the law of abstinence, so that when a holyday of obligation falls on Friday it is permissible to eat meat, there were those who said he had no right to make the change, and refused to eat meat on such days. That was due to prejudice and such people were wrong in their attitude. The same thing happened when children of seven years were permitted to receive Holy Communion; it took several years to break down the prejudice against this change of custom.

The fact that we tend to regard certain types of sin as being more grave than others results from our being influenced by the world's opinions. Hence prejudices are formed which are contrary to the teachings of the Church but very difficult to correct because we cling so closely to our formed opinions.

The needs of civilization make light of certain grave sins because modern conditions are said to demand a change. The Church is blamed for being old-fashioned when she con-demns such sins. Prejudice in favour of them is created by listening to the judgments of eminent, but irreligious, scient-ists rather than to what the 'old-fashioned' Church, the guar-dian of truth, teaches.

We judge people by the same standards. Certain sins have no attraction for us; but should others be guilty of them, we judge them harshly without any knowledge of the temptations they experience, the fight they put up against temptation, or other circumstances which lessen guilt on their part. We forget that only the grace of God keeps us free from sin. It may be that God keeps such temptations from us because of our weakness, maybe it is only want of opportunity that keeps us free from such sin. We have little claim to merit. Do we not judge others harshly when we find them in circumstances in which we ourselves would certainly have fallen into sin? We judge others by ourselves, but prejudiced in our favour we judge lightly of our own misdeeds while condemning others. Maybe the sin of pride which condemns is far more grave than the sin it condemns.

How are prejudices formed? Sometimes by family tradition which judges acts innocent in themselves to be wrong; children are taught that things are not right because the parents are of that opinion without sufficient reason. The children grow up with this prejudice firmly fixed and condemn all who do such acts as guilty of sin. Such ideas take a lot of uprooting. For example, a father may on one occasion go to a place of amusement where he witnesses some performance which he considers indecent. He judges the place by that one incident, tells the family that it is an indecent place of amusement and the family tradition is formed. The children see other people going to this place and judge them guilty of enjoying indecent shows. Later they may go themselves and believe themselves guilty of sin in so doing because of family prejudice. It is the old story of giving a dog a bad name.

Environment gives rise to prejudice. A boy brought up in the slums is taught to regard the rich as oppressors, grows up hating them, and thinks nothing of stealing from them if the chance of so doing occurs. How can we blame him when we realise that he acts from prejudice formed at home?

When our prejudices begin to affect the liberty of others, it is time we looked into them and uprooted them. Prejudice too often sets up a standard of conduct which we expect all to follow. What right have we to set ourselves up as the judges of what others should or should not do? We are moved largely by our prejudices, which militate against our ability to form a correct judgment and are a sign of ignorance.

Prejudice may be the outcome of a false conscience making lawful things sinful or sinful things lawful. The bad example of parents may be a cause of prejudice in the children. If parents do wrong, children imitate them in ignorance and so form a false conscience. If parents condemn innocent things, children do likewise. Hence the need of adequate knowledge before we can judge rightly. Especially in matters of conscience must we be on our guard against forming opinions without sufficient knowledge or judgments based on the prejudices of others. We cannot afford to make grave mistakes in matters of conscience which is the final guide to all action. Strange it is how we cling to the opinions of others, no better informed than ourselves and utterly unfitted to give counsel on matters affecting the soul. It is but common sense to inquire from a priest whose knowledge fits him to give true advice, what is to be done when we are in doubt about matters affecting the moral or religious life. We should not be lax-minded, without guiding principles, nor should we be narrow-minded which is the effect of ignorance; but we ought to be open-minded, willing to learn truth and be guided by the proper authorities before we presume to form judgments, and when authority has spoken to be convinced and unprejudiced.

In the Epistle to the Romans, St Paul writes: 'One believeth that he may eat all things, but he that is weak let him eat herbs. Let not him that eateth dispise him that eateth not... Who art thou that judgest another man's servant?... For one judgeth between day and day; and another judgeth every day... let us not therefore judge one another any more... I know, and I am confident in the Lord Jesus, that nothing is unclean of itself; but to him that esteemeth anything to be unclean, to him it is unclean.'

Here we see the workings of prejudice. The Jewish converts still retained their prejudice against eating 'unclean meats' such as pork, but the Gentile converts ate all kinds of meat. For this they were condemned by the prejudice of the Jewish converts who still clung to the old regime though it had been abolished by the New Law. St Paul has to admonish them, since they were condemning each other in their ignorance as being guilty of evil ways. Other laws which had been changed also caused prejudices and dissensions among early converts to christianity. We must learn not to be influenced by what is simply prejudice and avoid passing judgment on the actions of others unless we are certain that we have adequate knowledge on which to form a true opinion. We must be quite certain that our judgments are not the result of personal prejudices.

'Let not then our good be evil spoken of.' (Rom. XIV).

LXI   CRITICISM

The word 'critic' is taken from the Greek and signifies a 'judge'; hence to criticise is to pass judgment. Originally it was applied solely to art and literature, now it applies almost to everything, work, personalities, achievements. Criticism may have far reaching effects, therefore it is wise to consider what may result from our criticisms, since either good or evil may be produced. We are all apt to criticise without giving sufficient thought as to the possible consequences that may follow therefrom. Unfortunately criticism is usually associated with something harsh and unpalatable, though this need not be so. True criticism is not merely depreciation of some person or his achievements, which too often is simply fault-finding, the lowest form and the most harmful type of criticism since it goes no further than to expose defects or mistakes without any recognition of the beauty or worth that there may be in the thing criticised. True criticism goes much deeper than the discovery of defects. Faults are found indeed, but only that these may be removed and improvement be made. Mere fault-finding is of little value and may do harm, but the discovery of real underlying value is of real worth.

Each soul is endowed with the faculty of criticism, or passing of judgment on merit or demerit, for its own safeguard. Too often it is used from motives of pride, vanity, jealousy or displeasure and not from any desire of discovering truth or beauty. To follow blindly in any path is unwise, wherefore the faculty of judging comes into play as a guide to what is best and thus helps to the making of a wise choice. Thus hero-worship is unwise unless a true judgment is formed in regard to the character of the hero. Is he worth following? What are his good points? What are his weaknesses, faults or defects? These must be weighed in the balance and judgment made as to the probable outcome, good or bad, of the influence he will exert on our own character through proximity to him or admiration of him. True criticism will thus be a safeguard against giving our allegiance to one who is unworthy. Before we can truly criticise we must have sufficient knowledge of the subject or our judgment will be faulty. Too often we criticise without requisite knowledge and a 'rash judgment' is formed. Ignorance produces a judgment that is unbalanced or possibly quite erroneous; we are not in a position to judge if we are ignorant of the subject. A wise man keeps silent when he is conscious of ignorance of the topic under discussion. Sufficient knowledge is a primary requisite of any criticism; if we criticise in ignorance we are guilty of rash judgment and when this concerns the good name or character of another it may be sinful; restitution will be of obligation if harm has been caused.

Criticism is of two kinds. One is helpful, creative and encouraging; the other is mere fault-finding, disheartening and destructive. Unfortunately destructive criticism is by far the more prevalent; it is easy to find fault, difficult to be helpful. It is mostly the result of presuming to criticise without having sufficient knowledge of the subject to be helpful. Fault-finding usually gets a person's back up, discourages and destroys effort, and achieves no good. Here is an example: A young artist painted a picture, which was admittedly crude and poor as most first attempts are, but it showed budding talent. He asked another artist to criticise it. This latter, fully aware of the defects, saw the underlying possibilities, and gave the picture a certain amount of praise as a first attempt, then in a kindly way showed how it could be improved and weak points avoided, and encouraged the young artist to go on to better work. A few years later, when much progress had been made, the young man desiring more help and advice showed his work to another artist who said after a cursory glance at the work, 'You do not know the first principles of drawing' and dismissed the matter. Can we blame the young artist for putting this churlish criticism down to jealousy? Here was a case of harsh fault-finding, no attempt to help of any sort, and not productive of any good at all. Suppose the young artist had met with this sort of criticism at the outset of his career, he would probably have been too discouraged to continue painting and the world would have been deprived of some great masterpiece.

Kindly criticism can be of the greatest service and give encouragement to persevere in any work, but fault-finding merely discourages and prevents further attempt at achievement. How do we usually criticise? Do we help others or throw cold water on their attempts and make them feel that they can do no good? If one person strike another, he can be brought up for assault; but if he gives a mental 'knock-out' no remedy is available. Bodily injury may soon be cured and forgotten, but a mental injury causing discouragement and producing perhaps an 'inferiority complex' often affects a whole life and puts a stop to any future career. Such complexes are often the result of harsh criticisms which are a species of mental knock-out. We do not realise how adverse criticism may affect the whole of another's life and prospects, making him fear to attempt certain things which they could so easily do with practice and experience. It produces nervousness when in the company of others and timidity when asked to do anything; it gives a feeling of uselessness at least in one sphere of action and may prevent much good work from being accomplished.

In one of our large cities a grave tragedy resulted from unkind fault-finding and ridicule. A young girl working in a factory was untidy and slovenly in dress and deportment. Her work-mates criticised her unmercifully about her appearance; this she took to heart very much and made some attempts to improve her appearance. These attempts were greeted with scorn and derisive laughter. A few days later she did not turn up to work and was later found drowned in a canal. The verdict was suicide whilst of unsound mind. No one was punished. There was no way of fixing the guilt on any party. But what was God's verdict? There was a definite moral responsibility for a lost life resulting from adverse criticism without any consideration of possible results.

This is an extreme example, but it serves to show to what lengths a person may be driven by criticism of the wrong kind, criticism that we should not care to have on our conscience could we know the result. The law of charity demands that we shall help and encourage, not dishearten or drive to despair. In the above case a word or two of encouragement, a little kindly help, might have saved a life; but no one gave it, no one was wise enough to see the underlying good shown by the serious attempt to improve.

The poet Longfellow wrote: 'Many critics are like wood-peckers, who, instead of enjoying the fruit and shadow of a tree, hop incessantly around the trunk, pecking holes in the bark to discover some little worm or other.' How very true! We are ready to seek out blemishes, to find the worm, but fail to see the good that lies around or beneath. If criticise we must, then let us first fit ourselves with the knowledge necessary to pass a true judgment. The true critic has not only sight, but insight or discernment, can see not only the obvious on the surface but also what is hidden under the exterior however unprepossessing it may appear. Here is one trying to do good work in some cause. Do we see more than the mistakes made? If not then we are not fit to criticise. There must be some good, otherwise that person would not try to help; there is enthusiasm which if directed in the proper way, will be a great asset. Why quench this ardour by finding fault when a little direction kindly given may produce fine results? Some need to have mistakes pointed out in a kindly way; they are anxious to give of their best. If harshly criticised they will give up all effort and feel useless. Particularly with young people must we be careful how we criticise their efforts. They are sure to make mistakes through want of experience, but they have enthusiasm which needs to be directed into the right channel. They have a creative instinct which is unformed, and an unkindly criticism may kill this desire of achievement and destroy all incentive to produce anything with their many talents.

We meet people who have a dread of doing some certain thing which others do without concern. If we could peer into the past, it might be seen to be the result of destructive criticism. If a duty obliges such a one to do what he dreads so greatly, it means untold agony to him because of the complex formed, and someone is responsible before God for this needless burden of fear. We must always remember that our criticism may do untold harm which can never be effaced. We should never cast down what we cannot rebuild in a better way. Anyone can knock a building down, but it takes skill to build any structure. It takes a steady hand to build a house

300

with a pack of cards, a mere breath will destroy it; so a mere word unkindly spoken may destroy what it takes a skilful mind to produce. When we do criticise we should always try to help, not to hinder; to encourage, not to dishearten; to create not to destroy. Look for the hidden good; it is always there if we will seek it; and when found, give it praise. The pharisees were always criticising our Lord; he never pleased them; they found fault with all he did. Shall we imitate them? Our Lord would not 'quench the smoking flax'—he saw good in all and tried to bring it out. That is what we also must do, giving encouragement to all to use their talents to the best of their ability. Fault-finding is never a true judgment; it is uncharitable, productive of harm, and unworthy of a reasonable being.

LXII TRUST

'Can you be trusted?' Were we asked that question, most of us would at once reply 'of course I can.' We might even feel it to be an aspersion on our honour to be asked such a question. We pride ourselves on being trustworthy because we should not dream of taking what belongs to another—our idea of trust generally concerns material possessions, and we forget there are other things more precious which may be entrusted to our keeping. It is not so certain as we imagine, perhaps, that we are worthy of being trusted. Thus spiritual things demand a far greater trust than the money we would scorn to filch. Character, reputation, confidences, secrets, are all very precious possessions which cannot be bought at any price. Dare we trust such things to another? Dare we trust even our best friend with the secrets of the heart? Dare he trust us? Many fail very lamentably in such matters. Trust means feeling secure about the veracity, probity, sympathy and prudence of another.

Personal secrets and confidences are sacred things too often lightly regarded and made the subject of gossip. We do not mean to be traitors to truth and the innocence of others; we do not rate such things very highly or else excuse ourselves on the plea that no promise of secrecy was given or asked for, not recognising that no promise of secrecy was exacted because we were wrongly thought to be trustworthy. This faith, this belief in our honesty should have been its best security and our failure under the test is proof that we are not trustworthy.

In business affairs there is often much more probity and trust than in personal confidences. 'The children of this world are wiser in their generation.' Business men will have no dealings with one who is unable to keep information to himself; there are too many business secrets which may not be made public to trust anyone without certainty of his keeping such matters secret; much harm might be done to hundreds of investors if secret transactions leaked out before the time. In the realm of confidences, friendship and love, our conscience is not so sensitive; confidences of priceless worth to a soul are given to us because we are deemed worthy of trust, but too frequently such trust is misplaced. Maybe one has a heavy burden to carry, too heavy to bear alone; advice is needed, or it will help to confide in another and discuss the matter. A bitter burden shared with a sympathetic friend takes away much of the bitterness and makes it easier to bear; such is the ideal. Alas, how often it turns out to be the opposite and the bitterness is increased when it is discovered that gossip has made the secret known to others. The temptation to tell what we know is strong, the fact that a secret is not our property but another's quite forgotten; we 'did not mean any harm,' but another soul is disillusioned, has lost faith in us and will not trust us again. He is, perhaps, condemned always to keep his secrets locked in his own breast, suffering from anxieties and sorrows that may not be shared, because we failed to be worthy of trust and he dare not risk another such betrayal. The older one grows, the more reticent one becomes about much that would be better shared with a friend, but it is kept hidden through such a fear. Should another wish to relate to you a matter 'in strict confidence' which he himself has received 'in strict confidence' also, refuse to listen; but mark that person down as untrustworthy since he obviously cannot keep faith with another. To be worthy of trust needs sympathy and understanding; it is a part of charity to bear another's burden, share another's trouble, but it must be kept locked in the heart as a sacred trust that may on no account be divulged. There is a moral aspect to this question involving grave sin. Just as sincerity and fidelity are forms of truth, so a violation of a promise is a defect of truth and to divulge a secret by an unjustifiable disclosure is in excess of truth; both are sinful.

A secret may be defined as a matter known by one person, or by so few that it is not public. It is of various kinds.

(a) *A natural secret*, i.e. one that cannot be divulged without causing harm, injury, or annoyance to another. To reveal hidden defects of character, or what may tarnish reputation, is to divulge a natural secret, since every one has a right to his good name; it belongs to him as much as any material goods; hence such hidden defects may not be disclosed except for public good.

(b) *A promised secret*, i.e. one which a person has learnt, no matter how, but promised not to disclose. Thus if two people were overheard talking together, themselves unaware that they could be overheard, and if we promise to keep secret what we have learnt we are strictly bound by such a promise.

(c) *An entrusted or committed secret*, i.e. when a promise is given to observe secrecy before the secret is made known. This may be 'implicit' i.e. not expressed but intended; or 'explicit' i.e. definitely promised. Implicit secrecy is demanded by the very nature of the case in secrets between friends or relations as well as in secrets entrusted by clients to professional men, such as priests, doctors, or lawyers, who by their position are bound to strict secrecy without any promise being given or exacted.

A secret is as much the property of its owner as his money or other goods; he has a strict right in justice to possession. It is no more lawful to tell a secret than to steal money, and both demand restitution.

To use fraud, force, or illegal means to deprive another of his secret is to violate the virtue of justice. Tc use a secret to the detriment of its owner's rights is unjust. To pry into secrets is unlawful, unless one has the right to knowledge because of authority of position and provided only honest means are used.

A practical application arises with regard to letters. These are written secrets and whatever is written belongs to the writer; it may not be made known, unless it is certain that the writer has no objection to the contents of the letter being made public. The recipient does not become the owner of the written matter but simply the confidant; hence he may not speak of what is in a letter unless he is quite sure that the writer does not mind others knowing. Post-cards are usually not considered to contain any secret, nor a letter left lying about open in a public place, thrown away or abandoned. One must take care that letters are not left lying about unless they may be made public. A sealed letter, one left in a private room, one lost in public, or torn into pieces, must be regarded as secret; it is wrong to piece together a torn-up letter, since the tearing indicates that it is not to become public knowledge. We are therefore bound to consider a letter as a written secret belonging to the writer alone. We have no right to read a letter sent to some other person and letters we receive should be considered as secrets of the writer, unless we are certain he will not object to the contents being made known to others. To do otherwise must be regarded as sinful, the gravity of the sin depending on the harm done, which, however, in many cases it is impossible to calculate.

The keeping of a secret is binding under pain of sin, even of mortal sin in some instances, since its violation offends against charity and against justice. This is especially the case with an entrusted secret which of itself obliges under sin. The violator of an entrusted secret injures private good by disregard of the contract, and injures public good by weakening confidence in officials to whom others must go for advice.

To betray a secret or a confidence may be a grave sin, even though it was given without explicit promise but with reliance on our honour. Everyone has a strict right in justice to his own secrets and we own nothing so completely as the secrets of the heart. Should another entrust such precious things to us, then in justice and charity we are bound to keep them inviolate. In a moment of weakness and temptation we might steal a sum of money, but it could be easily restored and restitution thus made; but if in a moment of thoughtlessness we steal a secret or confidence by disclosing it to others how shall we assess the damage and how make restitution? Once we have spoken we have lost all control of what has been said; we do not know where it will be repeated or how far it will spread abroad; we do not know what harm or injury may result to the person concerned, especially if it is a matter affecting his reputation; we cannot tell what anxiety or sadness we may have caused. How then can we make restitution or know when it has been completed? Yet we are responsible for all the effects brought about by our want of trustworthiness.

Promises should be given only if it is our intention to keep them honourably as obligations willingly taken upon ourselves;

otherwise they are little better than lies. Many are too casual in making promises and failing to keep them without just reason. Such people are unworthy of trust, their word is of no value and reliance cannot be placed on them.

'Can you be trusted?' A better answer may now be given after the above has been digested. Do we gossip about secrets or confidences? Do we keep our promises faithfully? If not, then we must admit that we are not to be trusted as far as our word is concerned. Ecclesiasticus says 'He that discloseth the secret of a friend loseth his credit and shall never find a friend to his mind. To disclose secrets leaveth no hope to an unhappy soul.'

LXIII PRIDE

Pride is a vice that our Lord always condemned most severely, yet few indeed can be found without some pride even though they refuse to admit the presence of this vice, which being difficult to detect, blinds us to its existence in ourselves. So deceptive is pride that it often poses as virtue, as zeal for good, even as humility; but it can be detected by its effects, by the faults and sins that spring from it.

What is pride? Pride is the inordinate love of one's own excellence; having too good an opinion of one's own self or capabilities. It should not be confused with self-respect, that recognition of moral responsibility or personal conduct which guards us from saying or doing what is disreputable and mean.

To admit ability is not pride; if there is something that we can do well, it is untrue to say that we cannot do it. Yet some hide their abilities lest another be found to do the same thing more perfectly; others belittle their talents in order to gain more praise or a reputation for modesty. That is pride! Fear of criticism is often due to pride. Taking credit to oneself for good done instead of referring all good to God is also an effect of pride and steals from God the glory due to him.

Pride is the cause and root of evil in the world. It was the first of all sins, bringing the downfall even of angels; it was at the root of man's first sin of disobedience to God; it lies hidden and unsuspected, the cause of much sin and a dangerous vice in us. Of the capital sins it is the first and probably the most common. It is hateful to both God and man. 'Pride loves no man, is loved by none.' The proud man is always discontented, feeling that he is not receiving his due from others. 'Pride goeth before a fall.' Those who, because of pride, exalt themselves are always humbled in the end. The world in its tenets is always opposed to the teaching of Christ, hence we are not surprised to find the world advising one to exalt oneself, to blow one's trumpet, to advertise oneself before men and not to cheapen oneself in any way. The worldly-wise man exalts himself, wants to be exalted, thinks that to be humble is a sign of weakness and certainly not a means of exaltation.

Yet Christ has said: 'He that humbleth himself shall be exalted.' God's wisdom always opposes the wisdom of the world.

Pride can be detected in various ways by its effects in ourselves.

(1) *Pride of the mind*. This form of pride tends to credit whatever good there may be in us to our own effort and excellence; it hides defects of character and dislikes any form of correction from superiors or others. There is a common form of intellectual pride by which others are despised for ignorance or considered beneath notice. It causes obstinacy in holding to an opinion, stubbornness in argument, refusal to admit any error or that any other opinion is tenable, fear of admitting that another may be better informed. Yet one who can admit to being in the wrong and can give in gracefully is always admired. This form of pride brings about heresies and schisms in religion; causes apostasies and refusal to accept the decision of the Church in matters of faith or moral conduct. Young people 'wise in their own conceits' suffer from this form of pride, refuse to accept advice or profit by the experience of their elders. Much harm is done to religion by intellectual pride since it sets forth dangerous opinions which delude weaker brethren and cause scandal to many.

(2) *Pride of heart*. This type of pride is caused by desire of esteem and praise; it wants all credit for self. Consequently to hear others praised or rewarded brings unhappiness and jealousy to the heart-proud. Others are belittled and criticised, their faults disclosed lest they be more esteemed than oneself. Again, it shows itself by the pretence that our talent or ability is not so great as it really is, in order that greater praise may be gained by this false modesty. Other signs of this form of pride are too great an anxiety about success in achievement; fear of failure in any project; eagerness to gain the good opinion of others; yielding to human respect lest esteem be lost; and the desire to have our own way in everything.

(3) *Pride of speech*. This is really the outward expression of the former types of pride. We brag or boast of achievements, of what we can do or have done; we make excuses lest others might think less of the work performed; we judge and criticise

what others do to make them appear less capable in ability than we are ourselves and so exalt ourselves above others. Like the pharisee, we are models of conduct for others. 'Thank God I am not as other men.' Though we do not actually say such words, yet they are implied by the exposing of faults in others. We presume to correct equals; refuse to accept the rulings of superiors and persist in pointing out how they are mistaken in their judgments. Pious people, unaware of the pride underlying their attitude, cling to erroneous opinions and pass judgment on authority. Again, too often, otherwise pious people are busy setting others right, failing to see their own faults in so doing, and refusing to set aside their private prejudices in spite of adverse decisions of authority. No doubt it is difficult for us to admit that pride is the underlying cause of such conduct, since it is hard to detect how such apparent zeal for good and right springs from hidden pride.

(4) *Pride in action.* This means doing things to gain praise and esteem. Its chief evil is hypocrisy. Thus an alms may be given to some poor person not out of real charity, but so that it will be seen by others and a reputation for charity thus be won. One may kneel for a considerable time in apparent prayer, yet the underlying motive is the hope to be thought very pious. Hypocrisy is particularly odious to God. 'Woe to you scribes and pharisees, hypocrites.' One may refuse to give good advice lest another profit by it, or may not accept advice given through sense of superiority and better knowledge. At some charitable function we may offer to help, but if asked to do some menial though necessary task such as to wash up cups or plates or to clear away litter, we are offended at the very idea of being assigned what seems to us degrading work. We prefer to do what will bring us into the limelight where we shall win praise and esteem as a good worker in the cause, rather than to be hidden in the background where no one knows what we are doing.

Many refuse to speak to, or associate with, those who are not in their own 'class' or 'set'; avoid those who are not dressed in the latest fashion; are vain about appearance, position in society, or possessions. How often people 'swank' and exhibit a foolish pride that impresses no one, brings ridicule instead of esteem. The 'new-rich' are often given to this foolishness and disdain their former companions. Such persons surely forget that all they have or own is a gift from God; because they are thus more favoured (if it is a favour) through no merit of their own, they should not scorn those who are less favoured. Over-sensitiveness often springs from pride so that we feel neglected and passed over by others. We are wounded and hurt in our self-conceit because others are preferred, pained by neglect and want of appreciation of our worth, as we estimate it. Pride produces an unforgiving spirit, injured by a wrong too grievous to be forgiven, utterly forgetful of the sins committed against God by self. We cannot pocket our pride and forgive! Ambition has its origin in pride; an immoderate desire of honours, glory, position or greatness, to gain which we stoop to mean actions, harbour hate and override the good of others, seek insatiably after riches not caring by what means these are gained, even though others may be ruined by the process.

Uncharitable talk, backbiting, and such-like injuries to neighbours rise from pride which judges others, loves self inordinately and tramples others underfoot to rise higher in self-esteem. Pride has no respect for authority, seeks to revenge injuries, tells lies of excuse, remains obstinate in holding to opinions and prejudices even though these are known to be erroneous. It apes humility and modesty by hiding the truth of abilities to gain more praise or cover failure. These and a host of other faults are the effect of hidden pride. No wonder it is called a deadly sin when it is the prolific cause of so many other sins, yet itself contrives to be hidden and unrecognised for what it really is.

Pride is of itself a mortal sin; if it is more often in us a venial sin, this is only through want of grave matter. In any case it is a tremendous obstacle to any progress in virtue because it causes so many other faults and itself keeps hidden. It is well worth while to see whether we are being self-deluded in so grave a matter, to discover whether pride is really at the root of many of our sins. We cannot expect to lessen our faults unless we first uproot the cause of them. The only thing we can claim as entirely our own is sin, and there is not much to be proud of in that! All else, spiritual or corporal, worthy of possession is a gift from God, a token of his interest and love, which ought to make us grateful and modest rather than absurdly proud. If we take the credit of such things to ourselves, we rob God of his glory and of that praise and honour which belongs to him alone.

LXIV HUMILITY

Humility is widely misunderstood in its real essence and many mistaken ideas are held about it. It is a virtue very dear to our Lord and was taught by him in word and example; he lived in poverty and obscurity, met the ingratitude of men with meekness, and gave us this precept: 'Learn of me for I am meek and humble of heart.'

Humility is the foundation of all other virtues. A spiritual writer tells us: 'A flower depends on its roots and if cut off from these, withers and dies; so virtue of whatever kind, unless rooted in humility soon fails and disappears.' Pride is an over-estimate of one's own excellence; true humility, the opposite of pride, is a correct estimate of one's unworthiness in the sight of God, of utter helplessness in oneself and complete dependence on God. It is the consciousness of one's nothingness in relation to God and the realisation of the fact that all good in oneself comes entirely from God. This inward awareness of impotence, lowliness, and utter nothingness when left to oneself is the essence of humility. Hence this virtue has the following essential qualities: (1) Consciousness that all we possess, whether in the order of nature or of grace, comes from God alone on whom we are essentially dependent for all things, being in constant need of his help. 'If any think himself to be something, whereas he is nothing, he deceiveth himself' (Gal.). 'Not that we are sufficient to think anything of ourselves as of ourselves, but our sufficiency is from God' (II Cor. 2). (2) Charity in our dealings with, and judgments of, our neighbours. (3) Dislike of the praise and applause of men, joined to the desire of self-abasement and mortification.

Humility is a source of grace since 'God resisteth the proud and giveth grace to the humble' (St James). In order to understand the real meaning of humility it should be contrasted with pride, as our Lord pointed out in the parable of the pharisee and the publican. These two men go up into the Temple to pray; the pharisee stands before the altar, there praises his own goodness and thanks God that he not as other men full of sin 'as also is this publican.' He reminds God of all the good he does, full of self-complacency and claiming all the credit for his achievement. Self-praise is certainly no recommendation! We cannot help feeling a sense of disgust at this overweening pride, especially in the grave mistake (one that we too often make) of drawing a comparison between himself and the publican and judging the latter's spiritual state of soul. How different is the attitude of the publican! Standing afar off, not daring to approach the holy altar, he recognises his wretchedness and sinfulness in the sight of God, pleading for mercy. 'O God be merciful to me a sinner.' He makes no comparison between himself and any other, is concerned solely with his own personal relationship to God. Himself and God! Therein we have the true essence of humility —the immense contrast between what God is and what man is! Jesus tells us that this publican went down justified in the sight of God, but the pharisee was wholly condemned.

We are often under a delusion as to the real meaning of humility. We read of a saint who considers himself the worst and most sinful of men. How can he think this of himself? Surely it is not true and therefore is not humility! The reason is this: the saint realises all that God has done for him, the many graces offered with which he feels that he has not corresponded as he ought to have done, that had these same graces been offered to another there might have been much more compliance with them and the Holy Ghost. Hence the saint feels that he is less worthy than others because of his failure to make most use of all the graces given to him by God.

It is a fatal mistake for us to make comparisons between ourselves and any others—unless we also are already saints! One might ask 'Why should I consider myself worse than some notorious criminal? It does not seem fair to think of myself as worse than a man who has sinned so grievously.' Why indeed? We are totally unable to make any such comparison at all. We do not know that another's sins are more grave than our own; we know nothing of his spiritual state before God. We see only the externals, and cannot possibly form any judgment about the internal state; God alone can do that. Hence it is utterly impossible for us to compare ourselves with others, to think ourselves better or worse. We know nothing of one another. What do we know of the hopes, fears, temptations, difficulties, struggles and desires of another, of his attitude to God? Nothing at all! He may love God far more than we do, make better use of graces offered, withstand greater temptations than we have ever known, and though he may appear to have fallen into graver sin that we have, yet we know nothing of the struggle made against sin which may have excused in the sight of God much that he has done. Knowing nothing of another we cannot make any comparison at all. The pharisee made that very grave mistake; the publican thought only of himself and God.

True humility is the recognition of one's own unworthiness in God's sight; of one's failure to correspond with grace; of the fact that we are not what we ought to be; of the want of gratitude for favours received; of the poverty of our love for God. Humility is the comparison between self and God alone; no other enters in. God is almighty; I am weak helpless and totally dependent on God. God is infinitely holy; I am a weak miserable sinner. God is the creator; I am his creature. God is life and being itself; I am but dust and ashes. The only thing I claim for my very own work is SIN! What is there to be proud of in this? To realise such truths about oneself ought to make one utterly abased before God, to make one feel very small and worthless, to give one a poor opinion of oneself and to prevent judgment of others. Job realised this when he exclaimed 'I will speak with my God, whereas I am but dust and ashes.'

What wonderful lessons of humility were given to us by our divine teacher. He chose to be born in a stable in poverty, who might have been born in the palaces of kings; to show the uselessness of worldly honours or wealth, the greater part of his life was spent hidden and obscure as a working man labouring with his sacred hands for the necessities of life, sanctifying life by work and ennobling the dignity of labour. He disdains not to wash the feet of his rude and ignorant disciples (a service in his days done only by slaves for their masters) and bids them serve each other likewise. If he, whom they called master, can so demean himself to this lowly service, then they too must imitate his example. If he, being God, could show such true humility, how shall we dare to exalt ourselves above others? Why shall we despise the labouring man considering his work to be beneath our dignity, why refuse to serve others in the lowliest of offices if need be, when he who is Lord and Master, God himself, did not consider it beneath him to labour with his hands and to wash the feet of his disciples? 'Learn of me for I am meek and humble of heart!'

Humility can be gained only by the realisation of what we are in the sight of God. It does not mean self-depreciation in comparison with others; we cannot make any such comparison, so let us leave others alone. It does not even mean thinking oneself the worst of sinners, neither does it mean belittling our talents given by God, but using them in all charity to benefit others. We must keep our self-respect and honour before all men. Even the Mother of God claims that she shall be acclaimed 'blessed' by all generations because of her humility. There is no pride in that; it is a simple statement of truth, giving all the glory of it to God 'because he hath regarded the humility of his handmaid.' Moreover it is the fulfilment of God's promise that the humble shall be exalted. Time has but proved the truth of Mary's claim to blessedness.

Humility does not concern itself with the possession of worldly wealth, honours, position in society or state of life; if any of these are possessed they should be recognised as gifts from the goodness of God. The poor man may be proud, the rich humble; a dustman may be proud, a king truly humble; it is a question solely of self and God. Not what others possess or what honours they have, nor yet what I have myself, but 'what I am before God,' is the foundation of humility. The recognition of the infinite difference between oneself and God, of the difference, between 'what I am' and 'what I ought to be' because of the numberless graces offered and perhaps disdained. To recognise our failure, the sins committed, so many fresh falls after repentance, so little done for God, does not give us much cause for pride in ourselves. How could we remain proud if we really considered our state in the sight of God, knowing what we really are in ourselves and our weakness?

St Bernard says that the humble are especially dear to the Mother of God because they are like herself through humility. How humble she was, how different we who claim to be her children.

It is not easy to be humble, it is not 'natural' to us; hence we must ask unceasingly for this lovely virtue which is the foundation of all others. It is difficult to love self-abasement and mortification, to accept sneers and insults without complaint, not to be anxious for success but to leave all to God. Yet humility brings its own reward: they that humble themselves shall be exalted! This virtue is loved and admired by all, it reveals its own excellence unconsciously, and brings peace of mind no matter what befall, for we cast all our care on God who will not fail us. Let us pray earnestly for true humility and it will be granted to us.

'The prayer of him that humbleth himself shall pierce the clouds.'

LXV HOME LIFE

'Home, sweet home!' Is it always sweet at home? It ought to be so, but much depends on the behaviour of those who live together in it. Theoretically home is the one place on earth to which we turn for understanding, sympathy, and the simple joys of life which no wealth can buy. Practically it is often the reverse, because at home we are our true selves without the veneer of politeness assumed in society. We speak of 'home truths' which usually means truths that are unpalatable, unvarnished, and bluntly told without feeling. Should it be so? The law of charity binds us to show kindness to kith and kin before all others; the closer the ties of relationship, the more binding is the law of charity. Yet too often it is in the home that ordinary courtesies demanded by charity are forgotten, selfish desires given full rein, and faults unchecked.

The home begins with marriage. Two persons, hitherto single and more or less free to please themselves in many ways, now become a composite unit, no longer two separate identities, but one life shared by two. Most couples pride themselves that their marriage is 'going to be different' but soon find themselves in the common rut, possibly asking 'is marriage a failure?' If it is, then the couple can blame only themselves. It is not marriage but the human element that fails. Marriage entails a complete change of outlook on life; if the two, being now one, still try to live a single selfish life instead of the unselfish composite life the marriage will fail. It is essential to the happiness of marriage that each be willing to 'give and take' in all, to sacrifice self, to make allowances for difference as to temperaments, likes and dislikes, fads and mannerisms, which though in the days of courtship may have seemed charming are apt to become irritating in the close contact of married life. Two persons can never know each other thoroughly until they live together; but once assumed, the bonds of marriage can never be broken until death breaks them.

Married life is not easy; hence the need of the special graces given by the sacrament of Matrimony to aid the parties in overcoming the many difficulties that arise. Marriage should be a matter of fervent prayer and grave consideration before it is assumed irrevocably for life. The romance of courtship inevitably dies a natural death and can only be replaced by true charity shown chiefly in forbearance to one another. Marriage entails grave responsibilities in the sight of God.

When the little ones come, entrusted to the parents by God to be brought up to love and serve him, how shall there be peace and good example unless husband and wife are one with each other in mutual charity? Children rely entirely on the parents for training both in the spiritual and in the natural life. Each child has an immortal soul to save; it must be taught to pray, to know the simple truths about God, to be corrected in faults of temper or selfishness, be taught to deny self and show charity as befits its tender years, since every child is 'prone to evil' by its own nature and is not naturally virtuous. All this is a grave responsibility which too often parents try to escape by leaving the child's training to school teachers or clergy.

The training of a child in ways of virtue should be commenced long before it reaches the age of going to school. The soul which has come into the world by the agency of the parents may be saved or lost eternally, and the way of salvation begins at home in the earliest years and may depend on parental training. Example counts for much. Children are natural imitators and religious training should be by example more than by word; family morning and evening prayers, now so much neglected, grace at meals, Mass on Sundays and holydays. Parents must pray with the children and take them to Mass, so they will learn far more than by merely being told to perform such duties. Children are what the parents make them; if they be ill-mannered, selfish and inconsiderate, then probably the parents are the same; like father like son—exceptions to this rule are rare. To know the children is to know the parents and parents are the makers of society for weal or woe. The eternal salvation of both parents and children has its roots in the home and parents are the stewards responsible to God for whatever evolves.

Parents are often heard to complain of the behaviour of their own children. Do they deserve any sympathy? It is very doubtful. They are reaping what they have sown for themselves by their own negligence in training their offspring, by their own selfishness and indolence in not correcting faults in the very earliest years of infancy when children are most pliable and easily taught. Parents who through their own selfishness and to save themselves from trouble allow the children to do just as they like, are asking for trouble; and they surely find it when the children grow up undisciplined and self-willed. 'Spare the rod and spoil the child' may be out-of-date, but remains woefully true.

In many homes charity is not marked by kindness and thoughtfulness for the comfort or happiness of others. A girl thought by her friends outside the home to be of charming disposition, obliging and eager to please, may prove to be just the opposite at home and truly selfish and ill-tempered. Courtesy is kept for the stranger; at home we are 'ourselves.' We are ready to oblige the casual caller, but not the home-folks; the stranger might think ill of us if we did not show courtesy, but the home-folk do not matter! Parents may perhaps have spent money in training a child to play the piano. Mother says 'Do play something for me' but the answer is 'Oh, I can't be bothered. I feel tired and want to read.' But let a stranger enter and at once the book is laid aside, the tired feeling disappears and should the caller ask for a tune, it is at once a pleasure to oblige; anything for the casual caller, nothing for mother! Who has the first right to consideration? Surely the home-folks should be considered before all others. The stranger leaves the home thinking 'What a sweet disposition that child has' but in truth the child is a fraud and a hypocrite.

At home we annoy and tease others in a manner in which we dare not treat any stranger; yet surely it is sinful to provoke anger in the home. Should we have any aches or pains we complain and expect sympathy and consideration. But do we show these to others in like circumstances? If another at home has a bad headache do we try to be quiet? Do we look after the needs and comfort of one who is sick or ailing in any way? The home-folk have the first claim on our sympathy and consideration. Are we cheerful at home, or just moody and difficult, displaying our temper? Thrice blessed are they who are pleasant to live with, a blessing to themselves, to those with whom they live, and to the world at large. As a writer has put it. 'There is a beautiful way and an ugly way in which to say almost all things and happiness depends on the way we take.' You can upset a person for a whole day by the harsh way in which you call him in a morning, or you may give him a beautiful start by the cheeriness of your greeting. So not only in words but in all the little common courtesies of life and its duties think of the beautiful way of doing each. Why give of our best to the stranger rather than to those with whom we live? The stranger has little of the interest or affection for us that our own folk have, yet we show more consideration to the stranger than to our own. Can this be from a motive of human respect, because we wish strangers to think well of us?

With the age of youth comes the question of obedience. Young folks are inclined to think that once they start work they are exempt from obedience; they want a key of the door to come in when they choose, they want to do as they please. Some measure of obedience binds all who live under the parental roof, no matter what age they may be. Our Lord himself sets the example: 'He went down to Nazareth and was subject to them' until he was thirty years of age and left his home. If God could so subject himself, his followers can do no less. Honour and obedience are demanded under grave sin. This implies respect, obedience and support to the extent needed. We owe respect because we received life from our parents; obedience because they were responsible for our training; support because they first supported us through their own sacrifices. This respect must be shown in word and deed, in bearing with defects and failings, in asking advice, in using, not despising, their mature experience of life. Obedience is due in all that is not sin nor the choice of a state of life.

What do the holy scriptures say on this point? St Paul writes to the Ephesians (Eph VI); 'Children obey your parents in the Lord, for this is just. *Honour thy father and thy mother*

320

which is the first commandment with a promise: *That it may be well with thee, and thou mayest be long-lived upon earth.* And you, fathers, provoke not your children to anger; but bring them up in the discipline and correction of the Lord.' In the Book of Ecclesiasticus (Ch. 3) it is written: 'Children hear the judgment of your fathers and so do that you may be saved. He that honoureth his mother is as one that layeth up a treasure. He that honoureth his father shall have joy in his own children. Honour thy father in word, in work, and all patience . . . of what an evil fame is he that forsaketh his father; and he cursed of God that angereth his mother.' Need we add more? Such words inspired by the Holy Ghost should impress on us the grave duty we owe to parents as children, and as parents to the children begotten; the law lays a definite duty on both. The nearer we are to people, the closer the ties that bind, the more we are bound to show charity in every way. It is in the home that we have the best chance of learning and practising real virtue. Stones are worn smooth by friction, and the frictions of family life wear away our faults and smooth away our vices if we use the opportunities given to practise real virtue.

Home ought to be the sweetest place on earth but it will be so only if all therein are really charitable and considerate for the needs of those with whom they live. 'Charity begins at home.'

LXVI PATIENCE

An old rhyme says 'Patience is a virtue, practise it if you can; it's seldom found in woman, and never in a man!' Yet the best known example of the virtue of patience is found in the man called Job, who was so patient that it has passed into a common saying, 'the patience of Job.' Job, who lived in the land of Hus, God-fearing and upright, had much wealth, counting his sheep, oxen, asses and camels in thousands; he has also seven sons and three daughters, with many servants. To prove Job's piety God delivered all his possessions into the power of Satan, the tempter, forbidding only harm to his own person. Satan deprived him of all his wealth, property and even his children; his wife alone remained to him. Being informed of these grievous losses, Job rose and rending his garments fell prostrate worshipping God, exclaiming: 'The Lord hath given and the Lord hath taken away, blessed be the name of the Lord.' In all these things Job sinned not by his lips nor spoke any foolish thing against God, who praised Job for his patience. Satan declared that if Job were afflicted in his own body, he would fail. God then permitted that Job should be afflicted with ulcers all over him. His wife taunted him, his friends accused him of evil-doing, advising him to make peace with God. In spite of all, Job kept unshaken patience and fidelity, so that God rewarded him with greater possessions even than he formerly had.

How should we have acted if afflicted so grievously as that? Should we still have been patient and faithful without murmuring? We have much that Job had not—sacraments to sustain us in virtue, the holy Mass to give us grace, and other helps from religion. Job was not even of the chosen race, yet his fear of God, his piety, were invincible; nothing could overcome his patience; yet we in spite of all our advantages repine over trifles and vent our displeasure in impatient words and acts.

Patience springs from fortitude and consists in supporting unceasingly the trials and troubles that life brings daily whether from the whims of others or from life's own hardships. It moderates the sadness we feel in evil days, enables us to practise virtue in difficulties. It must not be confounded with indifference or apathy which are akin to despair, nor is it a stoical attitude to life which puts all down to fate, saying 'What will be, will be, so why bother?' That is fatalism, which is wrong since it takes no account of free will. Neither is it longanimity or long-suffering which applies to the postponement of future joys and eternal life, since patience concerns only daily happenings. Impatience or want of patience is a vice and must be overcome. Many think that small failures in virtue are of no account, perhaps consider that patience is too small a matter for concern, but if we cannot keep patient in small difficulties, how shall we sustain the greater such as the onset of incurable disease, continual suffering, or loss of all wealth or friends? It is only by the practice of patience in small trials of daily life that we are able to sustain the greater evils should such befall. Even the small trials of life borne in patience merit a reward. The man who knows nothing of the novitiate of patience, who has passed through life without the chastening discipline of bodily pain, has missed one of the best parts of existence.

Patience is the ability to keep control over the impulses that rise suddenly when something disagreeable happens. Impatience is want of self-control and leads to other and perhaps greater faults. It may be that someone treads on our favourite corn; it hurts! What happens then? Do we vent our displeasure in an angry remark, 'You clumsy fool!' Or can we control our feelings and suppress the retort? It was an accident, and therefore excusable; it may have been our own fault for letting our foot sprawl in the passageway; but the impulse rises to say something very cutting about it, to give vent to our annoyance, and only patience can keep under control such sudden impulses. Again, it may happen on arrival at home that dinner is not ready and we have a good deal to say in the way of complaint, airing our grievance, blaming and hurting another. We take it as a personal grievance that our convenience is disturbed regardless of any difficulties there may have been; it matters nothing to us that the butcher's boy was late with the meat or that the fire refused to burn properly and so on. It is no concern of ours what others have had to put up with; our convenience has been disturbed and we make it known in no uncertain way. This means that we have no patience, that we are giving way to the vice of impatience. Often we get irritable and ill-tempered because things are not as we would have them to be, and it is just these tiny incidents which call for the exercise of patience, and which if patiently suffered would gain merit before God.

Impatience grows into anger, irritability, harsh words, unpleasantness towards others; it may anger others so that a quarrel ensues and peace is destroyed because we were wanting in self-control. If we fail in patience we may cause others to be impatient also and the responsibility for all that follows falls on us, for the loss of temper in others, for any quarrel arising out of it and so on. Impatience often arises through selfishness which demands that everything should be agreeable to our own desire, which insists that we have everything we want when we want it; we are not accustomed to self-denial and are wanting in self-control.

It is difficult to be patient when we are in a great hurry, irritating to be kept waiting for something needed; but making things awkward, causing confusion and irritating others will not help to get anything more quickly; it will rather cause more delay, and our impatience defeats itself. Bothers are often caused in family life by impatience in the members of the family. It breeds irritation, causes confusion, creates retaliation and is a cause of friction, all of which could be avoided by a little patience.

Some natures are more inclined to be hasty and impatient than others but that is no excuse for giving way. An impulsive nature is frequently an impatient one also. It is not wrong to be impulsive; many an impulse leads to good. But impulses need control; they must not be allowed to run away with us, for they may just as easily lead to evil as to good. Patience controls such impulses and directs them into the right path.

Want of perseverance in doing things is often the result of impatience. We want to progress too quickly, cannot trouble to learn and tire of the thing because we do not get along as quickly as we wish; we are too impatient to plod along slowly and carefully so we give up and fail to accomplish what we began. Some things can be learnt only by slow, painstaking methods, by diligently persevering through the various steps to success. This entails drudgery and hard work, continual striving, slow progress until the object is attained; but through impatience we become weary and tired of effort and weakly give in to ourselves. It is simply that we have not sufficient patience to endure the difficulties that arise and spoil things in our anxiety to get them done too quickly.

Usually young people are more impatient than older ones. Youth is impetuous, wants to progress quickly, to get things done; but as we grow older life forces us to be more patient; we learn that impatience rather hinders than helps progress; we learn that the old adage 'More haste, less speed' is true in fact. This of course is only natural since patience like all other good things has to be acquired slowly. It is not a 'natural' virtue by any means. There is an expression 'To get out of patience.' This usually means being bad-tempered, getting irritable, causing upsets, giving vent to angry words, and in general the want of self-control, the giving way to impulses that rise within us. We have to learn how to control ourselves and it can be done. We can feel 'boiling over' inside and yet smile, keep silent and avoid any outburst of feeling. It is not indeed easy and demands much watchfulness over our emotions and impulses.

The human need of patience is recognised quite apart from its spiritual aspect. Such old sayings as 'Rome wasn't built in a day,' 'Look before you leap,' or 'Safety first' all mean practising patience and self-control. Daily life teaches us the need of patience to avoid many accidents, to control our impulses lest they lead into danger.

Patience itself needs patience to acquire it! We cannot suddenly become patient by an act of the will. It is acquired, like other virtues that are not infused, by slow plodding, by continual repetition of patient control in spite of many failures. Just as courage is not mere recklessness and disregard of danger, but the effort to overcome fear of known danger, so patience is not just 'disregard and indifference to life's daily untoward happenings, but a real control of self, of one's feelings and impulses. It must be gradually acquired by growing self-control and watchfulness against giving way to any sudden onrush of some emotion within that seeks to vent itself in word or action. It does become in the end a second nature but it is only after many failures that we learn how to be on our guard against giving way. We must have patience with ourselves until we have learnt to be patient in reality. Our Lord tells us: 'In patience you shall possess your souls.' In other words patience teaches us not to be upset by trivial incidents however unpleasant in our daily lives and thus to keep peace within the soul.

LXVII   CHASTITY

Of all the virtues chastity is probably the most difficult
to keep unsullied, and sins against chastity are common. Our
Lord loved greatly this virtue and though he was accused of
crimes, of being a friend to sinners, a law-breaker, he never
allowed the least suspicion to tarnish his reputation in the
matter of perfect chastity. Not only is it hard to keep chastity
unsullied, it is also difficult even to write of it. How much
ought one to say, what leave unsaid? St Paul writes 'All
uncleanness, let it not be so much as named among you, as
becometh saints.' All scripture gives warnings against the sins
of the flesh; so the Church may not pass over in silence sins
against this virtue. It is necessary to consider what is involved
and by a better understanding safeguard this precious virtue
in so fragile a vessel. Ignorance is no safeguard and knowledge properly acquired is a great help.

Chastity is called by various names which do not strictly
give the true idea of this virtue. Thus purity is really freedom
from sin, a state of innocence, modesty concerns itself with
humility, outward behaviour, moderation and decency in dress,
but touches the matter of chastity since want of modesty is
an incentive to unchaste desire or act; want of decency in
dress can be and often is a grave temptation to others and
cannot be excused from blame. It is no use trying to shift the
blame on to the 'indecent minds of others.' It is human nature
to be affected by the immodest display of the human form and
no one has any right to put this danger in the way of another.

In what does chastity consist? It is the denial of consent to
the unlawful desire for, or the unlawful enjoyment of, that
pleasure attached to the acts necessary for the continuance
of the human race, together with all that constitutes a danger
of exciting or rousing desire for this pleasure. God has given
certain powers to ensure the continuance of the human race,
and as an incentive to their lawful exercise a definite pleasure
is attached to the necessary act. Only in valid marriage may
these powers be lawfully used and the pleasure enjoyed. In
no other case may this pleasure be desired or enjoyed, since

327

it is permitted for one specific purpose only and not for its own sake. So weak, though, is fallen nature that it is difficult to refrain from desire and act. The loss of control over the lower passions is the most grievous wound inflicted on our fallen nature by sin, so that the 'flesh lusteth against the spirit' throughout life.

As one grows to youth strange emotions are felt, passion seeks satisfaction, thoughts and desires rise from our very nature. This is not wrong in itself; it is a natural development of nature; such desires are as natural as hunger and thirst; we should hardly be human if we did not experience these effects of developing nature. Ignorance of our powers and their design in life is not innocence; to know the purpose of such powers, far from being sinful, is a safeguard to innocence. Too often parents neglect a grave duty in guiding their growing children through the difficult period of youth when nature is wakening to its fullest powers.

There is nothing nasty about sex. God made it. There is no reason why it should not be spoken of in a natural, matter-of-fact way; yet it must be treated with respect and reverence. The reason for not joking about sex is the same as the reason for not joking about sacred things. Too often youth is left to find out for itself, often in a dirty and foul way, what should be reverently explained in a clean and wholesome way by parents who are best fitted to make known the necessary facts of origin. There is nothing to be ashamed of in our mode of origin; it is God's ordinance and should be treated of decently and naturally so that knowledge may be kept free from shameful and indecent imaginings. Through ignorance of the purpose of these powers and their design in life, youths and maids may fall into unchaste habits without being aware of the sinfulness of such habits. Lack of knowledge is a source of curiosity and an incentive to experiment, with dire results. It is no use blinding ourselves to the facts of nature, which are good in themselves. But we must also know that the misuse and unlawful enjoyment of the God-given powers is grave sin.

In the matter of chastity everything is grave and any offence against it is of its nature mortally sinful. Thus, not only is the full enjoyment of the pleasure mortally sinful, but also all that may tend to excite passion such as thought, imaginings and desires, if deliberate, since these constitute a grave danger of full consent. Whether the individual is always guilty of mortal sin or not depends on circumstances which may lessen the guilt, such as violence of unprovoked temptation or passion, provided there is no clear consent of the will and that no bad habit has been already formed. But it must be understood that consent even to thoughts and desires constitutes a mortal sin. Such sins are usually followed by a sense of shame, but this is not contrition, being merely a natural effect which soon passes. Real sorrow for such sins is the sincere regret that nature has been indulged, combined with the determination to avoid the occasions and not to give way again by the help of God's grace. Temptations against chastity cannot be met as other temptations by fighting against them; we must run away! We must be cowards in the face of this enemy. To fight merely serves to impress the desire on us, to increase its violence; we must run away by changing our occupation, turning our thoughts to other ideas; if alone, by seeking the company of others that will deter us from the sin. The danger is within; we carry it everywhere with us. We tend naturally to desires and imaginations which are a powerful incentive to passion. So long as we are displeased at the presence of such thoughts or desires, they are but temptations, but as soon as we begin to enjoy them wilfully then we sin.

Thoughts and desires excite passion; passion seeks fulfilment; therefore anything which can excite the imagination, such as reading stories with suggestive descriptions or situations, looking at unchaste pictures, not keeping a guard over the eyes, must be shunned. Unchaste talk leads to unchaste desires and acts. 'Let not such things be so much as named amongst you.' There are times when it is necessary to speak for some useful purpose such as instruction, but talk of this nature for its own sake is strictly forbidden.

Idleness is a fertile source of temptation to be avoided at all costs; we are most vulnerable then. Lovers have an especial need of care and watchfulness. Human love is a great mystery which is liable to be profaned when passion enters in. Passion can seldom be wholly excluded from human love; it will accompany it, but should never be its essence. Love that leads to unchaste desires and acts is degrading to the immortal spirit of man, a defilement of the body which is the temple of the Holy Spirit. It is natural between those betrothed to give expression to love in kiss and embrace; but when these are too frequent or prolonged they become very dangerous to chastity; desire is roused and passion excited so that there is grave danger of mortal sin. If experience shows this danger (which differs in individuals) it is a proximate occasion of sin which must at all costs be avoided. Passion indulged between lovers causes loss of respect and often kills true love which is a divine gift to be kept spotless.

There is a law among the Romanys that 'No youth has any right to take what no maid has any right to give.' To use that function of our nature (i.e. sex pleasure) as an opportunity of passing amusement always involves treating another person as a plaything or toy. The greater the love, the more chaste it ought to be, the more carefully kept free from the indulgence of unlawful passion; true love is too sacred to be profaned.

It has been stated that only the 'lawful enjoyment' of this pleasure is permitted. Therefore even in the married state it is only lawful when the full divine purpose of these powers is intended and the possibility of reproduction is not hindered. Using as an excuse the economic difficulties caused by man himself through disregard of christian principles, many maintain nowadays that, in the enjoyment of this pleasure, it is lawful and even advisable to take precautions against its natural results, in other words to enjoy the pleasure for its own sake to the exclusion of the purpose for which it was given by the Creator. Others, quite apart from economic reasons and from purely selfish motives of self-indulgence, enjoy this pleasure for its own sake and take measures to prevent its resulting in offspring.

Such practices are definitely gravely sinful, contrary to the natural law and to the law of God. No state or law of civilization can alter that. 'Heaven and earth shall pass away but my word shall not pass.' Civilization, no matter what difficulties it may create, cannot change the law of God. The use of any preventive method to enjoy this pleasure without its natural results cannot under any circumstances be permitted. It always involves grave sin and is degrading to human nature. It results in loss of respect and reverence for the partner in marriage, will bring about destruction of love, and often breeds illness in the body or the mind.

The only permitted way of preventing births as a remedy for economic difficulty is self-control. Self-indulgence has no right to be considered at all. Self-control is admittedly difficult but where it is a question of eternal salvation, it is most surely necessary. The choice lies between self-indulgence and God. We must love God above all things, before husband or wife, and human love cannot excuse us from choosing God before all others. We may not commit unlawful acts to please one we love; to do so is to degrade love and to lower our human nature beneath that of the beasts who obey the natural law in their instincts.

What is needed above all is a greater faith and trust in the providence of God. He will never desert those who trust him and are faithful to his commands. But so many are afraid to trust God. Better to suffer the loss of luxuries, to struggle against poverty and hardship rather than risk eternal damnation for the sake of the passing indulgence of pleasure forbidden. 'Seek ye first the kingdom of God and these things shall be added unto you.' Trust God and he will not let you down in any way.

'Now the works of the flesh are manifest . . . fornication, uncleanness, immodesty . . . of the which I foretell you . . . that they who do such things shall not enter into the kingdom of heaven' (Gal. V. 21).

331

LXVIII OBEDIENCE

'Doth the Lord desire holocausts and victims, and not rather that the voice of God should be obeyed? For obedience is better than sacrifices' (I Kings XV, 22).

The foregoing text is explained thus by St Gregory: 'Obedience is rightly preferred to sacrifices because by sacrifices another's body is slain, whereas by obedience we slay our own will.' The chief merit in obedience lies just in that—the slaying of our will. Obedience entails the submission of one's own will to that of another and is a difficult form of self-denial. Other forms of self-denial may be of one's own choice and therefore less perfect, but obedience leaves no room for personal choice. This virtue, springing from justice at its root, gives to authority that submission which is its due.

St Thomas Aquinas teaches that obedience, whereby we contemn our own will for God's sake, is more praiseworthy than any other moral virtue which contemns other goods for God's sake. We find that obedience is laid down as of strict obligation; thus St Paul writes (Rom. XIII): 'Let every soul be subject to the higher powers: for there is no power but from God; and those that are, are ordained of God. Therefore he that resisteth the power, resisteth the ordinance of God. And they that resist purchase to themselves damnation.' To Titus (III) he writes: 'Admonish them to be subject to princes and powers, to obey at a word and to be ready to every good work.'

St Peter expounds the same theme (I Pet. II, 13-14): 'Be subject therefore to every human creature for God's sake: whether it be to the king as excelling; or to governors as sent by him . . . for so is the will of God.'

The greatest example of obedience is that given by our Lord himself who, though God, was yet subject to his parents till his thirtieth year. If he, being God, could so submit his will and obey creatures surely, we cannot refuse obedience to those set over us by God, since all authority is ordained of God.

There are various degrees of obedience: There is (a) *external obedience*, which does with exactness what is commanded though unwillingly; (b) *internal obedience*, which joins willingness to external obedience, even though the judgment or opinion doubts the wisdom, value, or good faith, of what is commanded; (c) *blind obedience* which submits the judgment as well and is virtuous so long as what is ordered is not clearly sinful.

The true virtue lies in the internal submission of the will, joined to the performance externally of the command. For this certain qualities are necessary: (1) The submission must be prompt and willing, so differing from a forced or unwilling submission, or from mere self-interest; (2) it must be shown to a superior, i.e. to one who has authority. Between equals there can be no question of obedience in the strict sense, though one may do what an equal commands through friendship or for the good of a common cause; (3) it must be in compliance with a command i.e. a law or precept imposed by authority; (4) the obedience is given solely because the will of authority has been expressed in a command.

One is not therefore strictly bound to do what is known to be merely a wish or a desire on the part of a superior when no expressed command has been given, nor is it want of obedience to neglect the advice given or a request made by a superior, provided that these are not of themselves of obligation nor in the nature of a command. At times a 'request' is a form of command which is more acceptable than an 'order' to do some thing; it is usually obvious when a request is in the nature of a command, and then it must be obeyed.

Obedience is of obligation only in those affairs which lie within the scope of the authority's powers. Thus the State cannot command the conscience of the individual in what pertains to spiritual or religious matters. In employment authorities may only demand obedience in what relates to the work to be done and the hours of employment. A foreman could not forbid an employee to go to the theatre during his leisure time. In the family the elder children have no authority and may not exact obedience from the younger children since all are equal, unless in their absence the parents specially put in charge one of the others, who then acts 'in loco parentis.'

All lawful authority comes from God and is a delegation of his own authority to others in various spheres of action—to obey authority in its own particular sphere of action, is to obey God. That is why St Peter and St Paul insist on submission to authority: 'Servants be subject to your masters.' The higher the authority the greater right it has to obedience, and lower authority may only command what is in accordance with the will of the higher; hence if a lower authority commands what is known to be contrary to the will of a higher authority it may not be obeyed, since the command is unlawful and has no force. Thus if a father has forbidden his boy to slide down the stair banisters, an elder child left in charge may not order the boy to do it.

How is authority acquired? There are two powers that confer moral authority over others and give the right to demand obedience. These are (a) *jurisdiction* and (b) *dominative power*. Jurisdiction is held by one who rules in a complete society, such as the Church or the State which have supreme power in their own spheres and the right to impose laws on all subjects. Dominative power is held by one who is at the head of an incomplete society and is a dependent authority with the right to issue precepts only but not to make laws. This power rises from the nature of the society or body composed of a superior and subjects, such as the family in which children are necessarily subject to the father; or from an agreement between the parties concerned, as in marriage in which the wife becomes subject to the husband; or in employment where the servant by accepting service becomes subject to the employer.

As in other virtues one may offend against obedience by excess or by defect. Excessive obedience is shown by obeying an order that is unlawful as when a child steals because ordered to do so by a parent; or if obedience is mere servility or fear of one who goes beyond the scope of his power or has not the right to command. Thus an employee may obey a foreman in matters outside the scope of his job, through fear of being victimized by the foreman.

Defect in obedience or disobedience is either the voluntary

neglect or refusal to do what is ordered, or the doing what is forbidden, against a lawful command particular or general, of authority. As was noticed above, it is not disobedience to ignore advice or requests not in the nature of a command, unless they be of obligation from some other cause. Formal disobedience may be a grave sin.

We can easily see the need for obedience, since there would be chaos if lawful authority were disregarded and commands not obeyed. It is the chief ingredient of all discipline. How could an army fight with any chance of success if the commands of officers were not obeyed? How could any business be run successfully if employees refused to obey orders? How could there be any order in family life if parents were not obeyed? Nothing in life would run smoothly without due obedience to authority; there could be nothing but confusion and cross-purposes unless respect were given to the orders of those above who have the responsibility of directing the means to whatever is to be achieved.

But the virtue of obedience goes far beyond being a convenience to the ordering of social affairs. It is a precept imposed on us by our Lord: 'If any man will come after me, let him deny himself.' There is no way of self-denial more perfect than that of obedience to authority for God's sake. It strikes at the very root of self since it entails giving up one's own personal desires in order to do the will of another and there can be no greater mortification than to obey or submit to the will of another, especially when what is ordered runs contrary to one's own will or desire.

Obedience is the only means of authority in religious life, without it there could be no religious life at all. Obedience is the essence of all discipline and the most perfect form of self-discipline and self-denial.

Obedience is admittedly difficult to human nature. We would rather please ourselves in everything we do; hence the vital need of this virtue. The habit of prompt obedience, like other virtues, can be acquired only by the frequent repetition of submission to authority.

Since obedience does not come naturally to us, parents have

a grave obligation of teaching their children to obey and of punishing them accordingly if they are not obedient; they must be taught that disobedience is sinful. It is much easier for a child to learn obedience than for an adult, and the earlier a child is trained in this important matter the better it is for his whole future career, for no matter what position in life he may hold, no matter what form of work he may choose, at least in the beginning he must obey those over him; beginning at school and for many years in his working life, he will be under the orders of others and he must learn to obey before he can himself be fit to have authority entrusted to him. Being so essential in all walks of life, it should be the chief lesson of childhood when it may be the more easily acquired, and the child who is taught to obey from his infancy will find it a blessing throughout life.

The example of the child Jesus should always be kept before children and the story of his submission to his parents told to them, that they may strive to imitate his perfect example. 'Who going to Nazareth was subject to them.' Just as Jesus was obedient to Mary and Joseph, so all children must be taught to subject their own wills to their parents', and thus learn the lesson of self-denial and self-discipline for their own spiritual good and for their success in material affairs of life.

Obedience is better than sacrifices.'

LXIX LEADERSHIP

Many have the desire to lead others, to be first in importance, to 'boss the show,' though they may have no qualifications for such a post nor even know the qualities needed for leadership. They imagine that it just means being at the head and telling others what they are to do, giving orders for others to carry out. Our Lord said: 'Whosoever among you will be the greater, let him be your minister; he that will be first among you, shall be your servant.' The Holy Father's most prized title is 'Servant of the servants of God.' Unless one is willing to serve, he cannot lead, but how many of those who hanker after leadership have any intention of being the servants of others? How many know the essential qualities that a leader must possess? Too often one who seeks to lead does so from mere pride and not because he is fit to be the leader. We should all try to fit ourselves for the post of leader, since there may come an occasion when we shall be asked to take charge of some work or organisation. Some are born leaders and seem to have a special flair for being at the head. Among a group of boys one will naturally assume leadership by some innate power which others are led to follow and obey. Born leaders are very few, but it is possible to train oneself to be fitted for leadership if the occasion arises. It often happens in church affairs that one may be asked to be at the head of a guild, society, or other organisation, to take charge of some special work such as a bazaar. If we know something of what is needful in a leader, we may be able to make good at the head; otherwise it may be a complete failure.

As in most things, one must begin at the bottom and work up step by step. The first step is to learn discipline. No one is fit to lead until he has learnt to obey; that is the first necessity. We have no right to expect obedience from others unless we have learnt obedience ourselves. This does not come naturally; it is a virtue that entails much self-denial in subordinating our own will to that of another. Blessed are the parents who teach their children to obey in their earliest years and fit them for the future.

The next step is to be 'keen and enthusiastic' about whatever is to be done. The leader must be keen in order to inspire others. This means conscientious, hard and unremitting work, a close attention to details, taking trouble over the small items, as well as the bigger ones, making everything as good as one can make it, and this can be done only by having a great interest; there is no room for slipshod or careless work. It is this attention to detail, foresight of difficulties to be overcome, planning out to the best advantage, and unremitting perseverance until the job is done that mark the budding leader; it is the only way to successful leadership.

Having acquired these two qualities, the next step is the subordination of self-interest, learning to suppress one's own desires for the good of the whole. Most people like to be in the limelight, to have the showy jobs, to gain praise for their efforts, to let others see that they are important. That is no way to lead. Suppression of self is necessary to be able to do the lesser humdrum work whilst others do the showy part. The lesser details are necessary for the success of the whole, and someone must give attention to these that the greater may also be done. Take a simple example. Perhaps a tea-party is being given and people are asked to help in the work. It will probably be easy to get volunteers to serve out the tea, to pass round the eatables and look after the guests. But it is usually a difficult matter to get helpers to wash up the cups and saucers, cut up the bread, see to the water boiling and other background jobs which are not seen; yet 'He that will be first, let him be your servant.' Unless such menial tasks are done, the other work cannot be a success, and it is in such things that the future leader develops the essential quality of self-subordination. Added to this must be a sense of responsibility.

What does this entail? It means that a person can be depended on to do whatever is put in his charge without having to be watched or reminded about his duty. It should be possible for the 'head' to feel certain that what he has put into the charge of another will be properly carried out and to have no anxiety about it; he can be sure that nothing will be forgotten or neglected. There are some who act on the principle that 'when

the cat's away the mice can play.' They have no sense of responsibility and are unreliable. Whether the head is present or
absent should make no difference whatever; if anything, one
should be more particular in the absence of the superior. It
is a compliment to be considered reliable, able to be trusted to
carry on without being watched all the time.

Having learnt self-discipline, self-subordination, keenness
and reliability, a man is then fit to take on himself the over-
seeing of others, but until all these qualities are acquired he
is unfitted to be a leader.

Now we must consider what a leader ought to do to lead.
Some think that to be a leader is just a matter of giving orders
and seeing that they are carried out, but doing nothing of the
work itself. That is driving, not leading. No one can get the
best out of others by driving methods. It is better to 'ask for a
thing to be done' than to 'order it to be done.' A leader does
not treat subordinates as slaves; that breeds resentment and
rebellion. Nor does leading mean prancing in front, making a
great fuss of dignity, being a figure-head, whilst others do the
work. It does not mean ruling by fear of punishments without
consideration for human weakness, without mercy; but it
does mean trying to understand the complex characters and
temperaments, the difficulties and abilities of subordinates.
To know of what any individual is capable, his likes and dislikes, and trying to give to each the job for which he is most
fitted or which is congenial to him, that is leadership. The art
of ruling is to acquire another to do the thing for which he
has most ability and which has some appeal for him. The
true leader knows how to develop that ability and foster that
appeal. He must encourage the faint-hearted, be approachable
on any matter, and be willing to listen to complaints or smooth
out difficulties. He must not be so autocratic that no one dares
to ask about any matter or suggest some alternative plan. A
leader cannot be always right, and should be willing to listen
to the other ideas that may be put before him though he may
not always see his way to comply. A leader should be loved
and respected, not hated by those under him; but this does not
mean ruling by pusillanimous kindness, by currying favour, by

seeking to be popular, or by having favourites; that makes a leader despised, causes jealousies and undermines his authority. People are quick to resent anything that smacks of favouritism. Fair dealing in every way must be the aim. Injustice is always hotly resented and causes murmuring among workers and a lessening of effort.

To be a leader it is necessary to have an understanding of human nature, of likes and dislikes, of prejudices and character; to know the value of a word of praise in season for work done, of encouragement in difficulties, of consideration for the needs of others. All are not formed in one common mould and each individual has peculiarities and differences; human beings are complex, not automatons, and need to be treated with due consideration for their characteristics and temperaments. Secondly it is necessary to have sympathy—that is the power of putting oneself in the other fellow's place and trying to understand how he feels about it; of appealing to his better nature and suggesting lofty ideals that can inspire him to aim at achieving the best of which he is capable. Thirdly there is need of ability to do what others are asked to do, so that one can step into the breach and get the job done. We can sympathise with a man who complains that he has 'to do jobs that the boss couldn't take on himself.' The subordinates ought to feel that the head has ability and readiness to do himself whatever he asks them to do. Lastly a leader must have intensity of purpose, or enthusiasm that does not wane but perseveres until the object is attained. He should have the power of decision, of making up his mind and sticking to it; a vacillating policy causes irritation, makes people feel that they do not know where they are and that the leader does not know his business; they lose interest or wait to see if he really means what he says or knows his own mind. A leader with such qualities will be followed by others who are inspired by his oneness of purpose, his determination to carry the project to its completion in spite of difficulties.

With good leadership necessarily goes discipline, which is not mere punishment for breaking petty regulations, but the doctrine of subordination of individuals for the good of the whole. Leadership means 'leading,' i.e. going before, not simply giving orders; it means 'playing the game' and not seeking self-gratification and kudos; it means being ready to bear the burden; it means an ability to find the best way; it means not being harsh and domineering, not imposing authority for its own sake, but being considerate and kindly.

Responsibility should be the guiding factor; to lead others to a sense of responsibility should be one of the leader's chief objects, to teach others to be reliable and trustworthy and not to do their duty through fear of being found out in neglect. Anything in the nature of nagging or bullying must be ruthlessly cut out; no one could hope to lead by such methods, which can only produce resentment and antagonism with a corresponding inclination to disobedience.

'He that will be first, let him become as a servant.'

LXX THANKSGIVING

Thanksgiving is the expression of gratitude for favours received, or being grateful. Too often this duty of returning thanks is ignored, or if expressed is mere lip-service. To be real, gratitude must come from the heart, must be the outcome of an underlying spirit of thankfulness and a recognition that a favour has been granted. Gratitude is for favours, for gifts to which we have no claim in right or justice. Thus a man has no need to be thankful for wages paid which are his due; he has a right to them in return for his own service given; but if through the generosity of his employer a bonus is added as a free gift, then for this he must be grateful, since he is presumably not entitled to it.

We notice how frequently our Lord returns thanks to his Father, thus teaching us the duty of thanksgiving for the many favours we receive. 'Father, I give thee thanks that thou hast heard me.' In the miracle describing the feeding of the five thousand with five loaves we read: 'When he had given thanks, he distributed them' (the loaves). At the Last Supper at the institution of the Blessed Sacrament, 'Taking bread he gave thanks . . . Taking the chalice, he gave thanks.' On the occasion when ten lepers came asking to be healed, our Lord sent them to see the priests and on the way all were made clean, but one only returned to give thanks. Our Lord complains of this want of gratitude, not for himself, but for God. 'Were not ten made clean? Where are the nine? There is no one found to give glory to God but this stranger.' (Stranger, because he was a Samaritan, not a Jew like the other nine ungratefuls.).

St Paul, in his Epistles, points out this duty of thanksgiving to God. To the Thessalonians he writes: 'We are bound to give thanks always.' To the Ephesians: 'But be ye filled with the Holy Spirit . . . giving thanks always for all things.' To the Philippians: 'By prayer and supplication with thanksgiving let your petitions be made known to God.' It is a serious duty to give thanks to God for the numberless favours given to us. Do we recognise and fulfil this duty? Many are careless about it, taking everything for granted as a matter of course, as though it were a natural right to receive all they need.

Gratitude is a virtue which should be spontaneous and natural to us; it is probably the easiest of virtues since it requires no difficult effort on our part. Ingratitude is an odious vice and no one can respect the ungrateful. We are irritated at finding our favours accepted without any thanks and judge that we have given to an unworthy recipient. But whereas usually we are grateful to one another for favours, to God we are too often indifferent and careless in this respect. Gratitude is the 'memory of the heart' joined to a desire of repaying in some way the favour shown; it is 'the poor man's payment.' No one, however poor he may be, is unable to be thankful; all can at least say 'thank you' and really mean it from the heart, even though it may not be possible to do anything else in return.

Among the ancient Persians ingratitude was a civil offence punishable in law by severe penalties. Pagan Rome detested the vice of ingratitude also. Pagan writers expressed this detestation in such phrases as the following: 'The world holds nothing worse than an ungrateful man.'—'Though we are grateful to a friend for a few acres or a little money, yet for the freedom of the world, the great benefits of our being, health or reason, we consider ourselves under no obligation to return thanks.' Thus even in the natural order ingratitude was considered hateful and odious; how much more so if it is shown to God!

It is unfortunately too true that we take God's gifts for granted as though we had a natural right to them. Were God to heal us by a miracle of some loathsome disease no doubt we should express gratitude for so signal a favour. Yet 'prevention is better than cure' and day by day through God's providence we enjoy good health but we seldom think of returning thanks. Imagine what it would be like to be deprived of one of the senses, to be deaf so that the harmony of music or a loved voice could no longer delight us; to be blind seeing neither light nor colour, to be unable to read or look on the face of a friend; to lose taste so that food had no savour. We enjoy these things. Are they not worth some thanks to

God since they are his gifts to us? Some do lose these benefits; it may happen to us also. Some are even born without them, never know what it is to enjoy sight or sound.

Everything is a gift from God, given to us and preserved by his fatherly care, and for this we have a definite duty of returning thanks. What of the spiritual gifts? Especially faith! This is a gift; we have no right or claim to it; it is not given to all, but is a mark of God's special favour; but it is not always appreciated by those who have never known what it means to grope in the outer darkness of error, doubt, prejudice, and false teachings, nor do they realise the immense comfort of having been spared those doubts and anxieties which beset those who have not the light of true faith. Truly for this gift alone we owe a very great debt of thanks to God.

How often do we plead forgiveness of our sins? We cannot claim forgiveness as a right. Do we show any real gratitude for forgiveness and prove it by an amendment of life and a greater love for God? What of the gift of the body and blood of our Lord in Holy Communion? Are we really grateful for this astounding condescension and do we prove it by the frequent acceptance of this most holy food of the soul? Not to make use of a gift for the purpose intended by the giver is want of gratitude. Grace, without which we cannot save our souls, is another of God's most precious gifts freely given for our eternal salvation. The gifts of God are so many, he is so prodigal in giving, that we forget the immense debt of thanksgiving that we owe for such a great multitude of gifts showered upon us, all unworthy though we are. We forget that these are 'gifts,' and not 'rights' to which we have a claim.

Gratitude is the 'memory of the heart.' Too often gratitude is mere lip-service; there is no real underlying spirit to give it life. It is so easy to say 'thank you' but is it really meant? Do we show our thanks in some tangible way? Do we long to give some real proof of gratitude and feel distressed because we can do it so inadequately? Gratitude, like love, is not mere sentiment; it seeks to do something to prove itself. Mere words are of no value unless the heart being truly thankful desires to express itself in action. How often do we do what we are not bound to, out of a sense of gratitude? When we pray, is our prayer asking for more favours or do we 'give thanks' in prayer? It is noticeable that many Masses are offered to ask for favours and benefits, but that very few in proportion are offered in thanksgiving. Surely if favours are granted through Mass, we ought to offer thanksgiving through the same offering.

Holy Mother Church never forgets this duty of thanking God for benefits. Many times in the divine office through the day, her ministers say 'Deo gratias'—thanks be to God. One of the chief ends of Mass is thanksgiving and the very word 'Eucharist' means thanksgiving. In the Mass the prayer before the Canon, known as the Preface, is a hymn of thanksgiving. The priest says 'let us give thanks to the Lord.' The answer comes: 'It is truly meet and just.' The Preface continues: 'It is truly meet and just, right and salutary that we should always and in all places give thanks to thee, O Holy Lord, Father Almighty, eternal God.' Because of this grave duty the Canon of the Mass begins 'Therefore we offer these gifts . . .' The Mass is amongst other things the Church's expression of thanksgiving to God for his favours.

Shall we, the children of the Church, neglect this grave duty which is laid on us of showing gratitude to God? How shall we most fitly do it? Surely by a great fidelity in serving God, by striving against our many faults and sins, our un-ending infidelities to God. If our thanksgiving means any-thing at all, it will show itself in some tangible form, in leading a better life, in more faithful service, in fewer lapses into sin. Gratitude is active, it does something to prove itself, and the only proof possible to us is a more fervent love and service of God.

In spite of our ingratitude God still showers his gifts upon us; but though God is patient he will not always suffer in-gratitude to pass. His gifts may grow fewer, graces may be offered less frequently, if we fail to have a spirit of thankful-ness manifested in our ready compliance with the opportunities offered us. Probably it is thoughtlessness on our part, but that is no valid excuse for neglect. If we are hurt by the ingratitude of those to whom we have shown favour, we should be all the more ready to show gratitude to God and not neglect him in that way. If pagans thought ingratitude so odious a vice when shown to men, is it not infinitely more odious when shown to God? We must not take God's gifts as a matter of course, as a right to which we are entitled. We have no claim at all on God in strict justice. All that we have has been given to us by God. The very prodigality of his gifts should not make us forgetful but rather fill us with humility that we so unworthy should be so greatly favoured in spite of our past failures, that we who are so utterly incapable of returning adequate thanks should receive so much. Though we can indeed do little in return, we can at least utter a fervent 'Deo gratias' from a spirit of gratitude deep in the heart and soul.

'Truly it is meet and just, right and salutary that we should always and in all places give thanks to thee, O holy Lord Father Almighty, eternal God!' 'Give thanks whilst thou art living, whilst thou art alive and in health thou shalt give thanks and shalt praise God and shalt glory in his mercies' (Eccles.: Ch. XVII, V. 27).

LXXI SUCCESS

Emerson wrote 'One thing is for ever good, that one thing is success.' This may or may not be true; it depends on what is meant by success and by the methods used to obtain it. The world recognises success as something to be sought after, but does not feel concerned about how this is achieved so long as nothing criminal is found out in gaining it. Moreover worldly success must be obvious, the glittering prize must be flaunted for the world to recognise it. The business magnate, the conquering general, the champion athlete, those who win fame and glory, these are considered successful in the eyes of the world. But the race is not always to the swift nor the battle to the strong. Many a true hero has been dubbed coward by the world which judges from outward appearance alone.

What is success? It may be defined as the achievement of the desired end, the attainment of a definite object. Hence it is plain that success cannot always be perceived outwardly. There may be many a hidden victory of which nothing is known or apparent. Sir Walter Scott summed this up in the words 'He, who having unlimited power to do evil, doeth good, deserveth credit not only for the good which he does, but also for the evil from which he forbears.' Each time we are tempted to sin but resist the temptation a victory unseen has been won, known only to God's grace, but it must surely be counted as success.

All want to make a success of life and, since success is the achievement of the desired end, it depends entirely on our estimate of the meaning of life and its purpose whether that success is to be real or no. If we make our object the attainment of wealth or honours, we shall miss success. If we consider life to be a preparation for the life of eternity to be achieved by striving after the conquest of self, then our success will be assured by our efforts in overcoming faults and increasing in the love of God and our neighbour. That is the success recognised by God; what else matters?

What the world considers success may well be failure in God's sight, and failure judged by the worldly standards may equally well be a success before God. The world wants to see outward results; God looks at the efforts made and the motives which spur us on, rather than at our actual achievements. I may wish to do all in my power to accomplish charitable work, only to find that it is impossible. Is this failure? In a worldly sense, yes; before God, who knows all motives, it may well be a success worthy of reward and merit.

Consider our Lord himself. Was he a success? The world of his day thought him a complete failure. He came on earth to draw all men to himself, to found a new religion of love, to teach new doctrines. But the multitude heard and went on its way unheeding; his only followers were a few ignorant men. He proved the truth of his mission by miracles, which were accepted by those helped, but forgotten by almost all. He turned those in authority against himself. They crushed him and condemned him to a disgraceful death between thieves. His followers fled in terror of their lives, only a poor handful remained faithful. His chief disciple denied all knowledge of him. What an utter failure! Yet 'It is consummated,' he said. What was consummated? All that he came to do, to fulfil the prophecies, to found his Church, to satisfy for sin and to open the gates of heaven to man, to gain the victory over the powers of darkness and sin. Jesus Christ, the world's failure, was infinitely successful in all that he came to achieve.

Judge success, therefore, not by outward results but by the motive and object. Only now do we begin fully to understand the complete success of our Lord's mission on earth, undreamt of by the people of his day. When one's name is written in the Book of Life, and one hears the words 'Well done good and faithful servant,' then is success achieved and life's object attained. That is what we must strive for, to win the victory over self and the passions of nature, to despise the attractions of the world, and to live unto God alone. Such a success will be ours only if we apply to our souls the copious and all-powerful means given by God to assure it.

Success, either in the natural life or in the spiritual life, is not to be gained by sitting down and waiting for it to come. It is no use merely wishing for success; it requires valiant efforts to gain it. The saying that 'everything comes to him who waits' certainly does not apply to success. We must go all out after it, win it with much striving and perseverance. There is no such thing as certain and automatic progress. Success depends on unceasing effort, on conscientious hard work, on attention to details; it will not come by wishing for it. The smallest details are as important as the greatest, and only by a slow, painful progress step by step until the end will success be attained.

An athlete desiring to win a race does not sit idly waiting for the day to come; he gets into training, gives up desirable things, practises self-restraint in food and drink, and perseveres until he is as fit as he can make himself, ready to meet his rivals who also train in like manner. If a student wants to pass an examination, he does not spend the day in frivolous amusement, but studies hard to prepare himself, otherwise he knows that failure will result. Such things are such obvious common sense that they are hardly worth mention; but do we apply such methods to our spiritual combat? Mostly we are indolent, content to do only what we are bound to do, to trust to luck to get us through when assailed by temptation. Is it any wonder that we fail? Nothing is so difficult as victory over self, yet we are apathetic, easily taken unaware by temptation, and fall into sin almost before we realise that a temptation is upon us. Each has his own particular weakness to overcome ; it needs watchful and unceasing effort to win the victory. We take things too easily, we are not on our guard, do not attend to the small details and so are easily overcome.

Let us take temper or irritability as an example. No matter how easily we tend to get into a temper, it can and must be overcome. But we shall not do it by just wishing to be good-tempered; it will need determination, watchfulness, and unremitting effort to overcome this fault. If we are inclined to blurt out harsh words when things upset us, we must be determined to shut our mouth and clench our teeth so that nothing is said till the anger or temper subsides. It requires determination, but it can be done. By the grace of God we can gain control over our inclinations. The same applies to any besetting sin or bad habit; any fault can be overcome by

God's grace, coupled with determination to succeed. There will be frequent falls at first, but these must be followed by patient risings without undue discouragement.

The mere avoidance of evil, though, will not constitute complete success. St Peter bids us 'avoid evil and do good.' One is negative, the other positive. Yet care is needed in doing good lest it be ruined by unworthy motives. God looks at our motives as well as our acts, the reason why we do things, our intention; and though through inability we may not achieve all the good we intend, yet God gives us credit for our good intentions. Thus I may intend to give an alms to some poor person, only to find that I have forgotten my purse and cannot give an alms, but the good desire has won merit in God's estimation, though I failed to perform the actual good work. In the same way a good act can be ruined by a bad motive; thus if I give an alms in actual fact because I was being noticed by others and wanted to create a good impression. 'Amen. I say you have had your reward.' You have succeeded in attaining your object of being noticed, but it was unworthy of any reward in God's sight; it is a success of the world, but a failure of the spirit, and therefore worthless. We must watch our motives lest they ruin all success.

We need a very clear idea of what success means in the sight of God. Life will be a success only when the spirit is master of the flesh and self-control is achieved; when all the good we do is done for the love of God, and not for mean personal advancement; when we learn to do the will of God in all things. God judges success by a different standard from that set by the world, which is always contrary to God, and we shall not know the success or the failure of life until we are judged.

Here are two parables. A certain preacher by his eloquence and reputation attracted great crowds. He was acclaimed as a great orator with a command of fine language; many came to hear him, charmed by his eloquence; but they heard and went their way without being moved to learn or profit by eloquence that was merely pleasing to the ear. Another preacher, a simple man without any command of fine language or eloquence, spoke sincerely from his heart, few went to hear him, but they were impressed by his sincerity and conviction, so that they were drawn to repentance and a better life. Which, think you, was the successful preacher? Two writers published books. One wrote a best-seller, but its theme made vice appear virtuous, described situations calculated to incite evil desire; it was eagerly read by many and the author made much money and was acclaimed a successful novelist. The other writer sold few of his books and made no profit, but a few souls found inspiration to better things and encouragement to fight evil through his writings. Which was the successful writer? Your decision will depend on your outlook on life and its meaning.

The secret of success is 'to watch and pray'—watch in order to be always ready to detect the hidden snare in temptation; pray in order to obtain the grace of God without which all effort is in vain, then count nothing too small to be noticed and so progress slowly step by step until the end is gained and victory won.

'I can do all things in him who strengtheneth me.'

LXXII PERSEVERANCE

The greatest of all graces is the gift of final perseverance. After warning the apostles of the hardships they must face, our Lord said: 'He that shall persevere to the end, he shall be saved.' One of the chief weaknesses of human nature is that prolonged difficulties cause a slackening off of effort, carelessness and final cessation of endeavour through weariness. If this is true of the natural order, much more is it applicable to the spiritual order of grace.

Life is one continued struggle between good and evil, between the spirit and the flesh, and the natural tendency is always towards evil, to give in to temptation rather than to resist it; we are 'prone to evil.' This ceaseless conflict throughout life causes weariness of spirit and temptation to relax effort; there seems to be no end to it, no respite, no peace, so that the tendency to grow slack, though imperceptible, is none the less sure. We really desire to be good, begin with enthusiasm to do good works, to strive against natural tendencies to evil, but after a period of combat we begin to relax, to get slack, until we are back again with all the bad habits in full sway.

It is an axiom of the religious life that we cannot remain in the same state of soul; either we are progressing, or we are slipping back into evil ways. Take an example; I am rowing a boat up stream against a strong current and so must keep on rowing all the time without slackening effort. If I cease rowing, the current at once takes charge and sweeps the boat back down the stream; even to keep in the same spot needs effort, to make progress still greater effort. It is the same in the spiritual endeavour to advance; any slackening in the fight against the current of natural inclination means being swept back into old habits and evil ways get an even stronger hold on us.

Take another example from nature. Certain trees in the natural state are of little use, such as the apple or the rose. To get good fruit, or a lovely bloom, the natural stock must have grafted on to it a branch from a tree or bush producing good fruit or flower. When this is done we get the desired result in

352

fruit and flower. However this is not all that must be done. The good tree or bush has the tendency to revert to nature; severe pruning and attention are needed to prevent deterioration, for if left to itself the tree reverts to the crab-apple, the bush to the briar.

By baptism the spiritual life is grafted on to the natural stock, but the tendency is always there to revert to nature, so we must be continually pruning our evil tendencies, ruthlessly cutting back the passion that rises within, keeping in check the propensity to evil, lest we drift back to bad habits or contract new ones so that our state becomes worse than it was formerly. At times a person who has felt a strong attraction to religious life has given it a trial, and failing to persevere has returned to worldly ways and ceased in the end to practise religion at all. Some who have been educated in convent schools give up the practice of their religion when the influence of the convent is taken away. They will excuse this as a natural reaction on the plea of having been oversatiated with religion that had been thrust on them. There is undoubtedly a danger in forcing the youthful to attend services and prayers willy-nilly. Nevertheless to give it all up afterwards is a sign of great weakness of character. It is the old story of the devil cast out of a man, taking with him seven other devils and re-entering, the last state of that man becoming worse than the first.

Perseverance means a sustained effort in the practice of the virtuous life, notwithstanding fatigue through the unceasing struggle, with no opportunity of rest until life is over. Death alone can end the effort of perseverance; that is what makes it so difficult to keep unflagging zeal. If one could say 'I must fight for five years, then I can rest' there would be a definite limit to aim at, but the indefinite period of life and the unending conflict is the difficulty.

When, perhaps, grace moves us to desire a more holy way of life, we respond to the call by joining, it may be, some guild or sodality. Full of enthusiasm we look forward to the day when having fulfilled the time of probation we are admitted to full membership. We are assiduous in attending the meetings and carrying out the rules and duties. Gradually enthusiasm begins to wane; we miss a meeting or two; then the rules or duties become tiresome and inconvenient so they are gradually neglected, until we cease to have any further interest. It is a common tale of failure to persevere, the wearisomeness of repetition and routine is allowed to destroy enthusiasm. Possibly we thought that to join a guild would prove an easy way to become holy; but we did not reckon with the assault of the devil, forgetting that the greater the effort we make to progress in holiness, the more the devil will strive to hinder and dissuade us, the more he will tempt us to give up. But God also, having prompted us to begin the good work, gives greater graces to aid us; if we correspond with those offered graces all will be well.

Why is it that we fail so easily? Simply because of lack of resistance, we submit too readily to weariness of spirit. There is a natural propensity to slide back into old easy ways, to revert to nature. Always we must be on our guard against taking things easily, giving way to natural indolence and ceasing to strive against our proneness to evil.

How are we to gain this precious gift of perseverance?

(1) *By fervent prayer.* Perseverance is essentially a gift from God and is received in answer to prayer. Prayer is the means of winning that grace without which we can do nothing. We must ask God to help us in our efforts since by our own power we are quite unable to sustain any good work.

(2) *By renewal of good intentions.* It often happens, in the beginning of the turning to God, that a sensible sweetness is felt in devotion; it is that 'first fervour' which springs from a new-found enthusiasm and interest. But this inevitably wanes leaving only the grim reality to be faced. This sensible devotion, given as an encouragement at first, is later withdrawn as a test of our devotion and selflessness in the service of God. It may come again with a renewal of good intentions, by making a fresh start with new enthusiasm. St Philip Neri recommends this renewal of good intentions from time to time as a means of encouragement to waning enthusiasm. A new start is a great help to perseverance.

(3) *By not undertaking too much at once.* It is a failing of enthusiasm to be carried away by itself and undertake more than

is reasonable; we want to run before we have learnt to walk.
Soon the burden becomes too heavy for us to carry and we
end by dropping the whole. It would be far better to undertake
a little and persevere in that little, rather than try to do more
than is feasible and risk accomplishing nothing at all. St
John Berchmans says: 'However little, so long as it is constant.'
It is the constant striving that is the chief worth in our effort.

It needs prudence in our choice of undertaking; we must
consider what is possible, the difficulties to be overcome, the
length of time to be faced, the duties involved and having
given due consideration to the intention, make a decision
about it and then persevere in it once it is made. Often we
begin under impulse without due thought only to find that
'we have bitten off more than we can chew' and are forced
to give up.

Consider therefore well all that is entailed before making a
decision and then, having decided, stick to it in spite of weariness and fatigue. Do not attempt to correct all bad habits
at once; one at a time is sufficient and will keep us busy. We
must take the worst evil first and when we have succeeded in
ridding ourselves of that particular vice, then we can begin on
the next. Let us not be in a hurry, it is the work of a lifetime.

We must not be discouraged by failures; they are bound to
come. We cannot get rid of long-standing habits in a day or
two; we must be patient and always distrustful of self. It is
our fatal tendency to give up the effort, to slide back into old
ways. We need a deep humility, a knowledge of our own weakness; hence we must lean on God. We must respect his laws,
hate sin, distrust worldly maxims or suggestions of what is
convenient to modern life. Catholics too often allow themselves
to be influenced by arguments advocating evil practices on
the ground of the present conditions of life, conditions due
to ignoring those very laws of God. 'Heaven and earth shall
pass, but my word shall not pass.' No condition of society
can change the law of God. Faithfulness to the teachings of
the Church is vital for perseverance; to consider the Church
'old-fashioned' or 'out-of-date' is a grave danger, it is the thin
end of the wedge driven between our allegiance and God.

Obstinacy must not be confused with perseverance. It may happen that, through circumstances over which we have no control, it becomes unwise to persevere in some form of good work because it is adverse to health. If one in authority bids us desist, then to persevere in it becomes sheer obstinacy and self-will and is contrary to obedience. By obeying authority we are safeguarded and gain greater merit. To pursue our own will is a choice of self as against the will of God made known to us through authority. Obedience relieves us of responsibility, and by giving up our own will we please God.

Be prudent in deciding what is to be done, consider the difficulties, start with a little rather than undertake too much, but above all, persevere in that little. Pray always for this greatest of all graces, the best of God's gifts, the certainty of eternal life, and the winning of the crown of glory.

'Be ye faithful unto death and I will give thee the crown of life . . . He that shall persevere to the end, he shall be saved.'

LXXIII LIVING BY FAITH

Faith plays a much greater part in life than is realised; it is the first necessity of life. In the natural order man lives by faith and his normal condition is one of trust and dependence on others. We rely on the laws of nature; if the seasons did not keep to a certain sequence, we should not dare set seeds for food; if we could not trust to gravity we could not build. We have to trust one another, too, in spite of the fact that we know so little of anyone beyond what he chooses to tell us; the commercial business of the world rests on continual and amazing faith in the probity of mankind. Education is simply a matter of faith, and blind faith too, since we rely entirely on the presumed experts in knowledge for facts which we are unable to verify for ourselves. Science is in the hands of a few experts and our knowledge of scientific facts is almost wholly gained from them, by reading or by word of mouth. How credulous people are in accepting whatever the daily papers print, without requiring any proof of the truth of the matters printed therein.

Religious faith is along the same lines as this natural faith, insofar as it demands the acceptance of truth and knowledge on the authority of another. But this supernatural faith has an infinitely greater compelling motive. As St Paul writes: 'If we accept the testimony of men, the testimony of God is greater,' infinitely more reliable. God cannot deceive since he *is* TRUTH, and in the person of Jesus Christ he has told us not only truths beyond our intelligence about himself, but also the true way of life that alone will bring happiness on earth and through eternity. He has given us the principles of conduct to guide us in every sphere of daily action, in every circumstance to ensure happiness and salvation.

Faith is not simply a matter of giving intellectual assent to truths which are mysteries beyond the power of human intelligence to fathom, but it entails the application of the teachings of faith to every event of life so that we act in accordance with them. Far too many try to divide life into separate compartments with little or no connection between them. Thus business forms one part, social life or pleasure another; a third part is religion, another politics. To divide life thus into unconnected sections is to have a totally false view of life as a whole, and of the meaning and influence of faith and religion in life. Our catholic faith should be the dominant factor in every section of life; the principles of faith can give the solution to every problem that arises. Faith must be the rule by which every judgment is made before action, it must be the chief influence in our mental attitude to whatever is proposed to our intelligence.

In business, as is well known, there is much to be deplored from the moral point of view; though business has its own standard of integrity, yet there is much 'sharp practice' also which is nothing less than a hidden way of cheating. Is this in accordance with faith? When there is a chance of 'easy money' that has a hint of fraud about it, does faith bid us reject it? If we are employed, do we feel that as catholics we are bound in conscience to give full value in time and work to our employer? That is how to live by faith, to bring faith to bear on every aspect of our working time and by it to judge the morality of our actions in every situation according to the teachings of Christ.

In social life are we influenced by the outlook of the world on moral problems presented to us. Take the cinema as an example. Too often unsavoury triangle dramas are represented, exalting illicit love and advocating divorce as the best solution of this human problem. What is our reaction? Do we feel that there is something to be said for divorce, that perhaps it is the only solution that fits the case? Do we have a disloyal feeling that the Church is behind the times and too strict in its decisions? Or do we immediately revolt in protest against this degrading of the sanctity of marriage? Our answer to these questions will give us the measure and sincerity of our faith. It is to be applied to all the many shady teachings of our modern corrupt society.

Politics need a deal of watching; we cannot accept the view of any political party without putting its proposals beneath the microscope of faith to see how their views and principles accord with catholic teaching. Unfortunately in these days we are faced with a universally humanitarian outlook on the problems of life, each party deciding, offering their solution, without reference to the laws of God. God is treated to a very large extent, even by the best of them, as though he had no rights or interests in human affairs. The important question of education has come to be regarded as a purely secular affair in which religion, if it is allowed to enter at all, must be of so general and indefinite a character that it cannot offend anyone's susceptibilities—as though it were the right of politics to accept or reject any truth or moral law according to convenience.

Faith must come into everything that touches human rights and liberties and freedom of conscience to worship God as far as the light of God is given. It must rule in economics which affect family life. The living wage is a matter of the moral law, not a political plank. If economic conditions result in the limitation of families by artificial means the government responsible is self-condemned as a traitor to God and man. It is, in any case, a tragedy that the 'standard of living' is of far more importance to the majority nowadays than the law of God and any excuse is taken for disregarding that law. A man thinks it his duty to his children to give them an expensive secular education; but since an increase in his family would make his means insufficient for this, he is unwilling to risk such an increase, though he does not intend to deny himself the pleasures of marriage for self-gratification and will maintain that he is quite within his rights in so doing. To the woman, it may be a plea of health, or fear of losing her good figure; maybe she wants a 'good time' without the hindrance which children cause. Any reason which appeals to personal convenience is sufficient to do away with all moral responsibility in these matters.

How does faith enter into the question? Surely if we profess to believe in the teachings of Jesus Christ, which must be the case if we are catholic in anything but name only, there cannot be the least doubt in our judgment about such obvious disregard of the moral law and the divine purposes. Faith should at once revolt against the suggestions of the world and the flesh that natural advantages outweigh the claims of the supernatural life. If it is a matter of choosing a school for the children, what influences the catholic parents most in deciding? Is it where they will get the best secular education to fit them for a business career or worldly advancement? Or is it where they will get the best foundation in religious knowledge? Would they consider the advantages of a non-catholic as compared with a catholic school? Or would faith immediately decide that only the best religious instruction is worthy of the children's salvation?

If we rely on human faith, should we not have infinitely more reliance on divine faith in every matter that affects life? Yet is it true that the majority of catholics do not use life properly because they do not judge by the principles of faith in deciding matters affecting social, economic or political aspects of life in general? They are apt to look on faith rather as a hindrance than as a sure guide in the making of decisions, to regard it as a drag upon their activities, putting them at a disadvantage with their fellow-men who are untrammelled by any such limitations in their moral conduct. Hence there is a sense of dissatisfaction with what they consider the hampering restrictions of faith. They fail to see how faith safeguards them in every decision so that they are saved from the fatal mistake of taking things on the world's valuation rather than on God's.

Faith must vitalize every thought, word, and deed. If the truths of faith are not linked with acts founded on these truths and so raised to a supernatural level, then our faith is not a 'living faith' but a mere intellectual acceptance of religious truths without any relation to reality. We need a very clear perception of the purposes of life as a preparation for the eternal happiness planned for us by God. We know, by our faith, that Mary the Mother of God, St Joseph, St Peter and St Paul, St John and the other apostles, all human beings like ourselves, after their short span of life on earth now enjoy the eternal bliss of heaven and have been enjoying that bliss for well-nigh 2,000 years! But what is 2,000 years in eternity? A mere moment! If we ponder on this fact, it may bring our short span of life into a truer perspective and prove the utter worthlessness of all schemes for secular advantage obtained by a disregard of our faith with a risk of eternal damnation. 'What doth it profit a man if he gain the whole world and lose his own soul?' What is earthly life in comparison to eternity? It is less than a drop of water in the ocean! If we live by faith we make certain of eternal life; and even though we lose much in this world by so doing, we shall lose nothing of any worth by our fidelity to God.

'Be ye faithful into death and I will give thee the crown of life.' Faith should enable us to weigh the transient events of mortal life against the eternal verities and make our decisions according to the law of God.

LXXIV SAINTS

What is meant by a 'saint'? Actually the real meaning of the term has been lost and now it is used only in a restricted sense that creates a false impression.

The word is really French and probably came into use in England when the Normans came in. It is derived from the Latin *sanctus* meaning 'holy' and the same idea is found in 'sanctification' or 'holiness' and in the phrase 'sanctifying grace,' which is 'saint-making' grace or the grace that makes us holy in the sight of God. The general meaning of the term is no longer generally understood and it is normally used in the restricted sense of one who is canonized by the Church, i.e. officially declared to be in the possession of eternal bliss in heaven. Yet the number of known saints must be very small compared with the immense multitude of souls in heaven. It is doubtful whether anyone could mention more than a hundred saints by name. The Roman Martyrology or list of saints mentions some 6,000 and these are always increasing. Other sources put the number at about 70,000 but even this must be but a minute portion of the saints in heaven. In the Apocalypse St John describes his vision of heaven: 'I heard the number of them that were signed, an hundred and forty thousand of all the tribes of Israel . . . After this I saw a great multitude which no man could number of all the nations and tribes and peoples and tongues standing before the throne in the sight of the Lamb clothed with white robes and palms in their hands.' This gives some idea of the immense multitude of souls in heaven, a multitude which is daily increasing as the mystical body of Christ grows towards perfection.

Strangely enough the greatest of all the saints, Mary the Mother of God, is not given the title of 'saint' by catholics in England. (The Anglican Church seems to have appropriated the title 'Saint Mary, the Virgin,' though this is of course a relic of pre-reformation days). We always refer to Mary as the Blessed Virgin and invoke her as holy Mary. It would seem strange to address her as Saint Mary, as though putting her on a par with the other saints of the same name. Yet in

Latin she is invoked as Sancta Maria just as the other saints are Sancta Rosa, Sancta Maria Magdalena, Sancta Anna. But we seem to prefer the English term 'holy' in referring to our Lady by name.

Where is this leading? I am trying to show how little we appreciate the true meaning of the word in its general sense; because we use a French term instead of the English one, the proper meaning of 'saint' is largely lost. St Paul as can be seen in the English version of his epistles uses the word very frequently to designate the faithful living in the world. Thus he tells them that they are called to be 'saints' in more than one epistle. He bids the Romans 'Receive Phoebe as becometh saints!, (XVI, 2), and tells them to 'salute Philologus and Julia, Nereus . . . and all the saints that are with them' (XVI, 15). To the Corinthians he writes: 'I teach in all the churches of the saints' (I XIV, 33) and 'now concerning the collections that are made for the saints as I have given order' (XVI,1). He begins his second epistle to them as 'To the church of God that is at Corinth with all the saints that are in Achaia' (I, 1) and bids them 'Salute one another with a holy kiss' adding 'All the saints salute you'(XIII,12).There are so many of these references to 'the saints' that it is difficult to choose from them, but they are found in nearly all the epistles. He tells the Ephesians about certain vices 'Let not such things be spoken of among you as becometh saints' (V.3), and the Philippians are told to 'Salute every saint in Jesus Christ. All the saints salute you especially they that are of the household of Caesar' (IV.21). To Timothy he writes: 'Let a widow be chosen having testimony of her good works . . . if she have washed the feet of the saints' (I, V. 9). The Hebrews are told to 'Salute all your prelates and all the saints.' The same phrases keep occurring as though it were the ordinary thing to call the faithful 'saints.'

St Paul obviously considers all christians living in the faith to be 'saints' as their normal state of soul; for him to be a christian is to be a saint. This shows how the failure to put this word into English misleads us as to its proper significance. It would be more properly rendered as 'holy people' and every person in a state of grace is truly a 'holy person' since sanctifying grace—saint-making grace—does give holiness to the soul. Hence for St Paul every christian in the grace and friendship of God is a 'saint,' i.e. a holy person. But now we seldom realise that fact owing to the term having been restricted to the blessed in heaven. In the German vernacular, the last phrase of the divine praises rendered into English would read: 'Blessed be God in his angels and in his holy ones.' thus including all people on earth in a state of grace. Our versions seem only to refer to the saints in heaven, yet God is glorified by his holy people on earth also. In very early times this land of ours was known as 'The Island of Saints,' yet the greater number of these saints have never been canonized by the Church, but showed themselves such by the holiness of their lives and were venerated as saints by the people. In life they were respected as friends of God and at death were acclaimed holy and worthy of veneration. The places where they lived were called after them and there are many such still perpetuated. Thus we have St Ives, St Neots, St Austell, St Bees, St Just in Roseland, St Buryan, St Aubins, and St Kevern and a host of others. There were many other saints such as Wilfrid, Ceolfrid, Caedmon, Hilda, Bede, Cuthbert, Ethelfrida, Petroc, Frideswide, Gilbert. Some few have been canonized by the Church but the greater number are simply canonized by popular veneration. This points to the recognition of personal holiness in a marked degree. It is doubtful whether all these saints would now receive the official canonization of the Church; not that they are unworthy, but because the standard of heroic sanctity now demanded is so high and normally the proof of miracles worked by the holy person concerned, is required. But it does serve to show that a high degree of holiness can be attained to by many, and not merely by the few. It also suggests that perhaps we do not recognise holiness in others as readily as we should, not realising the power of sanctifying grace and its 'saint-making' action in the soul. We are much too apt to see the faults in others rather than their virtues, to criticise and find fault with human frailty in 'holy people' out of all proportion to their sterling virtues. Hence we do not give them that reverence and respect that is their due, forgetting that by the second commandment we are bound to speak with respect of all holy persons.

It is also probable that we do not realise this possibility of holiness for ourselves. There is no doubt that our early fore-fathers had the same idea of personal holiness as had St Paul when he wrote to the 'saints' in various localities. For St Paul a true christian was a 'saint'; it should be so for us also. We fail to recognise the dignity of a soul made holy by the 'saint-making' grace which, as St Peter declares (II Pet. I, 4), makes us 'partakers of the divine nature.' This is assuredly a dignity so tremendous that we cannot hope to appreciate it fully; yet we have to recognise that it is the state offered to all of us by God through sanctifying grace.

Were anyone to enter a church during Holy Mass and see numbers receiving the body and blood of Jesus Christ in Holy Communion, he would rightly presume that all these communi-cants were in a state of grace and therefore 'saints,' as St Paul would call them. To come into such intimate contact with God himself, the author of all holiness, must surely make these people holy and worthy of respect and reverence. This will certainly be so in fact when they correspond in every way to the grace they have received. They do then indeed become saints. The realisation of this should be a great incentive to cling fast to the grace given, to keep ourselves from losing by sin the holiness that is imparted to us, to avoid lowering the dignity that is ours by petty acts of meanness. Yet we are so apt to criticise and find fault with the human frailties of holy people, and irritated by their weaknesses, exaggerate their failings and blind ourselves to their virtues and real goodness of heart. They may fail at times, but always rise again to con-tinue their efforts in seeking God, desiring to be in his friend-ship and give glory to him as his holy people; they are the 'saints' on earth.

We ourselves can also regard ourselves as 'saints' when we are in a state of grace, this cannot be in any spirit of pride since any holiness we have is due solely to the action of God in our souls. The great dignity thus bestowed on us should make us truly humble. It should make us careful of the in-herent weakness and meanness of our nature, as well as keep us free from loss of this high estate by deliberate sin. We should 'act as becometh saints,' as we are bidden to do by St Paul, and strive to increase daily in holiness before God and ·our fellow-men. In these days we seldom think of any person as a 'saint' in the way our forefathers did, and hence we have not that respect or reverence for others which may be due to them, we have lost, too, the sense of our own dignity. 'Recognise, O christian, thy dignity,' cries St Ambrose.

'Be you as living stones built up, a spiritual house, a holy priesthood to offer up spiritual sacrifices acceptable to God by Jesus Christ.'

LXXV SANCTITY

It should be evident that 'sanctity' is not to be considered as the concern only of the few who are chosen by God to be canonized saints and therefore of little or no immediate interest to the many. All followers of our blessed Lord are called to be saints, that is to lead a holy life. The precept 'Be ye perfect even as your heavenly Father is perfect' is given to all without exception, and since it is given by God it must be within the power of all to achieve in some degree by his grace.

Sanctity or holiness of life is simply the continual presence of the divine life of grace in the soul and the gradual increase of that grace through our efforts combined with God's generosity. These efforts consist in doing God's will at all times as far as we can discern it, whether it be pleasant to us or disagreeable. God created man to know, love, and serve him according to the divine plan by free subjection of his will, and in return to be rewarded for faithful service by eternal happiness.

We must realise, however, that each individual soul is marked out for definite service which no other soul can give; each must glorify God in his own life by serving him in the particular way God himself has determined, not in the way the individual chooses for himself.

Sanctity is achieved in general by following the spirit of Christ not so much following him in his actions as in his spirit of subjection to God's will in all things. 'I came to do the will of him that sent me.' Sanctity is determined not so much by *what* is done as by *why* it is done; the motive or the intention counts far more than the actual accomplishment itself. God may not desire us to perform great deeds for him but that we should do little things for his sake as well as we can. The deed is always secondary to motive in the sight of God. We must do whatever he wills, however trivial it may appear, however disagreeable or uninviting it may be; the fact that God wills it is sufficient. All activity, whether great or small is to be governed by the will of God whether such acts be great or small. There is no other way to sanctity or perfection; God's will must be the beginning and the end of all. The secret of sanctity, therefore, is simple—to do God's will; but growth in sanctity is difficult because of our wayward nature and self-seeking.

How am I to discern what God wills for me?

In the first place, we know God's will in a general way by the teaching of the Church. The laws of God are to be obeyed in the least detail to avoid sin. The regulations of the Church regarding worship and moral behaviour all show the will of God to us: 'He that heareth you, heareth me.' In carrying out any duty imposed by the Church we can be certain that we are doing God's will. In all the problems of life the teaching of faith is our guide and the application of the principles of faith to each detail of life is clearly God's will; faith must be the dominant factor in all decisions we have to make, true faith which is not merely the intellectual acceptance of truths, but the 'way of life' as taught by our Lord in word and example.

We come now to the more individual or particular know-ledge of God's will as it affects each of us personally in the state of life to which we have been called by God. It must be understood that our state of life is not a haphazard matter; it is God's will for us. Thus a married man or woman has certain definite obligations imposed by the state of marriage, mutual love to be fostered and forbearance to be shown. If there are children these have to be fed, clothed and helped in all the needs of childhood, trained in the knowledge of God, corrected of faults and advised as needed; children have a right to love and care from parents who must be worthy of respect in themselves. All this is God's will for married people and must be accepted. Again, in the matter of employment, an employer has certain duties to his workmen; he must pay a living wage, give suitable conditions in which to work, be kind, charitable and forbearing towards all. The one employed has likewise obligations arising out of acceptance of service; he must give just value in time and work, render obedience to masters in a reasonable way and be conscientious. All this is God's will for those people. Soldiers and sailors owe obedience to their officers as an essential element in such a state of life. This is more clearly and obviously true of those in the religious

state who fulfil God's will by obedience to their rule of life
and the commands of their superiors. In whatever state of
life one may be, from the king to the meanest subject, there
are found certain obligations and duties connected with that
state and the observance of these is God's will.

Now the question arises how, apart from such known duties
or obligations, one is to know God's will in particular instances
when there is no visible indication of it. Everyone has a certain
amount of free time during which he is left to his own resources,
when he can be his own master and act according to choice.
How can one be sure that one is acting in accordance with
God's will at such times? The answer is that God's will is done
by acting reasonably, as a creature endowed with reason
should act. God has given reason to be a guide to action,
conscience as the judge of right or wrong, and in making
man a reasonable being God intended that man should
glorify him by reasonable service. Faith guides us in giving
the principles of action, reason applies such principles to any
given moment and a reasonable man acts in accordance with
the decision made after prudent consideration of all that is
involved. Moreover we are helped more than we often realise
by the guidance and inspiration of the Holy Spirit who dwells
within us and by the spiritual gifts that he has brought to us.

Many things are left to our discretion such as eating,
drinking, sleep, recreation and all these are used in moderation
by a reasonable man. It is a principle that virtue always takes
the middle way, neither too much nor too little. Take sleep as
an example. God gave sleep to restore the body from the
fatigue of the day so that a man is able to carry out his duties
again after sleep. To prolong the period of sleep beyond what
is sufficient to restore nature to its vigour is foolish and imprudent. It must be God's will that we normally take sufficient
sleep. If a man carries on with his pleasures long into the night
so that he must rise for his duties without sufficient rest to
enable him to do his work properly the next day, he is not
acting in a reasonable way and therefore is not doing the
will of God. Again it is not reasonable to make pleasure or
recreation a chief thing in life, to consider work only a burden,

369   AA

to be got rid of so that one can return to pleasure as soon as possible. Work is God's will for every man.

That principle can be applied universally. What is merely self-indulgence is excessive and unreasonable; moreover a man is bound to 'deny himself' as a duty imposed by God. Hence the rule to follow is to use all things according to reason helped and fortified by grace, as a means of furthering the real object of life which is to become holy and worthy of God.

Our Lord in his human nature gave us an example that we should follow. If we do that we shall do God's will. In considering that example we are to consider the whole life of Jesus especially as it can be adapted to our own circumstances according to his spirit. Jesus lived about thirty three years on earth; of that period a comparatively short time was spent in his public life of teaching. The years of his hidden life are an important element of that example, therefore. How was this life spent? The answer is given in the simple words: 'He went down to Nazareth and was subject to them.' What a wonderful thought! God subject in his humanity to his creatures! As a child he obeyed his parents; for all children that is the will of God, for to obey parents is to obey God, it is his will that children be subject to their parents. As a youth he would have learnt the trade of his foster-parent, made tables, chairs, yokes for oxen and all the objects of a carpenter's craft. He would have helped to keep the house going by his labours. As a man he became the sole support of his widowed mother. His work would always be well done nor would he charge more than a just price for his labour.

Is not our Lord's hidden life a picture of the normal life of most men? It can easily be adapted to fit any sort of life. He accepted his state of life as the will of God. Work is not simply a means of gaining a livelihood; it is God's will that a certain individual shall do certain work according to his state in life and there lies the way to salvation. All one has to be concerned about is carrying out to the best of one's ability whatever work is to be done, doing it in the way a reasonable man should do it.

Sanctity is, therefore, simply serving God willingly in the

small details of life no matter how trivial they may be, no matter how difficult it may be to see the relation of such things to holiness of life. They may be hard and toilsome, distasteful or disagreeable, but it is the acceptance of them as the will of God that sanctifies life and increases holiness in the soul.

This secret of sanctity is not just wanting to do great things for God, but actually doing small things well; it is not found in doing great penances or mortifications but in discerning God's will according to one's state of life and carrying out our duties in a spirit of subjection to God. There is no other road to holiness of life. It is the spirit of Christ pervading all: 'I came to do the will of him that sent me.' To love God with our whole being so that his will becomes the dominant power in all activity, the acceptance of all that may befall in joy or sorrow as God's will,—therein is sanctity to be achieved.

LXXVI GIVE AN ACCOUNT

'Remember thy last end and thou shalt never sin.' Many fear to think of their last end as though thinking might bring it sooner, and also because to think of the final things would involve a change in life that they are unwilling to make. Nevertheless we are advised to think of our last end, of death, of judgment, of hell and of heaven. Such thoughts will not avoid the final reckoning but will at least prepare us for it; surely it is wise to prepare for the most inevitable and most important thing in life—death, and after that the judgment. We are the stewards of God, entrusted with various properties for which a strict account must be given. The duty of a steward is to care for what is under his charge, to use all in accordance with the will of the owner, and to give a strict account of his dealings at the end. That is our position in regard to all the things we seem to own.

Time, one of God's gifts to be used in his service not in the service of self alone, must be accounted for. We must account for each hour, each minute of work, of leisure, of repose, of enjoyment. Did we use these in the service of God? The goods we possess, property, riches, honours, these are under our care, not ours to do with as we please but to use according to God's will. These things bring obligations to our fellow-men; the poor have a claim on our charity, the Church for its support and the furtherance of religion. Property may not be squandered in riotous living or for self alone. These possessions are not 'ours' in an absolute sense but are entrusted by God to whom we must render account. Talents, mental and physical, are not to lie idle but to be used for the common good. A singer should not use his gift solely for personal gain, but for the glory of God in singing his praises. Some will use this gift only if paid to do so, even when it is a question of singing in the service of the Church, in praise of God.

Spiritual gifts, grace, the virtues, the sacraments, the power of prayer, all are to be used for our soul's benefit. What responsibilities are ours in the use of all these gifts of God, such precious possessions. Do we value them, use them to the best of our ability according to God's purpose? Give an account of thy stewardship! Dare we even give an account to ourselves, much less to God, for the use of these tokens of God's love to us? Are we not conscious of the little appreciation we have for such precious benefits?

God will judge every thought, word and deed, each omission of duty, at the moment of death, deciding once for all our eternal happiness or woe. Fearful indeed is this thought. Preachers sometimes impress on us the final efforts of the devil to drive us to despair, the agony and loneliness of death, the terror of this awful judgment. One wonders if it is wise to paint so horrible a picture of these inevitable moments, as if by fear to drive us to serve God. May not this defeat its own end and induce an unwillingness to face up to the inevitable? Is it good to fear death in terror when it ought to be a happy release from this 'vale of tears,' the opening of the door to eternal happiness? Is it good to begin to despair in life about salvation? If we despair in life we are already prepared to be overcome by the temptation at death, for as a man lives so shall he die!

It would be better, perhaps, to insist on this certain fact, that we can only fail to secure salvation by our own deliberate choice, by being willing to commit grievous sin, by refusing to serve God, by spurning his love and friendship, by wilful aversion from him. Hell was made for the devil and his angels—not for man! If man goes there it is through his own choice in rejecting the grace of God. The Church teaches that at the moment of death the soul receives a perfect illumination of its state. Should it be in a state of grace and innocence it will wing its flight at once to heaven; if it be stained with venial sin or owe a debt of temporal punishment, it will choose to be purified by the flame of purgatory; if it be totally averted from God by unrepented mortal sin, by final impenitence, then it will choose hell by its own act. God does not send the soul to hell; its fixed unchanging hatred of God is hell. Thus we shall give the account of our stewardship.

Often it is said that few will be saved, the many lost. Is it so? Actually we know nothing at all about that; God alone knows; it has not been revealed to us. Yet it would seem to be entirely contrary to the infinite mercy of God who wills not the death of the sinner but that he be converted and live. It would appear to make the redemption almost a failure if the greater number were lost and few saved, since Christ died to save all men. By all means we must have a wholesome fear of God's judgments, not presuming on his divine mercy; but one who is honestly trying as best he can to love and serve God need not, in spite of many falls, despair of salvation. The Church can tell us but little of those who have gone before. She declares that certain souls are in possession of eternal bliss; she has never declared that any soul is definitely lost—not even Judas, the son of perdition. We have no knowledge of the power of grace to save at the last moment by a swift act of repentance in turning to God. The one great folly would be to rely on this and so presume on the mercy of God as to care little how we offend his justice.

Our Lord gives us a glimpse of the judgment and the sins that will be most severely condemned, all of which seem to affect the law of charity to others. This bears out the teaching: 'Judge not, and you shall not be judged.' 'Forgive and you shall be forgiven.' Scandal in the true sense, i.e. leading another into sin, is severely condemned: 'If thy right hand scandalise thee, cut if off, it is better to enter heaven maimed.' 'If anyone scandalise one of these little ones it were better for him that a millstone should be hanged about his neck and that he were cast into the sea.' Beware of bad example! Hypocrisy is condemned: 'Woe unto ye scribes and pharisees, hypocrites' who try to impress others with a false appearance of piety, yet condemn others. Want of charity is singled out for blame. At the judgment the Son of man shall say to those on the right hand; 'Come ye blessed of my Father possess ye the kingdom of heaven, for I was hungry and ye gave me to eat, thirsty and ye gave me to drink.' Then shall the just answer: 'Lord when did we see thee hungry and gave thee to eat, thirsty and gave thee to drink?' The Lord will answer: 'As long as ye did it to one of these my least brethren, ye did it to me.' To those on the left, he will say: 'Depart from me ye cursed into everlasting fire because I was hungry and ye gave me not to eat.' They will ask: 'Lord when did we see thee hungry and gave thee not to eat?' Then will come the indictment: 'Amen, I say to you so long as ye did it not to one of these my least brethren ye did it not to me.' Thus does our Lord identify himself with each soul, and whatsoever is done to another in word or deed, for or against a neighbour is taken by our Lord as done to himself and will be rewarded or punished accordingly.

A certain man asked our Lord: 'Lord will they be few who are saved?' No definite answer is given but he is bidden to 'strive to enter by the narrow way, for many shall seek to enter and shall not be able.' The parable of the wedding garment seems to suggest that the greater number will be saved. The kingdom of heaven is likened to a marriage feast but those who were invited (i.e. the Jews) refused to come. The servants were sent out into the lanes and byways to compel the beggars, the blind and the lame to come in to the feast, and it was filled with guests of all kinds. Of these only one is found not wearing the marriage garment. That was entirely his own fault since these garments were provided and needed only to be asked for to be obtained; to fail to get one was an insult to the giver of the feast. This one was cast out into the exterior darkness entirely through his own fault. This wedding garment means the grace of God without which none can enter heaven. The number at this feast was great, but one only was found without the garment. If this refers to the number who will be saved, then few will be lost—because of the infinite value of the redemption and its continuance in the multitude of Masses offered daily, and because of the infinite mercy of God who gives grace to all who truly seek it. When we consider that the mercy of God persists to the last moment of life, that the good shepherd goes out after the lost sheep, that Christ died to save all men, it seems no extravagant claim that the greater number will be saved and few lost.

It is the very ignorance of man, his want of understanding of the mystery of sin which excuses much that is done in evil. 'Father forgive them, they know not what they do.' Thus Christ prays for the ignorance of men who offend against

God not realising their enormous guilt. Sin alone can bring about damnation and sin is the deliberate choice of the will; we cannot commit mortal sin by accident, nor be unaware that we have sinned grievously, since it is the deliberate choice of what we know to be a grave offence against God. Mortal sin unrepented is the sole cause of damnation, we cannot be forced to sin against our will; hence it is entirely our own choice if we are lost. We must have a wholesome filial fear of God, not a servile fear; we shall be punished according to our just deserts, no more, no less, to the uttermost farthing. If we keep the thought of judgment always before us, it will surely deter us from grave sin. At the same time we must not allow that fear which drives to despair; rather we must have an intense love for God who shows such infinite mercy to man. We must avoid sin not through fear of judgment, but from love for God who so deserves all our love and every sacrifice that we can make for him. If we love God we cannot be lost; no friend of God will lose his soul.

'Give an account of thy stewardship for now thou canst be steward no longer.'